THE
UNITED SYNAGOGUE
1870–1970

בס"ד

ככה יעשה לאיש אשר המלך חפץ ביקרו

To Nicola and Anthony
on their marriage
with the very best wishes
for joy and happiness

מזל טוב

From Rabbi Dr and Mrs H Rabinowicz
12 July 1987

THE
UNITED
SYNAGOGUE
1870–1970

AUBREY NEWMAN

ROUTLEDGE & KEGAN PAUL
LONDON, HENLEY AND BOSTON

First published in 1976
by Routledge & Kegan Paul Ltd
39 Store Street,
London WC1E 7DD,
Broadway House,
Newtown Road,
Henley-on-Thames,
Oxon RG9 1EN and
9 Park Street,
Boston, Mass. 02108, USA
Set in Photon Bembo
and printed in Great Britain by
The Camelot Press Ltd, Southampton
© The United Synagogue 1976

ISBN 0 7100 8456 0

Dedicated to all who unite to form Synagogues for prayer, and all such as occupy themselves in faithfulness with the wants of the Congregation.

Owing to production
delays this book was
published in 1977

CONTENTS

ILLUSTRATIONS

ix

TABLES *page*

FIGURE

MAPS OF CONGREGATIONS IN THE UNITED SYNAGOGUE

FOREWORD

It was essential to create a record of the United Synagogue to mark its centenary year in 1970. What was required was a standard work by a distinguished professional historian. And so the invitation to write this history was extended to Dr Aubrey Newman. It should be noted at once that no conditions were laid down which might limit the scope of our historian; nothing was to be concealed that might add to the knowledge of our institution and its significance in the life of Anglo-Jewry.

This history appears at a time which may well be described as a watershed for the United Synagogue and the Jewish community as a whole in these islands. Looking back, one can discern the successive periods in its story. The Union in 1870 of the 'City Synagogues' of the eighteenth century was followed in the nineteenth century and the early part of the twentieth century by a large Jewish immigration to these shores from Eastern Europe, and later by a substantial immigration from Nazi Europe. So Anglo-Jewry reached its maximum development, the United Synagogue itself becoming a union of some 80 synagogues, with 30,000 male and 10,000 female members.

Much of this was achieved under a paternalistic rule of wise, able and sincere men, but in time the rule of the 'grand dukes' gave way to government essentially democratic as power spread to the grass roots. It is now wielded by the children and grandchildren of the early immigrants who participate to the full in the life of this great country. They have enjoyed the benefits of its education and the fruits of its industry, and they in turn help to bear the burdens of the nation, and of the Jewish community within it.

Within the United Synagogue today, far-reaching changes are taking place. The present Council of Constituent Synagogues is changing to include the representatives of the District Synagogues. The District Synagogues, formed in 1926 to help new congregations develop in membership and means until they were fully able to play their part, will now cease to be a separate body. The District Synagogues have largely represented the growth of the United Synagogue, as Jews spread from the East End and the inner metropolitan boroughs to the outer areas of the metropolis, where the future of the United Synagogue will be found.

Great tasks lie ahead for the new Council, particularly in the field of youth and education, to ensure that future. Though we now stand at a pinnacle, a look into the future reveals a scene of sombre hue. There is little likelihood of further immigration of Jews into this country to increase, or even maintain our numbers. Assimilation, inter-marriage and low fertility are beginning to take their toll. Despair, however, is contrary to Jewish belief, and the resolve must surely be to save every Jewish soul so that our community shall remain substantial and viable.

It is to be hoped that this volume will contribute to that end by inspiring in its readers a sense of pride in the institution which carries so many of the burdens of Anglo-Jewry, including the Chief Rabbinate, the Beth Din, the Board of Deputies, making at the same time a massive contribution to the State of Israel.

We should express gratitude to leaders, lay and spiritual, who, in the past, have created our institution, and to those who sustain it today. It remains most heartily to thank Sir Isaac Wolfson, who was president of the United Synagogue during the centenary year, for his generous donation towards the publication of this volume.

Salmond S. Levin

Chairman – Centenary Exhibition and

Publication Committee

May 1976

INTRODUCTION

This is not a history of London Jewry, nor even a history of London Jewry between 1870 and 1970. It is the study of an institution which has, during that century, served the Jewish community in London, Anglo-Jewry, and Jewry as a whole. In the telling of that story an attempt has been made to put the United Synagogue into its context, and to relate its growth to the development of the Jewish community and to that of the wider scene in which London Jewry was set. It has not been the intention here to tell the story of each individual synagogue within that institution, but rather to select instances from individual congregations to shed light upon the workings of the community as a whole. That is not to denigrate any individual congregation, nor to cast doubt upon those whose congregational piety has led them to write the history of their individual communities. All such histories are of value, and indeed it is to be hoped that this work might inspire the writing of others. There are other aspects of London Jewry which have not been developed in detail. The Beth Din and the Shechita Board appear only in passing, and despite the close connection between the United Synagogue and the Board of Deputies that is an independent body which deserves a history of its own.

In its writing the story of the United Synagogue has developed into a study of the way in which the London Jewish community has changed in its pattern of leadership, in its pattern of membership, and in its pattern of physical and geographical spread over the metropolitan area. It has also illustrated a most interesting phenomenon: the way in which the Jewish immigrant community has managed to adopt, chameleon-like, many of the characteristics of its host. Whether the host be the small Anglo-

Jewish community which received into its midst the vast volume of immigrants at the turn of the century or, in a wider sense, the whole non-Jewish community, it still remains true that Anglo-Jewry has managed to adapt itself to its surroundings. A hundred years ago the United Synagogue existed to serve a small London Jewish community. During the next century that community expanded virtually tenfold, but when the dust had settled and the next generation had come to maturity, the institution remained. It was recognisably the same, and still tried to maintain the same standards of service to the community. That has always been the strength of the United Synagogue, and it is that which, it is hoped, this history will serve to illustrate.

This volume has not been conceived as a work merely to give praise, credit, or gratitude to those who founded the institution, or who continue to bear its burden. The history was commissioned, but the author was left to execute his task as he saw fit; at no stage did the officers of the United Synagogue ever try to influence him other than by encouraging him to complete his work, and by giving him unrestricted access to every possible piece of paper which he might have wanted.

The author acknowledges gratefully the help of all ranks of the officers of the United Synagogue, honorary and full-time alike. They, and Mr Salmond S. Levin in particular, have discovered that the task of writing a history is much lengthier than they had envisaged. Having originally hoped that the book would be ready before the end of the centenary year, they must have wondered whether it would appear before the next centenary was due. They have, however, been very forbearing, and for this understanding deserve especial thanks. The Secretary, Mr Nathan Rubin, and his various officers have been of immense assistance; particularisation is invidious, but it would be churlish not to mention Mr W. Norwood who has been extremely helpful in his general comments on the last twenty years, and Mr S. Rosenberg who has unfailingly produced manuscripts, files, reports, and photocopies with constant courtesy and effectiveness. Many others, officers past and present, have been delighted to help, to offer suggestions, and to answer long series of questions. All have been anxious to be of assistance in telling the story of how the institution has developed and worked in practice. To all these individuals, named and unnamed, the author offers his most grateful thanks and his hopes that this work matches their expectations.

Two particular thanks must be expressed. The first is to my research assistant, Helen Levin. During the years of research she developed an instinct for relevant material and a willingness to delve – physically on occasion – into files of records undisturbed for many years. The foundations of this book rest very solidly upon the information she gathered and passed on to me, and without her work this book would have been impossible. The second is to my wife who for years has had to put up with United Synagogue politics. Many wives are accustomed to this, but at least their husbands are involved in the politics of the present; there can be few who have to worry about the closure of synagogues that have for long been but a distant memory.

University of Leicester
March 1976

CHAPTER 1

THE FOUNDATION

The history of modern Jewry in England begins with the Resettlement in the middle of the seventeenth century, and London Jewry is as old as the Resettlement itself. Starting originally with a small congregation of Jews of Spanish and Portuguese origins, the Sephardim, worshipping eventually in the Bevis Marks Synagogue, and expanding by the end of the century to include also a congregation of Jews of German and Polish origins, the Ashkenazim, London Jewry had grown steadily during the eighteenth century until it contained at least three major Ashkenazi congregations – the Great Synagogue, the Hambro' Synagogue, and the New Synagogue.[1] These synagogues, which among them contained over 1,000 seatholders (between 7,000 and 8,000 individuals), had been founded to serve Jewish congregants living in the east side of the City of London, Houndsditch, and Goodman's Fields, and provided a multitude of services for their members. So long as these members remained static the communal organisations which served them remained adequate. London Jewry, however, was at this time very far indeed from being a static community. Both geographically and socially London Jews were on the move, and in consequence these communal institutions were faced with a series of crises. Many Jews were moving out of the older city areas towards new centres such as Bloomsbury, Marylebone, Westminster, or Bayswater in the west, Islington or Stepney in the north or east, and this weakened the congregations and their associated bodies.[2] Movement was of course selective, and those who were left behind were increasingly either the poor who could not afford to move or the elderly who retained a sentimental attachment to the scenes of their youth. On the other hand those who moved away still demanded a continuance of what they had enjoyed previously, not merely the privileges of membership of the congregation but more particularly the opportunity of attending divine service on a Sabbath. Since moving to the West End did not involve also the sloughing off of orthodoxy, the only alternative to a long walk on a Sabbath or Festival day with all its attendant hardships even in a normal English summer (to say nothing of a winter) was the opening of new synagogues in the new centres of population. This, however, was easier said than done, for it ran counter to the traditions and the laws of the existing bodies.

Common to all the synagogues in London, Sephardi and Ashkenazi, was the forbidding of services other than in the parent synagogue. Members were not allowed to hold or even attend services elsewhere. These laws represented an attempt to hold the congregation together spiritually and physically in order to avoid the very real danger of a fragmented community becoming too small and impoverished to maintain collective responsibility for poor relief, burial of the dead, or even the upkeep of its buildings. These formed part of the congregation's responsibilities to its own members and also to the community as a whole. Each synagogue had in fact a partial responsibility for the welfare of the entire London Jewish community. The poor had to be given relief, even when the individuals were not members of any of the synagogues, and in addition there was responsibility for the finances of the Chief Rabbinate and, in conjunction with the Sephardi congregation of Bevis Marks, for the supervision of the provision of kosher meat and the providing of Passover matzoth. A series of agreements among the three leading Ashkenazi synagogues from the late eighteenth century had culminated, by the 'Treaty' of 1834, in the recognition of the 'conjoint synagogues', and had provided for the financing of communal responsibilities in agreed proportions among these congregations. The 'Treaty' had also made provision to prevent the poaching of members by any other synagogue within the organisation. Any member who might feel a diminution of his loyalty to his parent synagogue would none the less find it very difficult to break away and establish a valid connection with another; indeed it was very likely that it was this section of the 'Treaty' of 1834 which made the new formal organisation palatable to all three congregations.

It is clear then that there were conflicting pressures in the middle of the nineteenth century; the new 'suburbanites' were asking for their own religious facilities closer at hand while the extant congregations were seeking to forbid or at least to limit any growth in the number of synagogues. Close examination, for instance, of the literature issued by all sides during the struggle over the formation of the West London Synagogue of British Jews shows how much emphasis was put on the problems of attending service. The founding fathers of the new congregation complained of 'the distance of the existing Synagogues from the places of our residence', while the authorities of Bevis Marks themselves came to recognise the need to permit the holding of regular services elsewhere than in the parent synagogue. This particular incident had affected the Sephardim more than the Ashkenazim; only five or six of the founders had been members of Ashkenazi congregations. But it was very soon afterwards, on 7 November 1848, that the Committee of the Great Synagogue resolved that 'it being considered of the utmost importance that a place of worship in connection with this synagogue be established at the West End of the Metropolis, this Committee do take the subject into consideration at the next meeting'.[3] The results of this consideration were eventually the decisions to set up a 'branch' synagogue to the west of Regent Street, and to invite the other two congregations to participate. Neither one was prepared to accept, for reasons which were largely financial, so that the final arrangements were for a synagogue entirely dependent on the Great alone, with a membership restricted to members of the Great. From the outset it was made clear that the new building was not intended as the home of a new congregation, and when it was ready for consecration proclamation was made from the reading desk that 'notice is hereby given that this building now about to be consecrated is a Branch of the Great Synagogue situate in Duke's Place, in the parish of St James' Aldgate, in the City of London'.[4] It was the Jewish equivalent of a 'chapel of ease', set up to meet conditions parallel within the parish organisation of the Church of England; no marriages could be solemnised in it; it could have no honorary officers of its own save those appointed for it by the parent congregation; its financial affairs were strictly controlled by the Great; and although its members, if otherwise qualified, could vote for the officers of the Great, the votes had to be taken to Duke's Place for counting. Even so, the branch proved highly popular, and within a short time the building was insufficient to meet the demand for 'western' accommodation which had to be met, partly by an enlargement of the existing building and partly by a further one even more to the west.

The demand for a further branch gave rise once again to the suggestion that all three 'conjoint' members should act as sponsors; but whereas the earlier suggestion had met with little response from either the New or the Hambro' there was now a rather surprising reaction. On 24 March 1859 the Board of Management of the New Synagogue resolved that 'with a view of preventing the necessity of this congregation having a Branch synagogue of their own . . . some endeavours be made with the Great and Hambro' Synagogues to effect an amalgamation'[5] and these two agreed to appoint delegates to a meeting of the three. On 27 April the delegate committee resolved:[6]

> Considering the present social conditions of the Jewish community in London – and with a view of their future well-doing – and to afford to the respective members and their families residing at the West End of the Metropolis increased accommodation by the establishment of another synagogue, it is the opinion of this committee that before entering into the details for building the said branch Synagogue there should first be an amalgamation of the three City and such other Metropolitan synagogues as may desire to unite with them.

Suggestions for amalgamation of functions were in the air already, for the minutes of the three conjoint synagogues at this very time contain the details of the way in which they were agreeing to set up the Board of Guardians, combining the work that each was already doing to alleviate distress among the poor,[7] but this resolution was the first suggestion of a further union that seems to have had the support of the governing bodies of any of the major synagogues, and there was probably a connection between the financial weaknesses of both the Hambro' and New Synagogues and this possibility of retaining some hold over their suburban members without an undue cost. Discussions were continued, but by 1861 the Hambro' had withdrawn from participation in the scheme for a new branch and was more interested in questions of survival. In the meantime the development of the Bayswater branch had proceeded apace under the joint sponsorship of the other two, the Great and the New. This scheme followed, more or less, the same lines as the Central branch, with one essential difference. Since this new branch was dependent on two parents, it could not be under the same strict surveillance. It had, for example, to be allowed its own honorary officers and a certain degree of financial independence, and the residence in the area of such strong-minded individuals as Samuel Montagu almost inevitably meant that even from the beginning the congregation would be difficult to handle. It made demands to which the parent bodies took considerable exception. It refused, for example, to be treated merely as a 'chapel', and its president Lewis Jacobs applied to the Board of Deputies for the recognition of the Bayswater Synagogue's secretary as an independent marriage secretary and registrar. For over a year the arguments went backwards and forwards between the parent synagogues and the Board, the Great even having a case sent for the consideration of the Attorney-General, but eventually the Bayswater branch had to be given its own way. None the less this overall control by the two founding congregations could not remain effective for long. As the report of the Charity Commissioners explained in 1870:[8]

> The accidental circumstances of the principal members of this Branch Synagogue having seats at the parent boards has, hitherto, prevented any grave inconvenience from this constitution; but it cannot be forgotten that when this tie lapses, a natural consequence in the course of years, it will be difficult to reconcile the members of this and other synagogues, which may hereafter be similarly established, to the fact that they have no control over the administration of the funds to which they contribute.

Demands for the building of 'branches' were not the only signs of the changes caused by population movements. Other, older communities sought help for their building programmes from individual prominent figures in Anglo-Jewry, through the advertisement columns of the *Jewish Chronicle*, and also directly from the major London bodies and particularly the Great Synagogue. Leeds and Dover outside London, the Borough congregation inside London, were all told that there were no funds available, but when the committee of a proposed North London synagogue approached the Great the response was much more favourable, the difference being that such a building might be of direct use to members of the Great. At all events, negotiations were opened in March 1864, and on 9 February 1865 an agreement was outlined laying down clearly the terms on which the Great was prepared to lend £1,100 for the new building. The proposals declared firmly 'that the said proposed synagogue shall not be a Branch of the Great Synagogue',[9] but went on to tie the two very closely together, insisting on a continued conformity of ritual and customs between the new congregation and the Great, and indicating the terms on which members of the Great could join this new body. The terms also insisted that the loan was to be strictly secured, and the ground on which the synagogue was to be built was to be vested in the trusteeship of nominees of the Great. It became apparent, however, that there was more to the agreement than the expressed terms, for in July 1869 a special meeting of the Great Synagogue Vestry was held to discuss possible variations in the agreement. In practice the details by which money had been raised had differed from the way envisaged and as a consequence the North London congregation wished to have the Treaty declared lapsed. The Great refused to agree on the grounds that 'the North London synagogue had been founded plainly on the assumption of a permanent connection between the Synagogues'.[10] Clearly as early as 1864 the officers of the Great had had in mind some fundamental changes in the structure of London Jewry.

One such change had already been envisaged in 1859, when delegates had begun discussion of possible amalgamation. The suggestion had been canvassed at several meetings of the Hambro' governing body and in June 1861 was taken so far as to secure a legal opinion from Jacob Waley as to how such a union might be brought into being.[11] The case prepared for Waley indicated the connection between the growing difficulties of the Hambro' and the attractiveness of amalgamation.[12]

> For some time past owing to the decreasing number of seat-holders of the Hambro' Synagogue and its diminishing resources a wish has been entertained by some of its members to amalgamate with the Great and New Synagogues.

He was specifically asked 'if he would suggest some general features of a scheme for such an amalgamation'. In his reply he rejected one suggestion that a case would have to be brought into the Court of Chancery, but recommended that an approach could be made to the Charity Commissioners who could draw up a scheme which would be approved by Parliament 'as a matter of course'. His opinion continued:

> I should think that any plan having the approbation of the Governing Bodies and of the generality of the Congregations recommended by expediency, and calculated to promote the general interests of the Jewish worship and religion, and also to preserve in substance the special charitable trusts above mentioned, would probably meet with the sanction of the Board. I therefore think that the Board might be induced to approve of a sale of the buildings and lands of the Hambro' Synagogue with a dedication of the proceeds towards the purchase and erection of a new local synagogue in some other district or as a fund for enlargement or repairs of either of the other City Synagogues.

Negotiations continued over a further two years, until the Hambro' decided to concentrate on union with the Great; in April 1863 the Great and Hambro' set up committees to discuss the matter further. Nearly all points were capable of being agreed to by both sides, but the negotiations eventually broke down on the demand by the Hambro' that there should be an engagement to keep the building of the Hambro' open for daily worship. The Great would not accept the financial burden involved in this, and so the negotiations quietly lapsed.

It is in fact clear that the background to London Jewish life in the 1860s is one of growing co-operation between the leading communal institutions, and a feeling among their leading members that there ought to be closer ties than then existed. One important factor was the emergence on to the communal scene of a number of younger men who had the time and the desire to engage in communal work, and most prominent among them was Lionel Louis Cohen. He had been active in 1859 in the formation of the Board of Guardians, chairman of one of the committees discussing terms for amalgamation with the Hambro', and above all chairman of the committee which had drawn up the terms of agreement with the North London congregation. By the middle of the 1860s his was the rising star in the Great Synagogue, and his influence was certainly not weakened by the election of a new secretary of the Great in the spring of 1866. The successful candidate was Dr Asher Asher of Glasgow, who had come to London in 1862, and had become prominent in the work of the Board of Guardians where Lionel Louis Cohen was of course a prominent figure. Asher's election was in many ways a victory of the 'West' over the City within the Great, so that this was yet another pointer to the ways in which the old-established institutions were being brought to consider change.

The occasion for the closer union among the London synagogues was a renewal of membership problems. There had always been a certain amount of disagreement among the Conjoint synagogues about their claims to the allegiance of particular individuals, and about whether some person ought, or ought not, to have been enrolled in one or other of the older communities. Transfer of membership involved, if it were possible, a considerable degree of argument and bargaining, if only because there was a considerable amount of money at stake. The Treaty always provided for the discussion of such problems between the contracting parties, and the minutes of the board meetings of the synagogues reveal several such delegate meetings. In the summer of 1866 one such conference had to be arranged, the issues concerning two members of the New who had been given seats at the Great Synagogue's branch in Portland Street and a member of the New who had been allocated a seat at the Great and whose son was shortly to be *Bar Mitzvah* in the Great. The second case was easy of solution since the member in question was prepared to surrender his seat at the Great. But the first was much more difficult and it was agreed that a conference of the two synagogues be held. In the meantime a great deal of discussion had taken place and it was on that issue that Chief Rabbi Nathan Adler is said to have suggested at the celebrated *succah* breakfast of 24 September 1866 that it was time that the various London synagogues sank their various differences. It is the close connection between that breakfast and the conference on 5 November 1866 among delegates of the Great and New Synagogues which has led to the Chief Rabbi being given the credit for the initiative which gave rise to the United Synagogue. At the very least, however, he was pushing at an opening door, since Lionel Louis Cohen, who had been so involved with many uniting movements in London, was one of those at the breakfast. Indeed, it is not absolutely impossible that Cohen might have made a suggestion along these lines for Adler's own use. It remains quite certain that although after the November meeting the delegates' minute books record 'the business of the meeting having terminated the gentlemen present took the opportunity of discussing the question of the fusion of their respective congregations',[13] an examination of the minute books of the various committees of delegates entrusted with the discussion and drafting shows quite clearly that the idea of a union had been carefully thought out well in advance.

The officers of the Great and New Synagogues conveyed to their respective boards, and to that of the Hambro', the suggestion that a closer union be considered, and all three appointed delegates to a meeting which took place on 13 December 1866. The meetings of this committee and its sub-committee were held in a very efficient way, which in itself pays tribute to the effectiveness of their members but also indicates that there were people on the committee determined to push its business through. This is further evidenced by the very way in which the records of these discussions were kept. Each delegation kept minutes of the discussions, since each had to report back to its parent body. These books differ slightly in wording, but the differences are so slight as to suggest that the three secretaries had got together in order to draw up an agreed minute. Gradually, however, two of them fade away; the Hambro' minutes die away after a meeting on 27 December 1866 and while those of the New Synagogue continue until a meeting on 11 November 1867, the minute book thereafter contains only various copies of letters and printed circulars. Only the Great Synagogue copy shows a conscious attempt to present material in a chronological and methodical way. This was the official version; Asher, the secretary of the Great, was also the secretary to the delegates, and Lionel Louis Cohen, the chairman of the committee and drafting sub-committee, was also a leading member of the Great. It is therefore the more significant that the Great Synagogue's copy of the minutes begins not with the meeting of the delegates on 13 December (as does the Hambro'), nor with that on 5 November (as docs that of the New), but with file copies of pamphlets published in 1863 at the time of the abortive attempt to unite the Great and Hambro' Synagogues. It continues with the four letters from the secretary of the New to the secretary of the Great on the subject of the disputed members written between 16 May and 12 June 1866, minutes the early meetings between the Great and New Synagogues on this subject, and then leads directly into the meeting of the delegates themselves. In other words, no matter what anyone else thought, both Lionel Louis Cohen and Asher Asher had very distinct ideas, as early as May 1866, as to the direction in which they wished the discussions to go; indeed, their ideas may have been formulated earlier during the close association of Cohen and Asher through their work on the Board of Guardians, and this may have been why Asher stood as secretary. This was, at all events, well before any *succah* breakfasts. There is a long-standing tradition of a comment by the Chief Rabbi that morning about the desirability of a closer union – and indeed the tradition goes back to the 1880s; but the comment would only have had a response if those to whom the idea was mentioned were predisposed to pay attention.

The suggestion of 5 November having been communicated to each of the three synagogues, general meetings were held – at the Great on 29 November, the New on 22 November, and the Hambro' on 6 December – and, all having agreed to the amalgamation in principle, delegates were appointed to discuss the necessary details. The meetings began on 13 December and laid down the guidelines for their future discussions. The question of amalgamation was not, of course, in doubt but the delegates made one point clear:[14]

> While all the Synagogues they represent should be united as regards their pecuniary interest and the arrangement and expenditure of their income and also as regards matters of common concern, the internal management of each Synagogue should remain distinct, and existing arrangements should be as little as possible interfered with; and that the scheme for a fusion should proceed on this principle.

This issue of local autonomy was one which was to recur. The sub-committee which was set up – four representatives from the Great and three each from the other two synagogues – met a fortnight later, and even at that stage had so much of the final scheme ready prepared as to leave no doubt about the way in which the founding fathers knew exactly what they were doing. A series of resolutions approved the formation of the 'United Metropolitan Congregation of Jews' – a title later changed to 'United Synagogue' – the possibility of expansion through the addition of any other 'Metropolitan Congregation', the ecclesiastical authority of the Chief Rabbi and the maintenance of the Polish *Minhag*, and the machinery of government of the new body. Essentially, at this first meeting of the sub-committee there was laid down the basis of the scheme as carried through, although there were to be differences of opinion, complicated negotiations, and a certain amount of 'horse-trading' before agreement could be secured from all parties. The extent of the contentiousness of the business – and perhaps even the desire of the founding fathers to be able to return home at a reasonable hour after each meeting – may perhaps be gauged by the resolution that 'at all meetings of this sub-committee no fresh business be introduced after nine o'clock in the evening'.[15] The final report of the sub-committee was in print by 11 February 1867 when it was considered by the full delegate meeting, and the final report, as amended by the delegates, was in the hands of members of the various synagogues for consideration by the beginning of March. A point which goes some way towards assessing the part played by the Chief Rabbi in the detailed discussions is that it was only at the last of the first series of meetings that his intervention is recorded. At that, on 4 March, a letter from him was read to the delegates approving of the scheme but asking that no place of worship should be closed without his sanction. The delegates responded 'respectfully' that this was a matter 'on which they have no power to legislate'. None the less, nearly three months later, each synagogue did agree, under various conditions, that the new body ought to have power to close a synagogue if that was thought desirable.

Each congregation had now to make its decision, and each at a general meeting saw fit to make suggestions for changes. It was at this stage that both Lionel Louis Cohen and Asher Asher had perhaps the most difficult task – that of persuading some to drop their suggestions or others to accept alterations in order to make the scheme as a whole acceptable. The letter from Cohen to the New Synagogue illustrates clearly the courteous but firm way in which he dealt with objections and suggestions, always bearing in mind the future of this new institution. The suggestion had been made by the New Synagogue that the terms defining the *Minhag* should be dropped:

As this clause was originally drawn by an honorary member of your Board, he will have no difficulty in explaining to them that it was considered absolutely necessary to define the *Minhag* on which the institution is founded, and politic so to do, as removing from the future a Question which might, if unprovided for, lead to cavil and dissention. The Clause as drawn is the same as now in force in the Constituent Synagogues.

He explained the reasoning behind a broadening of the governing body from a fixed figure of twenty elected members of the Vestry to a number based on the membership of each constituent: 'By the Clause as originally drawn, the adhesion of a new Synagogue to the General body, or the growth of any present Synagogue, would have diminished pro tanto the representation of the rest.'[16]

One important change had, however, been made; the original scheme had wished to restrict the right of voting to 'privileged members', and although a concession had been made allowing all seat-holders to vote for the non-official members of the Vestry, but restricting voting rights in the constituent synagogues, pressure was now very firmly put on the delegates to extend this right more widely.

The first stage – of securing the broad agreement of the three conjoint synagogues – had thus, by the summer of 1867, been largely successful. Though minor difficulties still existed, and there were still to be differences of opinion among them, the major problems now lay elsewhere. The first of these concerned the Bayswater Synagogue. Having got its own way earlier over the celebration and registration of marriages, Bayswater was now prepared to secure its own way over the formation of the United Synagogue. Since, although only a 'branch', Bayswater stood in a different relationship to its two parents from that of the Central Branch to its one parent, there were special considerations, particularly in relation to the finances of the union. Bayswater in particular took strong exception to the extent of the powers given to the central government of the union, and proposed variations concerning finance and the relative part played by local and central committees in making local appointments. The delays were now being considered as vexatious by the public and by the *Jewish Chronicle*, whose editor, Michael Henry, published anonymously a pamphlet entitled *A Few Words on Jewish Congregational Union by a Victim of Jewish Congregational Disunion*, attacking the spirit of 'disunity' in the community and deploring the absence of a unified administrator. Asher wrote to Bayswater urging upon them the necessity 'out of deference to the voice of public opinion, of coming to some speedy and definitive settlement of the questions'.[17] The pressure had effect, and in April 1868 the revised scheme was put forward for approval by general meetings of the three synagogues. Broadly speaking, the major changes lay in three main areas

During the first stage of revision the executive committee of the union had been reconstituted in order to give more representation to the constituent synagogues; in place of eight elected members the honorary officers were to be joined by the wardens of each of the synagogues, and a small finance committee was set up in order to assist the treasurers. At the second stage this process was carried much further; the finance committee was much enlarged, and each synagogue nominated a financial representative to serve on it. Much more authority was also given to the individual congregations in preparing their budgets and raising their share of the communal taxation; locally prepared budgets were to come into effect unless the central body disapproved within a fixed time, and individual synagogues fixed the price of their own seats, subject to central approval. Above all, individual synagogues were given much more authority in the appointment of officers who were to be purely local in their work. All in all the changes at this second stage were largely along the lines of the relations between Bayswater and its parent bodies, and indicate not only the assiduity with which the Bayswater honorary officers had been pushing their opinions but the strong desire of the delegates as a whole to bring that synagogue into the general scheme. The changes were enshrined in a series of reports,[18] and in the process of change one other alteration had been made. An attempt had originally been made completely to remove from the synagogues any payments to the poor and to transfer the responsibility to the Board of Guardians, but that had met with opposition and it had had to be removed. On the other hand, a clause had been inserted permitting the new body to close any building if that was thought desirable. The third draft was now ready for submission to the various general meetings, and although some further changes were there suggested, these in their turn were agreed to by the other synagogues. Bayswater was now invited to nominate delegates – Samuel Montagu was one of them – and the way was clear for the final steps. The minutes of the meeting of the delegates on 27 October 1868 record that a resolution was passed that 'A special vote of thanks and the gratitude of the meeting was tendered to Mr Lionel L. Cohen for the earnestness, ability and perseverance with which he has conducted the business of the amalgamation and guided the deliberations of the Delegates.'

The agreement of the synagogues was not, however, enough in itself. There were trust funds and various charitable foundations involved, and so it was essential to secure the permission of the Charity Commissioners and the approval by them of a statutory scheme. Clause by clause, sentence by sentence, phrase by phrase the whole scheme had to be redrafted in a formal legal document for embodiment in an Act of Parliament, so that painfully, clause after clause, sentence after sentence, phrase after phrase had to be mulled over and given careful consideration. All the time counsel had to ensure that the draft of the bill coincided with the terms of the agreed scheme, so that, for example, when at one meeting it was agreed that the words 'who use the Polish or German ritual' be deleted they had to be put back into the clause at the subsequent meeting since, it was ruled, they were an integral part of the scheme.[19] This was the stage when the help of the lawyers was so important; Asher Asher himself was no lawyer and he had always to have spelled out for him by Algernon Sydney and Joseph Solomon the full implications of any decisions or suggestions. It was not until May 1869, nearly three years after the first discussions, that a full scheme could be presented to the Charity Commissioners with the assurance that the scheme had been put in detail to the synagogues and approved. The Commissioners made it clear in their reply that they could proceed only on the basis that there was no opposition to the scheme and sent copies of formal notices which, they pointed out, had to be fixed on or near the principal outer door of the synagogue and left for one full month. The notice for the Great Synagogue still preserves the marks of the original sealing wax used for this purpose.

Two objections were made – by Alfred Davis, who after having been spoken to by Sir Anthony de Rothschild (according to Lionel Louis Cohen, Sir Anthony had 'managed the negotiations with really great dexterity'), withdrew his objections, and by Judah Jacobs of the Hambro'. All but one of his objections were also withdrawn, but unless he could be persuaded to withdraw even that by the end of the year, the scheme would have to be dropped. Jacobs was invited to address a special meeting of the delegates, when it was decided to meet his point without, however, altering the scheme. It was agreed that if ever the Hambro' Synagogue should have to be closed, the first synagogue built within the jurisdiction of the United Synagogue after such closing should be designated the Hambro' and that this resolution was to be conveyed to the new body at its first meeting. The care which had to be taken in dealing with the Charity Commissioners is shown by the fact that on hearing of this meeting they insisted on knowing precisely what had been said and agreed to, in case it affected the scheme as a whole.

That should have been the end of the matter. A letter from the solicitors to Asher on 10 December 1869 informed him:[20]

The Scheme having been now approved and certified by the Board will be included in the next report to Parliament and no further action will be necessary on the part of the applicants.

In fact, however, the scheme was plagued once more with problems. Objections were raised by the Home Secretary, who had the formal responsibility for presenting the reports of the Charity Commissioners to Parliament. He felt a certain embarrassment about doing so on this occasion. The government of the day were fully engaged in disestablishing the Anglican Church of Ireland, and at a time when ministers were controversially taking away secular backing for ecclesiastical authorities in one sphere they could not, they felt, consistently incorporate it elsewhere. They declined, for example, to include references to 'the Chief Rabbi', preferring to use the phrase 'a Chief Rabbi'; it was pointed out that it was within the province of the synagogues to agree upon these matters for themselves but not to include it as parliamentary legislation. Once more the delegates had to meet, and they decided that since they had been given authority by their constituent bodies to 'take the necessary steps for bringing the scheme for the union into operation'[21] they could agree to the deletions desired by the government. On the other hand the scheme stood or fell as a whole, and so, in turn, they agreed further that all the deletions should be embodied in the laws and constitution of the United Synagogue. And so it was agreed, and a last meeting of the delegates was held and a last report was issued. Lionel Louis Cohen signed it as chairman, Asher Asher as secretary, but the last sentence was perhaps particularly appropriate for Cohen's signature, being as he was a Cohen and entitled to bestow a priestly benediction:[22]

In conclusion, the Delegates congratulate the congregations on the accomplishment of the Act of Union, which they regard as a most important event in the Communal life, calculated to increase the harmony and stability of the whole community, and to assist in the fulfilment and development of its sacred duties. They are convinced that union is strength, and that though each congregation can no more shine as a minor constellation, combined, they can and will diffuse light and warmth, in a degree formerly impossible, among the community. The Delegates pray Almighty God to cause His countenance ever to shine on His congregation; to bless this, the last work of its hands; and to vouchsafe to it and to all Israel peace in its religious and social life.

PART ONE

THE FIRST GENERATION 1870–1890

The first twenty years of the new United Synagogue found coming to the front problems that the founding fathers could never have imagined, as well as others that they had already foreseen. The years before 1890, and more especially before 1880, were crucial to its development, for these were the years in which patterns of working were laid down for the institution before the strains of the 'Great Immigration' of the end of the century came upon it. These were years in which London Jewry began to show the lines of that social and geographic development which was to become even more vital during the following century. This was the emergence of what has been termed 'Jewish suburbia'. The process had already been important and had resulted in the creation of the earlier 'branch' synagogues, but it accelerated thereafter and immediately presented problems. The total population of London, and the geographical area which it covered, was expanding, and the Jewish population expanded as well. From about 35,000 in 1870 the community increased in number to between 60,000 and 70,000 in 1890, and that in itself would have created difficulties. Much of this increase was of course concentrated into the East End of London, and its problems were of particular significance for the 'second generation' of United Synagogue leadership. Other problems were, however, more immediately pressing. The movement of population out of the older settled areas into others that were more salubrious, or more socially desirable, gathered momentum, and in the event even the recently founded Bayswater or North London suburbs began to overspill. Bayswater, for example, expanded into Maida Vale or into the fringes of Hyde Park, and various social surveys show the area round what was to become the New West

End Synagogue as 'affluent' and that around Maida Vale and St John's Wood as 'middle class to well-to-do'. As various elements of the Jewish population became more prosperous, they tended to move on into such suburbs and begin a process of looking for a new synagogue. A similar process, further down the social ladder, began by which Jews moved out of the earlier centres of settlement into North London, which in its turn became the suburb of the newer middle classes, the society so well portrayed by Israel Zangwill in his *Ghetto Tragedies*. Underlying these movements were the changes in transport patterns and housing development which were transforming late Victorian London. In this, as in so many ways, the changes in the Jewish population are understandable only in the context of similar changes among their hosts.

At the same time as these problems had to be faced the new organisation had to be formally brought into being. The foundation of any new organisation is inevitably accompanied by a series of compromises, by a series of assumptions, and by a series of hopes. However closely the founding fathers may have worked together, their relations become subtly different when the initial stage is over and the problems of adjustment to the new situation come to the surface. Any study, then, of this first generation of the United Synagogue must inevitably concentrate on the ways in which the organisation was brought into being, how it reacted to all the various new problems which were brought before it, and how far the founders could preserve their original vision. Certainly, it was as well that the institution was able to command the services of its original leaders for many years after its foundation, and that both Lionel Louis Cohen and Asher Asher were able to serve for nearly twenty years more.

CHAPTER 2

THE NEW
ORGANISATION

The passing into law of the Act of Parliament creating the United Synagogue was in itself only a beginning; much had to be done to give the organisation its being. The machinery of government had to be given form, and there were various promises, made during the last stages of the negotiations, which had to be implemented. Much, of course, had been laid down by the scheme of union itself. By the Act the future governing body was to consist of various elected members together with all those 'who, at the date of the passing of the Act, are entitled to Life Seats at the Governing Boards of their respective synagogues'. Until the former class had been elected the life members were to constitute the governing body, and it was to them (on 28 July 1870) that Asher sent notices convening a meeting of the provisional Vestry or Council.[1] His instructions had been 'to convene a meeting of the Provisional Governing Body with a view to their . . . providing for the appointment of the Definitive Governing Body, and for the intermediate management of the Synagogue'. The meeting was held on 11 August 1870, at 4.30 p.m., and immediately was thrown into the full consideration of a wide range of problems affecting fundamental issues in the new organisation. In themselves each of these problems was fairly routine, and indeed was largely the same sort of issue which had been separately decided by the individual boards of management in the past. What gave a new dimension, however, was that new precedents were being created for the future, and that the decisions were being taken by 'people from other synagogues', that it was no longer left solely to the people who had always dealt with them in the past. It was thus fortunate that the key members of the Council were precisely those who had worked so closely over the details of the union, and who therefore had trusted each other from long experience.

The first and most pressing task was to lay down the arrangements for the election of the balance of the members of the Council. Election day was fixed as 4 December, and on that day each constituent was to elect its wardens, committee men, financial representative, and Council members. Until that day the existing local honorary officers were to continue in office and each synagogue was to be governed by its own laws and by-laws. Accounts were to be made up to the end of 1870, and any surpluses – or liabilities – were then to be handed over to the new Treasurers of the United Synagogue. But other problems also appeared. The reader of the Great Synagogue wished to resign after thirty-nine years' service; was the cost of superannuation pensions to be borne by the United Synagogue as a whole or by the particular individual constituent? Furthermore, who was now to give immediate authority for filling vacancies? The High Holydays were close at hand, and there had been in the past 'overflow' services; who was to make the arrangements? Each of the conjoint synagogues had participated in the work of the Board of Guardians, the Shechita Board, the Passover Matzoth and Flour Committee, and indeed in all the other activities of the community. It was accepted that the new body should take over the obligations of the older ones, but the exact details had to be spelled out. Some of these decisions could be taken immediately. Individual synagogues, for example, could be told how many representatives they could elect.[2] Those who had been in charge of the High Holyday services (including, of course, Lionel Louis Cohen himself) could be invited to continue as before, with the difference that the synagogues were asked to ensure that publicity be given to the services as part of the 'combined' arrangements. The Conjoint Committee for the supply of flour and matzoth was asked to continue in office *ad interim*. But so far as possible, other problems which came up were put to one side for consideration by the new Council on its first full meeting; in the meantime the interim executive – Lionel Louis Cohen, Jacob Waley, Henry Isaacs, Henry Solomon, and Sampson Lucas – were considering what recommendations they should be making. That in itself was a precedent for the normal routines of the future.

Election Sunday, the first of them in the history of the United Synagogue, came and was fully reported. The *Jewish Chronicle* made a series of comments. Ten days before, on 25 November 1870, the leader declared:

Thoughtful men reasonably regard the United Synagogue as not only important in itself but as additionally important because it may be the nucleus of an accumulation of all, or nearly all, English Synagogues. The results of the exertions of such a linking can scarcely be exaggerated; but if the responsibility of the elected be great, scarcely less great will be the responsibilities of the electors. . . . Let us have men faithful to the traditions which have, humanely speaking, made Judaism; not men who are doctrinaires and imbued with new-fangled theories and untried hobbies; let us have men to whom for years past the country owes so much of its vitality and vigour.

The next week, 2 December, the *Jewish Chronicle* declared:

Next Sunday is the great Election Day. The Council of the greatest Congregation of the greatest people in the greatest City of the greatest Empire of the World will be appointed by the independent suffrages of the constituency.

And on 9 December, after the elections were over:

Sunday, the 4 December, 5631, will henceforth be a red letter day in the Anglo-Jewish Calendar . . . May the New Union prosper! May other Congregations join it! May it be guided by wise Counsels! May God be with it!

When the new Council met, on 14 December, there was a wide range of business already waiting for it. The treasurers and overseers had to be elected, as also had the seven elders; these plus the wardens of the constituent synagogues constituted the Executive Committee, from whom were unanimously elected the President and Vice-Presidents. Various other committees were also provided for by the Act of Parliament and had to be given formal existence. The Finance Committee was directly constituted by the Act, but a Committee for the Relief of the Poor had to be balloted for, and although the Act had laid down that there was to be a burial society the details had been left to the Council itself for decision as to 'the constitution of the society, and the conditions and privileges of membership'. All that could be done for the moment was to invite the existing societies to continue in being, and appoint a sub-committee to report back to the Council. For the rest, it was to be at a later meeting that the Bequests and Trusts Committee was constituted, and not until a year after the passing of the United Synagogue Act that it was felt necessary to set up a Building Committee. This too was to be one pattern of administration; no committee was ever set up until the need for it had been fully demonstrated.

None of this business was in any way contentious, but there was one piece of business that was very important – the implementation of the promise made earlier by the delegates setting up the union. Despite a certain amount of opposition, the Council agreed at its first meeting that the President, the Vice-President, and the Treasurers should execute a Deed of Trust incorporating the clauses deleted from the final scheme at the instance of the Home Secretary as head of the Charity Commissioners. Similarly the resolution of the delegates on 17 November 1869, with its safeguards as to the future of the Hambro' Synagogue and its name, was entered on to the Council's minutes.

In all this activity, however, there was a key figure who had as yet little official existence. At the first meeting of the Provisional Council Asher had been asked to act as *pro tem.* Secretary of the United Synagogue. Now the Executive, at the request of the Council, declared that there was a vacancy for the new post of Secretary and laid down the conditions under which the office was to be held. He was to be a full-time employee of the United Synagogue, and above all he was not allowed to hold the office of Secretary in conjunction with office in any of the constituent synagogues. His salary was fixed at £500 a year, a figure which compared favourably with official salaries paid at that date by other bodies, such as the civil service. It was obvious that the appointment would go to Asher, but the Act of Parliament had laid down the procedures for the filling of various posts, and so the formalities of declaring a vacancy, of inviting nominations, and proceeding formally to an election by all the seatholders had all to be gone through. In the meantime he had already been honoured by the Council, free membership having been presented to him and it being directed that his name was to be inserted first in the list of privileged members. On 5 March 1871 he was formally elected, unanimously, as the first Secretary of the United Synagogue.

Gradually over the next ten years a pattern of administration became fixed. Dates and places of meetings of the various committees settled down. The Executive Committee, for example, had tried to lay down at its first meeting that its regular monthly meetings would be held on the last Wednesday of the month, as nearly as possible at 8 p.m.; in practice, however, the meetings were held rather more often than that, and varied both in day and in time, summonses showing the time of meetings as anything between 5 p.m. and 7.30 p.m. Places of meeting varied as among committees, although each committee tended to stay at the same venue. The Council, and some of the other larger groups, met at the Central Synagogue, but others met at either the Great or the New. The official office of the United Synagogue remained off Portland Place, although the office of the Chief Rabbi remained fixed in Finsbury Square. What could not be varied was the burden of work. Comparison of dates of meetings, and the evidence of the letter-books of the Secretary, show how likely it was that in any one week there might well be several meetings falling together. From the beginning of the existence of the United Synagogue it was abundantly clear that the privilege of holding honorary – or even paid – office carried with it the overwhelming burden of innumerable hours spent in the service of the community. Some of the problems facing the new organisation have already been mentioned. The decision about the responsibility for the payment of pensions was taken, and these became a charge on the central funds of the United Synagogue itself. Equally important were the decisions about the appointment of new officials or the replacement of those who had retired. The Act had laid the formal responsibility for these appointments on the Council, but in practice, once the need to fill or create a vacancy had been accepted by the Council, the practical steps were left to the individual congregation, subject to the final and overriding need to secure the approval of the Chief Rabbi for all ecclesiastical appointments. All the time new situations emerged, and answers had to be found on a day-to-day pragmatic basis. The rule, for example, that new appointments of officials could not be made if candidates were over forty came from the need to secure insurance cover. The ruling that local congregations were responsible for the repair and maintenance of their buildings, coming to the United Synagogue's main funds only for major and structural changes, equally arose out of particular sets of circumstances. Gradually it became accepted that decisions of the Council normally were agreed to only after due notice had been given on the agenda paper and the Council meeting next following had had a further chance to deliberate. The practice too that all matters came originally to the Council, whence they were referred to the appropriate committee, equally grew up out of what seems obvious practice but could quite easily have gone a different way, direct to the Executive Committee.

Equally important was the way in which the United Synagogue accepted continued responsibility for membership of other communal institutions. The constituent synagogues had individually been members of various other communal institutions, and, now that they had formally been united into one, the new body might very well have been tempted to 'take over' these others. In practice, however, there is no evidence of this; instead the United Synagogue was continually at pains to maintain consultation with the other members of such bodies as the Board of Shechita and the Board of Deputies. Given the characters of the principal members of the United Synagogue this was only to be expected, and the Council indeed almost went out of its way to emphasise its extremely limited aims.

These had always been intimately concerned with the building of new synagogues and the provision of religious facilities for its members and would-be members. It is therefore not surprising to find that financial considerations dominated much of the routine and near-routine of its agendas. This went beyond the formal budget discussions each year; these were very far indeed from formal, and the Finance Committee went into synagogue budgets in enormous detail, instructing each congregation precisely how many seats should be let at each range of prices, querying items in the accounts, and often enough referring the budgets back for reconsideration. Over and over again, however, during the course of the year, additional items of expenditure, some of which could have been foreseen but many others which could not, appeared before the Council and received either approval or rejection by that body. This was not merely a case of 'surplus' synagogues securing approval and others being tightly scrutinised. Each of the constituents was expected to be in surplus, and the aim of the Treasurers was to secure a balance at all times, cutting out unnecessary wastage. Their reports draw attention to the undesirability of letting 'temporary seats' in the various synagogues at the High Holydays, this leading to possible loss of permanent membership. Another subject of attack was the practice of paying *minyan* men; the Treasurers could not but feel 'that the personal attendance of the Salaried Officers, and the influence of their example, should tend considerably to reduce this charge'.[3] But if this was the small change of Council meetings there were many items which represented important decisions, and outstanding among these were those which reflected the growing pressures of expanding London Jewry.

The greatest of these pressures was for new synagogues, and in the decade immediately following the union six congregations made application to join the United Synagogue. Two of these were not newly created: the Borough Synagogue had been founded in 1867, and indeed various congregations had had a long existence south of the river previously. The story of the North London Synagogue has already been in part discussed, its growth having played a part in the foundation of the United Synagogue. Neither of them found joining easy. An application came from the Borough almost immediately after the first elections to the Council, and for almost the whole of 1871 the negotiations continued, the main issues being the extent to which the Borough's building debt was to be taken over by the United Synagogue and the proportion of communal taxation which would have to be borne by the Borough. When the synagogue did come in, in February 1873, the union was accompanied by an appeal to wipe off the bulk of the capital debt. The North London congregation also needed convincing of the need to join the United Synagogue, and one trustee who refused to sign the deed transferring the property of the congregation to the United Synagogue delayed the union for a year and almost caused the whole application to fall through. Nevertheless it was almost inevitable that congregations already in existence would see various advantages in joining the United Synagogue, and, as will be shown, there were various congregations outside London who wished to secure the advantages of membership. What was new, however, was the way in which the other four congregations came into existence, and since this does throw considerable light on the attitude held by the officers and officials of the United Synagogue to their task a certain attention to their origins is warranted.

One of the fundamental issues was the extent to which the construction of synagogues and their admission to the United Synagogue should reflect the changing patterns of London Jewish settlement. Mention has already been made of the ways in which Jewish population was moving away from the older centres into newer suburbs, and indeed it had been such movement which had resulted in the establishment of the two branches already discussed. That movement had continued, and pressure came for either the erection of new buildings in totally new areas or for the replacement of older smaller ones by much bigger and grander structures. The result was that agitation came for the creation of three new congregations at the same time as it was being urged that the Bayswater Synagogue was too small. It was urged that the building in which the Bayswater congregation worshipped had become grossly inadequate for the demands being made upon it, and that there were vast numbers living in the vicinity who were unable to find accommodation in it. But an attempt to build a 'super' West End synagogue roused enormous opposition, partly from those members of Bayswater who disliked alteration in their already familiar building, partly from men like Samuel Montagu who were on record as disliking large synagogue buildings, and partly from those who felt that there was greater need for synagogue accommodation in the East End of London, particularly in the Stepney area. Demands for this had already been made. Editorials and letter-writers in the *Jewish Chronicle*, bitter speeches in the meetings of the United Synagogue Council, argued the issues backwards and forwards, rehearsing many of the arguments used in relation to later 'super-synagogue' plans, while commissions of enquiry succeeded each other with contradictory and bewildering recommendations. Within the Council of the United Synagogue itself the debates on the Bayswater and East London plans ran curiously side by side, beginning in the spring of 1873 and ending in the summer of 1876.

The Bayswater scheme foundered eventually on its financial aspects; it was altogether too grandiose, frightening even its sponsors, and the twin factors of strong internal opposition and the escalation of costs were sufficient to ensure its eventual withdrawal, even without the furore over the effect that an enlargement would have upon the 'Byzantine' structure of the edifice. The East London scheme, which had been first mooted at various public meetings in 1872, very nearly foundered on the same financial rock. After initial objections that it would be wrong to build another East London synagogue when the three that were in the City already were in need of further members, objections that were soon swept away by the physical problems for those in the East End of getting to the Hambro', the principal problem was that of financing the new venture. It was obviously unlikely that East London Jews would be able to finance such a building on their own account, but there was no precedent for the United Synagogue, as distinct from its constituents, providing grants as distinct from loans for the erection of the building. However, precedents had to be created, and the minutes of the Executive Committee of 18 March 1873 laid down a procedure to be followed thereafter. A deputation from the promoters was called into a meeting of the Executive Committee and the Chairman laid down several clear discussion points.

> It was an essential feature of the amalgamation that all Synagogues belonging to it are on a footing of absolute equality, that each must pay its own expenses, then its proportion of the communal burdens. These are about 50% on the seat rentals, plus a tax for the Burial Society. He further stated that it was impossible to go to the Council for support without definite statistics as to the prospects of the proposed Synagogues, and that the promoters must have a tangible amount of support before embarking in any schemes.

The deputation stated that they had canvassed the East London District: 500 circulars had been issued to the Jewish inhabitants residing within one mile North, South and East of Mile End Gate. They had not gone West of Mile End Gate so as not to interfere with the City Synagogues. Up to the present time, 100 Gentlemen's seats and 40 Ladies' seats have been applied for. They estimate the income of the proposed Synagogues to be from £400 to £500 per annum, and the expenditure at from £400 to £450. They consider that in order to stimulate subscriptions for erecting the Synagogues, a general meeting should be held, presided over by the President of the Council of the United Synagogue, and they anticipate that about £500 will be collected at that meeting. There is a suitable plot of ground vacant near Stepney Green, 1½ miles from the Great Synagogue, the freehold of which will cost about £600, and they estimate the erecting and fitting of the Synagogue at from £1,400 to £1,700: Total £2,000 to £2,300; and they state that these figures are based on the cost of the Stepney Schools, and are endorsed by a practical and experienced member of the proposed Synagogue.

The Chairman of the Executive Committee, Lionel Louis Cohen, proved to be a tower of strength for the would-be constituent synagogue. He backed the granting of money to the new group; he was reported in the *Jewish Chronicle* of 14 February 1873 as declaring that 'it was competent for the Council, by the terms of the Act of Union, to vote money to erect a Synagogue in a poor district where it was wanted, but certainly not to support a synagogue which all agreed was not wanted' – an obvious reference to the arguments over the future of the Hambro' and its threatened deficits; and he sponsored the appeal made on behalf of the congregation to the community at large. He was responsible for the raising at the consecration of the bulk of the balance needed to pay for the completion of the building, and it was he who ensured that the new congregation would become a constituent of the United Synagogue without a crushing burden of debt.

One of the arguments against the Bayswater enlargement had been that the bulk of those who would be accommodated by it would be just as well served by smaller establishments nearer to their own homes. It was as one result of that argument that the final collapse of the Bayswater scheme was accompanied by strong agitation for two new synagogues in its catchment area. The first of these to be opened was that in St John's Wood, which thus achieved the distinction of being the first constituent created and built as a constituent. The speed with which this congregation came into being is explained by the minute of the Executive Committee:[4]

The Executive Committee consider the new principle introduced by the Committee of the proposed Synagogue to be highly commendable. If the means were forthcoming it would undoubtedly be preferable at once to erect a permanent edifice; but the number of kindred claims concurrently pressing on the community is so great, that the modest plan of the Committee of St John's Wood is very praiseworthy. The iron structure proposed will be opened free from debt if the Council vote the sum of £1,000, and the founders hope, at a future period, to replace it by a permanent Synagogue.

The temporary structure was in use for only a few years, for in 1881 the United Synagogue was asked to provide the funds for a permanent structure. The basic principles were still being observed. A basic need was made evident, and the Council would respond to that need. The Council made a grant, but the balance had to be found from local sources. As Lionel Louis Cohen wrote in connection with the 1881 rebuilding scheme: 'the Executive Committee have anxiously desired that the building may be opened free from debt, so that the St John's Wood Synagogue may from its opening join in contributing to the relief of the ever-increasing Communal burdens.'[5] Since he was chairman of the sub-committee which had produced verdicts on the other synagogue building projects of this decade, his sentiments at this time may reasonably be taken as being those of his career in the United Synagogue.

The third synagogue resulting from the Bayswater agitation was for some time known as the Notting Hill Synagogue until it adopted the title of New West End, in St Petersburg Place. The Executive Committee report on this project throws considerable light on the way in which Lionel Louis Cohen and the rest of the Executive treated applicants, and this detail may also be connected with the prominent part played by Samuel Montagu in its foundation, and with the discontent revealed by the whole Bayswater controversy. The Executive showed itself very much alive to such problems as possible future needs of the building, the possible need for additional seating, and above all of the financial problems involved. Cohen wrote:[6]

The loan should be repaid by annual instalments, out of the surplus revenue accruing from the proposed Synagogue after payment of its local expenditure and of the Communal rate. It would be advisable to fix the amount of each obligatory annual repayment, retaining the power to increase the amount if the revenues of the new Synagogue should allow of such a course.

The Committee do not now propose any fixed annual sum to be applied in replacement of the stock sold out, nor do they recommend that any interest should be charged to the Constituent Synagogue in its local budget for the sum voted. There is, financially speaking, a wide distinction between advances made for the purpose of erecting Synagogues, and appropriations in redemption of annual existing charges on established Synagogues. The former, in their purpose of founding Synagogues, enlarge the already existing circle of congregants who contribute to the Communal burdens, and thus ultimately increase the stability of the institution; the latter, by commuting payments as convenience or exigency may require, do not lose or change their inherent character of burdens locally assumed, and chargeable as heretofore on the local budgets. But the principle of replacement of capital must nevertheless be inflexibly maintained; otherwise at the rate of decadence of its funded property in progress for the last twenty years, the United Synagogue will soon lose its power of aiding the religious movement of the community, and providing for its recurrent wants.

The building proved to be more costly than planned, costing £24,000 rather than £18,000, but the promoters raised more than had been promised, and in 1879 the New West End joined the United Synagogue, making up the *minyan* of constituents.

A last would-be synagogue was that proposed for Dalston. That project had first been discussed in May 1874, but the first formal application was made in the spring of 1876; it was considered by the same sub-committee considering the Notting Hill and North London projects. That comparison was not at all to the advantage of Dalston. The report cut the apparent pretensions of the promoters down to size, particularly concentrating on two points: the proposed financial basis of the congregation and the extent to which a demand had been made out. Its capital basis was particularly unsatisfactory: whereas other congregations had found two-thirds of the capital themselves, coming to the United Synagogue for only one-third, here the proportions had been completely reversed. Nor was the Committee willing to accept a situation where the financial balance necessary was achieved only because the first reader was to be paid an annual salary of £50. It was a constant feature of the Executive that although it never believed in princely salaries for ministers it refused to see the ecclesiastical officials underpaid. The report concluded:[7]

The Committee do not wish to deter the promoters of the Dalston Synagogue from every expectation of success. From the first inception of the idea that a Synagogue is necessary, to the period of its erection, a period of at least three years usually elapses. The present application from Dalston appears somewhat premature, and the Committee consider that at a future time, when the arrangements of the Committee are more matured, their prospects more defined, and the pecuniary support they have secured more commensurate with their undertaking, and when they can show more obviously than they have done at present the necessity for the establishment of a Synagogue, their application may be renewed, and that it will then meet with that consideration and encouragement at the hands of the Council which the establishment of a Synagogue always demands and receives.

The application was renewed in 1881, when the Council recorded that circumstances had changed as a result of the greatly enlarged Jewish population in the district; the Council welcomed the prospect of the new congregation, and in 1885 Dalston was formally admitted as the eleventh constituent synagogue.

It becomes clear, then, that the pattern was standard. The United Synagogue itself did not initiate any demand for a synagogue, nor indeed even suggest that a synagogue ought to be created in order to fill any presumed religious need. The initiative came from local residents who decided themselves that a need was already there and that there was a chance of a viable congregation – viable, that is, in terms of both religious and financial responsibilities. Having done so, these leaders turned to the United Synagogue to discover what help could be afforded or even, as in the case of the future Dalston congregation, for some suggestions as to the next step. Only then did the officers of the United Synagogue take any official part in the discussions, and their first endeavour was always to check the financial aspects of the new congregation. The story of these synagogues points certainly to the conclusion that there was never any suggestion of the recognition of a 'deficit' congregation, but that all were intended to be 'surplus' from the outset. The long and tangled history of the Hambro' would serve to emphasise this. The problems of the Hambro' stem from well before the foundation of the United Synagogue; so far was its future in doubt that the delegates recognised the possibility of its closure and bound themselves in those circumstances to transfer its name to the first synagogue to be founded after such closure took place. It has already been shown how a resolution to that effect was formally written into the minutes of the first Council meeting after the initial elections. There were several occasions when the condition of the Hambro' – physical, spiritual, and financial alike – gave cause for concern. In January 1872 the Treasurers refused to accept the draft budget of that synagogue and invited a general meeting of its members to consider the financial and structural condition of their building, extensive repairs being then necessary and the synagogue unable to bear the burden itself. But the projected amalgamation of the Beth Hamedrash with the Hambro' delayed any further consideration of the closure, and a series of loans from individual members of the community, including Samuel Montagu, led to the pressures for closure being diminished. In 1876 the seatholders held a meeting at which the synagogue's closure was actually approved, but a subsequent meeting, held as the Act laid down, disapproved of the closure by two votes. Each year the Treasurers had to draw attention to some deficiency or backsliding of the synagogue. It was rare, for example, for the synagogue to meet its full quota of communal burdens, while one way in which it made sure that there was no deficit on the year's workings was by a failure to pay its reader a sufficient salary. Almost every year the Council had to vote an additional sum of £100 to the unfortunate Reverend Gollancz, and in 1874 the Treasurers had to draw specific attention to this.[8] 'Notwithstanding its inability to contribute its fair proportion of the Communal burdens, the Treasurers are unable to endorse the recommendation that its principal officer should be inadequately remunerated for his services, which are admitted to be efficiently performed', and they proceeded to recommend the payment of an additional sum over and above the synagogue's own budget. In January 1877 the Treasurers recorded that the voluntary offerings during the year had considerably exceeded the receipts from taxation and seat rentals, and paid tribute to the 'open-handedness and generosity which was evinced by the Members of the Hambro' Synagogue in support of their place of worship'. As a result, when in March 1880 the Executive was directed by the Council 'to consider the present Financial Condition of the Hambro' Synagogue, and the desirability of its maintenance as a Place of Worship; and to report to the Council', the Council was bluntly informed that 'the conditions under which a Synagogue may be compulsorily closed by the Council do not exist'.[9] Even though it was by far the smallest of the constituent synagogues, with a budget in hundreds rather than in thousands, none the less it remained marginally viable. Had it not been regarded as such it would undoubtedly have been closed.

At all events financial pressures on the United Synagogue had shown themselves to be mounting, and the demand for sinking funds and for the creation of adequate financial reserves for future action show up as part of this. The overall financial position was certainly far from adequate, and the financial reports in the 1880s show continual warnings, further evidence, if it were needed, that each congregation was expected to maintain its own solvency. It was not, however, the need for solvency which made the United Synagogue turn down various requests for affiliation made to it. At various stages in the first two decades of its existence approaches were made by various provincial communities for some degree of co-operation. Dover asked for financial help, Leeds and Oxford asked to be allowed to join as constituent members, Falmouth asked the United Synagogue to take over as trustee of its properties lest there be no trustee at all of its possessions, and Middlesbrough asked the United Synagogue to take over its properties in order to prevent arguments among the various congregations there which had agreed to unite. To all these pleas the answer remained unvarying: the United Synagogue was a union of London congregations and it was not able to participate in the affairs of congregations outside the metropolis. Pressures in and from London were enough so far as the United Synagogue leaders were concerned, even had the Act permitted them to look further afield.

These pressures were not altogether financial, although the request by the trustees of the Beth Hamedrash for that institution to be absorbed within the United Synagogue had a great deal to do with the problems of financing that institution. There was the growing realisation in London that in matters affecting the wellbeing of London Jewry there was a special responsibility resting on the United Synagogue. In nothing was this shown more clearly than in the enquiry instituted by the United Synagogue into Jews' College and the training of future Jewish ministers.[10] The enquiry was certainly brought about in part for financial reasons. Jews' College had requested the continuation of a subvention hitherto paid to it, and the request then precipitated a general enquiry into the subject of 'the training of Jewish ministers'. The Committee restricted itself 'to the pulpit'; they 'endeavoured simply to point out a means whereby "Rabbi Preachers" will be provided, gentlemen who will be, at least, on the level educationally of their flock, who will be able to teach them the essentials of their faith, and who have the knowledge requisite for strengthening them in their religious belief.' The Committee saw quite clearly the various problems which faced the community. It objected to a Theological College as adopted by other denominations.

It is somewhat too monastic in principle to commend itself to Jewish sympathies, and it has the further drawback, besides that of cost, that the students are apt to become simply bookworms, without that knowledge of the world and its ways which is essential for their sacred calling.

On the other hand there was a need not

> to subject the Community to the dangerous hazard of drawing, from the Jewish public, men who may feel no calling for the profession which perhaps the poverty of parents in the first instance selected for them; men, who though highly gifted, may be otherwise totally unfitted for the proper discharge of the onerous functions of a Jewish minister, who may be good classic scholars, and know nothing of Hebrew literature or of Jewish theology, or who on the other hand, may be ripe Rabbinical 'schoolmen', but whose secular knowledge is deficient. Nor should the growing and advancing English community be dependent on extraneous sources for its Clergymen, who might in those circumstances be eminent Hebraists, but utterly ignorant of the vernacular.

The matter was not a purely theoretical problem; in November 1884 the New Synagogue, in asking permission to fill a vacancy of reader, specifically asked that the normal requirement of a knowledge of English be dispensed with in order to secure a better class of candidate. The United Synagogue Committee of Enquiry into Jews' College urged on the Council the need to support the activities of Jews' College; on the other hand it was reluctant to create a fund to offer subventions to students or augment salaries, this not being 'consonant with public policy': 'the Council in its corporate capacity could not call on the seatholders of its Constituent Synagogues to tax themselves, in order that Provincial Congregations may be relieved of their duties'. Some aspects of the report still ring true, and offer a basis for some aspects of Jewish humour. In reply to the question 'Are there any special circumstances in connection with the Orthodox Jewish practice which prevent members of the upper or middle-class from becoming candidates for the Jewish Ministry?' the Council of Jews' College replied:

> The simple and obvious reason which discourages members of the upper and middle-class from embracing the clerical career is the want of sufficient inducement. A Jewish youth, after long years spent in labour and study for the acquisition of the knowledge necessary for the Ministry, can aspire to no fortune, but at best, when successful, must be

content to run a course which offers scarcely any prizes, living on a bare pittance and bearing a grave moral responsibility. It is no wonder if a Jewish youth possessing some means and education, prefers one of the many professions open to him, which hold out inducements and attractions not to be found in the clerical or tutorial career.

However, one of the great pressures on the Council of the United Synagogue was not financial at all. Society was changing, and Jewish society was changing too. The Act had continued distinctions within the United Synagogue which were already being eroded in the constituent synagogues, and which indeed had already come under pressure during the negotiations leading to the formation of the United Synagogue itself. Privileged membership was no longer acceptable to the bulk of the membership of the United Synagogue and it came constantly under fire both in the press and in the Council itself. The first reaction of the press, and presumably the bulk of the United Synagogue leadership, was that of maintaining the distinction between privileged and non-privileged membership. On 2 December 1870 the *Jewish Chronicle* declared:

> A community like ours requires *invested capital* to support its institutions; especially to support its synagogues which ought not to depend on ephemeral contributions. Heaven forbid! Hence the obtaining of privileged members is a great advantage to those seat holders who are not privileged members, and who profit, in fact, by the investment and sunken capital of the privileged members. These surely are entitled to see advantages for their sacrifice of means. And he who shows his love of his synagogue by permanently endowing it, so as to help to maintain it; who proves his attachment for his congregation by permanently benefitting it; is just the man most fitted to protect the fabric of that synagogue and to represent the interests of that congregation.

In 1871 the *Jewish Chronicle* was still opposing the abolition of privileged membership because of the financial losses which such an abolition would entail. But thereafter the pressure for abolition grew steadily and the institution became almost indefensible following on the admission of the Borough and then the North London Synagogues. These synagogues made the request that all their seatholders, both then and in the future, should automatically become privileged members. The United Synagogue Council was unable to accept this, and was prepared only to permit all those who were seatholders at the time of union to become automatically privileged members. These vast expansions, however, made it impossible to differentiate between the two categories, and the attack upon its continued existence began not only in the Council of the United Synagogue but in the synagogues as well, especially in the Great Synagogue. In 1873, 1874, and 1875 the matter was raised in the Council and although in February 1874 the Executive Committee declared itself against changing privileged membership, by 1877 the Executive Committee had fully agreed to its abolition.

The reasons which induced this change of mind were fully set out in the report drawn up by Maurice Hart and presented in June 1877 to the Executive Committee.

It is difficult to decide with any certainty the objects which our predecessors had in mind when framing the distinction in question. The conditions of society were then widely different to those now existing, and probably it was intended to secure a governing class, consisting of those persons who . . . were 'masters of houses', described as 'domiciled in the Country', and having some social standing. That this governing class should in the process of time have constituted themselves a privileged class was, perhaps, a natural sequence of events. . . .

An investigation into the working of the present system leaves no doubt that much of these objects is now secured, that its maintenance will involve a gross injustice, and that at least equally advantageous financial results can be secured by much less objectionable means.

It is not pretended that the fact of being a Privileged Member is now any evidence of respectability. The indiscriminate admission of entire Congregations would of itself be a refutation of any such pretension. . . . It becomes, therefore, both just and necessary that our laws should be altered to meet the exigencies of the development and growth of the Union.

The report also went on not only to discuss the financial implications of the abolition – the annual levy of a sum ranging from one to three shillings on the seat rental of members – but also other more minor changes which experience had shown were needed in the structure of the union.

Once again changes took time. It was not until 2 July 1878 that the Council agreed to the changes, and not until December 1878 that Lionel Louis Cohen reported on the necessary procedure. It was decided to summon a special delegate meeting of the constituent synagogues as laid down in clause 67 of the Act of Union, and in 1880 this meeting fully approved the changes. These changes represented in practice, however, not merely a growing dislike of the old privileges and distinctions but more significantly a putting of greater authority into the hands of the governing body, now no longer officially the 'Vestry'. Various anomalies were dealt with; it was made clear, for example, that no one could hold elected office unless he was not only a full-price seat member but also not in arrears with his subscription. The most significant change was that the power to elect all of the salaried officers of the United Synagogue, other than the Chief Rabbi himself (who of course was not elected by the United Synagogue at all), was to be vested in the United Synagogue Council and not a meeting of the seatholders of all the constituent synagogues, while the Council was also given power to expel members. The effect was to put much more power into the hands of the Council as a body, and, in effect, into the hands of the Executive Committee. That was the more warranted since the Executive Committee during this first decade had shown itself fully capable of guiding and controlling the decisions of the Council of the United Synagogue.

These details might all seem, perhaps, pettifogging; administration would seem to have become bogged down in details of interest to the antiquarian rather than the historian or analyst of quasi-public bodies. But in fact they are of considerably more interest than appears on the surface. Gradually, at a time of a slow expansion of London Jewish life and numbers, the new body had begun to assume responsibilities and to lay down guidelines which were to be vital to future generations. Fundamental to that future was the entire attitude to synagogue building and expansion. The only effective organ of Jewish public opinion, the *Jewish Chronicle*, under the guidance of its energetic editor Michael Henry, had continually urged the United Synagogue not to restrict itself to the main concerns of the few constituent synagogues of the first foundation, but to expand its activities for the service of a growing community. It was the *Jewish Chronicle* that urged the United Synagogue to take an initiative in setting up new synagogues and indeed to build them not merely in London but in the provinces as well. Part of that advice was taken, although the United Synagogue maintained continually that it was not permitted to extend outside London. But there were other issues in these years, issues of debate with the Chief Rabbi, issues of debate with the other institutions of London Jewry, such as with the Board of Guardians, with the Board of Deputies, with the other synagogues, and with such bodies as those responsible for provision of matzoth and flour at Passover. The picture that emerges from these activities is not unlike the parallel one in contemporary English life.

This was the period of the Joseph Chamberlains, the period of the successful businessmen facing new social issues and putting their business experience to the service of their community. In Jewish life the experience of the Rothschilds, the Cohens, and the Montagus was vital for the continued extension of the community whose members, often enough near the poverty line, needed the financial acumen and direct support of these 'Grand Dukes'. The reports of the Visitation Committee, the Passover Matzoth and Flour Committee, and the Committee of Poverty reflect very strongly Victorian self-help attitudes. There was a report on Passover help which could well have emerged from the non-Jewish Poor Law Commissioners in an advocacy of self-help and the setting up of a friendly society for the financing of Passover flour distribution. Yet this was not an attitude which the Jewish recipients themselves resented; the Reverend Stallard's famous report on the poor of London[11] showed how the self-help of the Jewish Board of Guardians reflected the desires of the poor themselves.

There were in these years men without vision, competent administrators and men of business, on the committees of the United Synagogue. There were also men with considerable talent and acumen, men who knew what they wanted for the Jewish community and had no compunction about forcing those ideas on their colleagues. In these years these were the men, like Lionel Louis Cohen and Asher Asher, who ran the United Synagogue, and ultimately it was the character of these men who framed the organisation of the United Synagogue and made it strong enough to withstand the strains of the closing years of the nineteenth century.

CHAPTER 3

THE FINANCIAL STRUCTURE

The annual budgets and financial statements of the Treasurers even from the earliest years throw a great deal of light on the development of the United Synagogue. Obviously they can tell only a part of the whole story, since they are concerned only with sources of income and expenditure, yet even that part is central to the whole story since, as was emphasised over and over again, an essential factor bringing about the union had been the desire to bring all the financial resources of the individual synagogues together for the benefit of the whole London Jewish community. The early budgets are far from clear, and it is never very certain from the annual reports whether in fact, by standards of modern accounting, the United Synagogue 'broke even' on each year's operations. It was not until 1880 that Asher Asher had the accounts drawn up to include a summary of the overall expenditure and income of both the United Synagogue and the individual constituent synagogues. But even from the beginning the Treasurers felt bound to draw attention to the increased expenditure. After only one full year's operation they declared in 1872:[1]

> In their opinion the Council is not at present financially in a position to sanction any additional expenditure from income. The demands upon the resources of the United Synagogue are very unlikely to become diminished; and as the community becomes rapidly spread over various parts of the metropolis (its decentralisation involving increased expenditure for the establishment and maintenance of places for public worship) the most rigid economy, combined, however, with proper and efficient conduct of the internal affairs of the constituent Synagogues, will have to be observed.

The United Synagogue had already assumed additional responsibilities – such as hospital and prison visitation – which all, including the Treasurers, accepted as rightly falling within the desirable activities of the new institution. The assumption of these burdens did not preclude the Treasurers, therefore, from urging in almost every one of their reports the need to enlarge the basis of the United Synagogue by increasing the numbers of seatholders (and thus those paying seat rentals and contributions to the communal burdens) and by reducing the 'unnecessary' expenditure.

> As yet, there does not appear, unfortunately, to be any diminution in the number of Charity Funerals, although, with a view of placing Paid Funerals more within the means of the poorer classes (by bringing into practice what are termed 'Second Class Funerals'), the charges have been considerably reduced, this in many cases possibly obviating the necessity of recourse being had to charity, and promoting independence and self-reliance. It is to be regretted that so little aversion is shown by so many of the humbler classes to a Charity Funeral, and it is difficult to believe that the necessity exists for the numbers that have taken place . . . the earnest attention of the Burial Committee should continuously be given to this subject.

To the Treasurers the most unsatisfactory aspect of the general situation was the inadequate provision made for central burdens. When the Borough Synagogue was brought into the United Synagogue its budget was immediately debited with a tax of 30 per cent on the seat rentals, and the Treasurers brought pressure through the Finance Committee and the Executive on the various constituents to equalise rates of communal taxation on each of its members. The need for this taxation was made clear by the Treasurers when they pointed out, for example, in 1873 that whereas the net communal income was £1,938 the expenditure was rather more than £8,800, so that the constituent synagogues would have to find £6,727. The request for this equalisation of taxation was agreed to, but in fact two further questions came rapidly to the fore.

The first of these related to the extent of local control over local budgets. Even when the original terms of the amalgamation were under discussion some alteration had had to be made in order to give more freedom to boards of management, and in February 1878 the Executive was asked by the Council to consider and report on the possibilities of giving even more power to the constituent synagogues over items of local expenditure. That committee was unable to formulate anything, and the question was dropped. Two years earlier the Council had already taken up disquiet expressed by the Treasurers and appointed a sub-committee to report on whether any alterations in the financial regulations were desirable. Nothing, however, had been agreed to and no report had ever been made.

In their report for 1880 the Treasurers specifically raised the whole issue of the financial basis of the United Synagogue, turning to the general capital position as well as the basis of the various budgets of the constituent synagogues. On the first they pointed out how year after year considerable amounts of capital had had to be 'sold out' without any adequate provision being made for replacement; whatever was being paid back was done over such a long period of time that the chances of the United Synagogue's being able to meet a continuous series of demands for capital advances were not very good. On the second, however, they pointed to the summary of revenue and expenditure included for the first time and to the implications which they could perceive. Their report stated the position clearly and concisely in words which could have been repeated many times over:

> The Treasurers look with anything but complaisance on a condition of things which shows a gain, on an income of £22,700, of only £126. 0. 9d. It is true that the General Balance Sheet shows expenditure for a few items which were never thought of, and would have been impossible, when the Synagogues stood alone; and some of these items, such as that for the care of children in Reformatories, reflect the highest credit on the United Synagogue, which assumes charity and philanthropy as one of its most important and sacred duties. Nevertheless, it is clear that if the Synagogues were not amalgamated, their respective Boards of Management would look with something akin to dismay to an aggregate Balance, for the whole of them, of only £126. 0. 9d. There seems to be no doubt that the present system of book-keeping engenders in the Local Synagogue a false notion of financial security, brought about by the erroneous idea that the surplus shown at the end of the year in the Local Accounts is an *absolute* surplus, to be looked on as actual profit; and no note is taken of the fact that from these surpluses there must be paid all those items of communal expenditure which, prior to the amalgamation, were a charge upon and appeared in the local Balance Sheets.

The Treasurers went on to enlarge upon the effects of assessing each synagogue for repairs, upkeep of cemeteries, and a *pro rata* charge for communal expenditure. They even went so far as to charge each of the constituents with the appropriate share of capital repayments for those sums which had had to be advanced for initial building.

The Synagogues are held by the Council for the purposes and requirements of the worshippers only, and cannot, under any circumstances, be diverted by the Council from these purposes. Practically, therefore, they are the property of the Local bodies who use them; and in the event of the capital which they cost being required, however urgently, for other Communal purposes, it could not be realised.

On this new basis only four out of the ten synagogues were in surplus.

The following year the Treasurers repeated their warning. The same synagogues were in deficit as before, and the Treasurers reminded the Council that 'if these Synagogues stood alone, and under the same conditions of expenditure as are prescribed by the Act, namely, the support of the poor and contributions for general Communal purposes, they simply could not keep their doors open'. The Treasurers were even more alarmed by the fact that it was those very synagogues who were in deficit who were increasing their demands on the general funds of the United Synagogue.

By January 1886 the situation had become very serious, and the Treasurers wrote in measured terms in their report:

The Treasurers observe, with profound regret, that the financial prospects for 1886 are no better than the actuality was in 1885, and that, even by adopting the course pursued in that year of not funding anything towards the recoupment of Stock, there will again be a deficit at the end of the year. In the opinion of the Treasurers there is considerable extravagance in the outlay of the Local Synagogues, especially with regard to Choirs and Minyan Men; on the former item £1,885 was expended in the past year, and on the latter item £701. It is suggested that were the Synagogues to agree to have their Choirs trained together under one Choir Master, a great saving might be effected in this item. As to the Minyan Men, the Treasurers have more than once pointed out the absurdity of paying an individual to read prayers and paying others to come to listen to him. Were the attendance of the Salaried Officers at Synagogues more uniformly regular, the services of many of the Minyan Men might be dispensed with. As an instance, the Central Synagogue employs a Preacher, two Readers, two Beadles, and eight Minyan Men. Furthermore, the whole of the financial system of the United Synagogue seems to want revision. There should be regulations whereby the Local Synagogues' liability for Communal charges should be more clearly brought home to them than is the case at present; whereby Local Expenditure should be confined within a definite proportion of Local Income; and whereby some check should be placed upon the facility with which sums are voted by the Council. As the Treasurers have remarked in a previous Report, the Revenue side of the Synagogue's account seems for the present to have reached its utmost limit, while the Expenditure is an unknown quantity, boundless and ever increasing.

The Treasurers recommend that a Special Committee be appointed to consider and report on the Financial arrangements of the Synagogue.

The *Jewish Chronicle* on 29 January 1886 took up the Treasurers' report, less concerned about the details of the deficit – the Treasurers, it was agreed, had cried 'wolf' too often – than about the general relation between the centralised organisation of the United Synagogue and its constituent synagogues. It was clear that financial problems alone were not the only troubles bedevilling the United Synagogue. The editorial continued:

The General Council holds far too tight a grasp, too minute a scrutiny, over expenditure by the local Boards of Management and at the same time holds out no premium whatever to economical management. The Bayswater Synagogue, for instance, one of the main props of the Union, has to follow exactly the same procedure, say to obtain a trivial addition to the wages of its doorkeeper, as the Hambro' Synagogue with a large financial deficit and constituting a heavy financial burden despite the oft-repeated expressions of opinion by the Council that it should be closed. The whole question of the financial relations of the Constituent Synagogues to the general body must be reconsidered with a view to their equitable adjustment. It is intolerable that a manifestly partial and inequitable system should be continued merely owing to technical difficulties in modifying it.

The Council took the Treasurers' warning, and set up a committee to 'consider and report on the Financial arrangements of the United and Constituent synagogues'.

The preliminary report of the sub-committee was discussed by the Council in April 1886. The sub-committee had agreed on the general principles which it felt ought to guide their conclusions and therefore wished to have the opinion of the Council. The first of these guidelines was that after each synagogue had made due provision for general purposes, for local salaries, and for 'such other local expenses as the United Synagogue may be directly responsible for', whatever balance existed should thereafter be left to local control 'although such a measure is not in agreement with the financial arrangements under which the affairs of the United Synagogue have hitherto been administered'. In discussion an amendment was moved in direct contradiction, this recommendation being 'directly at variance with the recognised principle upon which the amalgamation of the synagogues is based, viz. using the surpluses of the strong for the assistance of the weaker congregations, and for other desirable purposes'. Only five voted for this amendment. The second of the guidelines was that proposals for meeting the deficiency of any synagogue from the general account should be put forward and voted on each year.

The report from the special committee, written largely by Lionel Louis Cohen, went fully into the financial situation, and it was adopted with comparatively little change. It laid down the details of the financial structure of the United Synagogue as it was to endure until after the First World War. The basic problem, as the Treasurers and Committee saw it, was the decline of that part of the income available for current expenditure; the opening of new synagogues had diverted revenue from the older congregations into the appropriated payment of salaries and repayment of debenture debt. The Treasurers not only saw the problem clearly enough but could also suggest a diagnosis.[2]

8. It is obvious that any substantial financial reform should be of a thorough nature, and should attain two objects; one, that of giving the Synagogues independent control over their miscellaneous local requirements, which, under the present system, have to be reviewed annually in the budgets by the Finance Committee and by the Council; and on the other, that of securing the Council from the consequences of passing Budgets without adequate means of meeting the requirements thereof. The process of selling Stock or of borrowing money to meet the exigencies of current expenditure must evidently have a proximate termination.

9. At the same time it is necessary that any new system should bring clearly under the notice of each Synagogue the burdens which it has to bear as a constituent of the general community, including communal duties to those Synagogues the resources of which are insufficient for their requirements, and which it is yet thought desirable to maintain; and including also the duty of assisting in the establishment of

Synagogues in London, in districts where Synagogue accommodation is required, but in which the inhabitants are unable to provide the necessary means. . . .

13. . . . the projected Scheme of course showed, as every scheme which combines the local and general obligations of each Synagogue in one view must show, that the deficiency which had existed for several years in the working of some of the Synagogues would be revealed as soon as their proportion of communal burdens was brought into their balance sheets.

The Treasurers recognised that a synagogue might well be in deficit for one of two reasons. It could well be the result of the inability of a constituent synagogue to pay all those charges regarded as 'primary' charges, or else because the synagogue had been too extravagant. It was the latter that the scheme was intended to curb, by giving all the other synagogues the opportunity of making observations on these expenditures.

20. . . . It cannot be considered otherwise than reasonable that where the requirements of any of the constituent Synagogues have to be met by an assessment on their sister Congregations, those Synagogues should have a direct voice in voting the expenditure for which they become responsible. This provision does not in any way place a Synagogue in a worse position than it is in at the present time. Every item of expenditure is now voted upon, and it is claimed as one of the merits of the present scheme that it affords a distinct premium to good and economical administration, and also holds out a tangible stimulus to the public spirit of the members of each Synagogue, inasmuch as by shaping their requirements in accordance with their means, they can at once escape from the examination of such requirements by any other body than their own local Board of Management, while at the same time Synagogues the financial position of which might temporarily be unsatisfactory will still be able to be strengthened by others more favourably circumstanced, and thus one of the main objects of the original founders of the Union will be preserved.

Changes were also to be made in the treatment of capital debt repayments, since surplus revenue was to be left to individual synagogues and thus not necessarily available to the Council as a replacement for the stocks previously sold out by order of the Council. When this part of the report was debated in the Council, opposition concentrated on the way in which, it was alleged, burdens would be shifted within the United Synagogue. Samuel Montagu argued against the idea that the richer synagogues should be allowed to retain some part of their surplus at the expense of those synagogues with deficits, managing at the same time to champion the cause of greater autonomy and the idea of transferring all surpluses from the richer synagogues for the benefit of those with deficits. He moved, unsuccessfully, that synagogues labouring under deficits should not be placed under special restrictions so long as their deficits were not increased. The brief report in the *Jewish Chronicle* on 15 October 1886 made quite clear the bitterness of the debate, commenting on how the Chairman 'peremptorily declined' to put one motion, and reported: 'a vote of thanks to the Chair concluded the proceedings which occasionally partook of a painfully recriminating character (as to "setting class against class" and "endeavouring to buy cheap popularity") between the noble Chairman and Mr. S. Montagu, M.P.'. The following week it publicly regretted the tone in which the discussions had been conducted.

The second section of the report marked an attempt to increase revenue. One way was to collect outstanding debts – unpaid synagogue accounts had reached the figure of £4,712; another was a more intensive canvass of potential members; and a third was an invitation to offer donations, to be sent to various relatives on occasions of family rejoicing or mourning. An attempt at increasing charges on female seatholders had to be dropped. Lastly, the Committee alluded to various causes of increased expenditure, and repeated earlier comments made by the Treasurers on such issues as paid *minyan* men – 'objectionable on religious grounds' – and professional choirs. More important was their comment on the maintenance of existing synagogues:

> If it is to be considered, it ought to be dealt with separately. The Committee, however, unanimously record their opinion that no religious purpose is served by the maintenance of several Synagogues within a very short distance of each other, there being ample accommodation for the worshippers without keeping up each separate establishment.

Almost immediately the new arrangements began to show results. There were increases in local revenues and reductions in local expenditures, so that by February 1888 only five of the synagogues were in deficit[3] and six showed surpluses.[4] The Treasurers in 1886 reported complacently that those synagogues with a surplus were husbanding their resources while many with deficits were trying to turn themselves into surplus synagogues. As they further reported in 1891, the new system had put the general financial position on a solid foundation.

> It has, moreover, enabled the local Boards of Management to exercise a direct control over their individual finances, and has removed that unseemly scramble for funds which was exercised alike by prosperous and unprosperous Synagogues and formed the usual accompaniment of Budget night at the Council.

The financial situation, as far as income and expenditure were concerned, had indeed been remedied by the new financial resolutions, and very small surpluses or deficits were replaced by a series of substantial balances on general account. None the less the improvement in itself was comparatively short-lived, once again deficits began to appear, and by 1910 the Treasurers were again sounding a note of alarm.

> The amount of the deficiency is one that calls for serious attention, and the Treasurers feel that the time is ripe – even if it is not long overdue – for the Council to deal with this deficit in its financial arrangements of the Synagogues. That some Synagogues must be carried on at a loss is undoubtedly unavoidable – it is the spirit in which the Union was formed that the wealthier bodies should come to the relief of the poorer ones – but it was never contemplated that such large individual deficits . . . should be allowed to accrue. And there seems a disposition on the part of deficit Synagogues to pile up expenditure upon expenditure without a thought as to the effect of their demands upon other Synagogues which are called upon to furnish the means. The sense of responsibility and self-reliance is destroyed by having a general fund to draw upon to make good deficiencies, and the Treasurers feel that some scheme might be devised for limiting Local Requirements to a fixed proportion of the income of the Synagogue concerned. Such a system would bring home to the Boards of Management the fact that expenditure could not be incurred without the means available for meeting it, and might be a stimulus for increasing Local Revenue.

Less easily solved, even on a short-term basis, was to be the capital basis of the United Synagogue. The United Synagogue had begun its corporate existence in 1870 with a funded property of £39,169, and in its first few years it had husbanded its resources carefully. When, for example, the ground for the Willesden Cemetery had been purchased, a large proportion of the capital required had been raised by direct application to the Jewish public, and it has already been shown how the first additional synagogues were largely free of capital debt on their admission as constituent synagogues. But there had been a change, and the Council had become more lavish in agreeing to sell out stock in order to finance various capital works. By 1890 the capital available had sunk to £29,498; there had been total sales of over £50,000, of which a reasonable proportion had been replaced over the years. More significantly, however, a total of £30,980 had been lent to various synagogues, of which £22,816 was outstanding. As the Treasurers pointed out, 'at the present rate of recoupment, the amount outstanding will not be liquidated within a period of about 25 years'. The dangers of an unchecked capital decline were clearly indicated. A reduction in the funded property meant a reduction in investment income on the general revenue of the United Synagogue 'and a proportionate increase of assessments upon the Constituent Synagogues for communal purposes'. There was also a more serious pointer to the future.

> With the large increase of population, and the continual migration of families to the extreme outward limits of the Metropolis, it is certain that applications for assistance to found new Synagogues will from time to time be made, and it is therefore of paramount importance that the Funded Property should be jealously guarded and preserved, so that when such applications are received the Council may be in a position to deal with them in the same just and liberal spirit as they have heretofore dealt with similar cases.

This problem of depletion of capital was one which became even more pressing with the great expansion between the wars, and later of course was to dominate not merely building policies but also day-to-day activities.

CHAPTER 4

THE FOUNDING FATHERS

The basic characteristic of the United Synagogue has always been the way in which it has reflected the strengths of the men who created it and then ran it. This has indeed been true of it over the century since it came into being. While it would not be true that the history of the institution could be written solely in terms of its honorary officers and its full-time administrative staff, their influence has always been outstanding, and that is particularly true of these early years when, as has been shown, no one was certain of why it had ever come into being. The formal circumstances of the union have already been analysed, and the mechanics of that union discussed, but there was something more to the creation of the new body, and for an understanding of that the personalities and backgrounds of the founding fathers are all-important.

The leading character among these 'fathers' was, as already demonstrated, Lionel Louis Cohen. Like many others prominent in London Jewish life in the second half of the nineteenth century he was a descendant of Levi Barent Cohen who had settled in London at the end of the eighteenth century, and was a prominent member of the so-called Cousinhood. Much has been written about the 'Grand Dukes' of Anglo-Jewry, but it was to be a factor of the greatest importance that the early leaders of the United Synagogue were nearly all to come from this narrow circle. It was not merely that they were all known to each other nor even that they were nearly all related. Indeed it was not even the fact that they all came from a particular group of London Jewish society that was important. What was extremely significant was that leadership in this first generation of the United Synagogue was in the hands of people accustomed to meeting informally at social gatherings as well as at the official meetings of the various committees and voluntary organisations in which they were involved, in the hands of people who had certain basic common assumptions about what they and their associates wanted in their religious organisations, and, above all, in the hands of people accustomed to making decisions in family and commercial concerns without having those decisions come under the scrutiny of many others. Lionel Louis Cohen was born in 1832 and entered the family firm of bankers and Stock Exchange members. He eventually became senior partner in the firm, entered politics – but as a Conservative, unlike others in his family who were strongly Liberals – and speedily gained a reputation in Parliament as an undoubted expert on financial and commercial matters. During his short time in politics he served on two Royal Commissions and an important Select Committee, so that his premature death at fifty-five stopped short what would have been an outstanding political career. By the age of twenty-eight he had already played a prominent part in the formation of the Board of Guardians of which he was the Honorary Secretary, and he had already become a leading figure among the leaders of the Great Synagogue. Some of his activities there – his part in the abortive negotiations for union with the Hambro' Synagogue and the special treaty with the North London Synagogue – have already been mentioned, and they go far towards indicating the tremendous activity and energy that seems to have characterised him. The obituary printed in the *Jewish Chronicle* makes this point clear, in dealing with his involvement over the foundation of the United Synagogue.[1]

Mr Cohen entered into the work with heart and soul, and an inspection of the documents relating to the proposed scheme will show how thoroughly he made the work his own. There is hardly a paper that does not bear notes in his handwriting and every report has his signature. At the memorable meeting held on 19th April 1868 [the meeting in the Great to approve the Union] . . . Mr Cohen proposed the first resolution embodying the principle of the Union. Those present at the meeting will recall how telling and convincing was Mr Cohen's speech. . . . It was Mr Cohen's tact and judgement – combined with the late Jacob Waley's legal experience and wise council – that carried the scheme through the opposition raised before the Charity Commissioners. . . . So indefatigable was he in doing work for the Congregation that it was a matter of frequent occurrence for him to leave a meeting of the Synagogue at eleven o'clock at night, and to forward by the first post the following morning 8 or 10 folios of closely written manuscript on the subject of that meeting.

Once the United Synagogue had been set up it was Lionel Louis Cohen who became the Chairman of the Executive Committee, and the records of Committee and Council meetings show over and over again how firmly he held the reins of power. Whenever there were particularly important decisions to be made by individual committees he was to be found present, often indeed invited to take the chair, and always ensuring that the 'right' decision was made in the way he thought best. Over and over again it was the imprint of his personality which marked out these early years; it was for example Lionel Cohen who drew up the first set of by-laws for the United Synagogue, as it was he who insisted that before any new synagogue could be brought into the United Synagogue it had to have sound finances and above all had to have paid off its foundation debt. It was under these circumstances that he brought the Borough and North London Synagogues into the union. But it was equally characteristic of him that he realised the unlikelihood of the East London Synagogue's ever managing to achieve this on its own account, even though a new synagogue in Stepney was absolutely essential. Accordingly he threw himself into the task of raising the money from the community at large, and always felt he had an especial tie with that synagogue. An anecdote after his death related that 'on several occasions, after the opening of the synagogue, Mr Cohen rode on horseback to the early week-day services and proceeded thence direct to his office in the City'.[2]

He has been described elsewhere as one of the great organisers of Anglo-Jewry,[3] and this was beyond all doubt true. But he was more than that. He possessed scholarship – he wrote long, learned, and anonymous articles in the *Jewish Chronicle* – and above all a burning commitment to involve himself personally, so that, for example, he not only played a prominent part in organising special services in the Jews' Free School over the High Holydays for those who could not find places in the synagogues of the United Synagogue but he also spent his time there as a warden in preference to attending at his own synagogue. His feeling for the community went even deeper, and justified the verdict that 'no one man among his contemporaries has left so deep an impress of his personality upon the inner life of the Anglo-Jewish body'. He was all too aware of the continual problem – even then – in the Anglo-Jewish community, a problem which was to be re-enunciated by a later member of his family. He wrote in 1878: 'I confess as I grow older I sometimes feel

48

anxious as to who will take up our hard dry and monotonous work, which indeed makes no stir and evokes little enthusiasm.' The need to find successors to carry on the administration of London Jewry was one to which he frequently returned; his obituarist recorded one of his comments: 'I want to make our community as an Englishman thinks his nation has been made, by teaching them how to govern themselves.'[4] In fact, of course, there are many close parallels to Lionel Cohen in the 'host community'. In personality very close to, say, the successful second-generation businessman of the calibre of Joseph Chamberlain, he wished to see the qualities which had enabled him to succeed in business applied to different activities. Educated privately, he had still managed to assume the characteristics of the native-born English gentleman, his effortless superiority and his assumptions that his own will was significant. And if he was right, if in fact the United Synagogue did reflect his desires and ambitions for it, that is an even surer indication of the way in which he had applied the *mores* of English upper-class society to this very un-English set of institutions.

Associated with him, of course, were men like Sir Anthony de Rothschild and his nephew, Nathaniel, the first Lord Rothschild. Despite their rank as Presidents, they were very much nominal figures, brought into the arena only when their immediate involvement was essential, or felt to be so by the Chairman of the Executive Committee. For much of this first century the President of the United Synagogue was not so much a figurehead as rather a passive figure, giving support and encouragement to the other honorary officers. The Rothschilds, for example, served as Presidents for nearly seventy years but were rarely involved in the day-to-day affairs of the United Synagogue; they preferred to keep an eye on the operation of the United Synagogue from behind their own office desks in New Court, whereas more recent leaders found themselves impelled frequently to be present at the headquarters of the organisation itself. Their eruptions into the United Synagogue had therefore much more effect when they occurred. On the other hand it tended much more to give to many, including those inside the United Synagogue, the feeling that the organisation was very much a benevolent dictatorship, a feeling which later generations tended to resent, particularly if later leaders did not possess the prestige of the Rothschilds, and since there was in any case pressure in the community at large for more 'open' government.

There were other leaders as well, men whose names appear over and over again among the mass of interconnecting committees and organisations in the broader London community. All these however were far less significant than either Lionel Louis Cohen or his right-hand man, Asher Asher.[5]

> In speaking of the United Synagogue, it is the custom to refer to it as the creation of Lionel Cohen. So in large measure it was, but if Lionel Cohen was the spirit that animated the movement, Asher Asher was the right hand that brought the movement into working order.

Elsewhere the *Jewish Chronicle* commented, in its obituary for Asher:[6]

> Into this work [the formation of the Union] Dr Asher threw his whole heart and soul. The idea might have been due to other minds, but to his was due the great work of giving it form and substance. No-one but those who were engaged in some part of this important work can conceive the gigantic labour it entailed. The late Mr Lionel Cohen and Dr Asher spent night and day in getting materials ready for the structure upon the design of which they were mutually engaged. . . . Great tact was displayed by Dr Asher in these personal negotiations which he conducted for the purpose of securing the support and goodwill of all parties – honorary and salaried – for the Union.

Asher, who was seven years younger than Lionel Louis Cohen, had qualified and practised shortly in Glasgow before he, like many other medically qualified Scots, came south to London. In 1862 the Board of Guardians had taken over the provision of medical attention to those receiving assistance from it, and Asher took up partnership with the medical officer to the City synagogues. He retired from this partnership when in 1866 he had stood as Secretary of the Great Synagogue. He was elected as the candidate of the 'western' element in the Synagogue's membership, and thus came even closer into contact with Lionel Louis Cohen without losing his links with the Board of Guardians, for he was appointed an honorary member of the Board's Medical and Sanitary Committees. He managed to spend a great deal of unpaid time on behalf of the Jewish poor. He was a prominent member of the Initiation Society, whose president lamented after Asher's death the loss of his personal services as well as of his substantial contributions. He was also the unpaid 'private almoner' to the Rothschild family; one writer of a posthumous tribute to him described him as virtually 'the manager of the "Charitable Department" of New Court', and recalled that a large basket with his name conspicuously displayed on it was generally filled with correspondence from all over the world. He had indeed developed very close ties of friendship with the Rothschild family, so close that on his death bed he managed to persuade to a reconciliation Lord

Rothschild and Samuel Montagu, with both of whom he had kept close touch. With all this he had still considerable scholastic interests and abilities. He wrote extensively for the *Jewish Chronicle* under the name of 'Aliquis', and a collection of his writings which was published privately in 1915 demonstrated the versatility of his learning in matters sacred and profane; he wrote in Hebrew – some of his letters for the United Synagogue were in Hebrew – and was reading shortly before his death a recently published novel in Hebrew.[7]

His deepest interest, however, was the foundation of the United Synagogue and an indication has been given earlier of the extent to which he was concerned both in the mechanics of the negotiations involved and, more important, in the spirit with which leaders such as Lionel Louis Cohen had embarked on the move. But once the union had been agreed it was virtually on him alone that the task of implementation fell. His official correspondence book shows clearly the amount of paper that passed through his hands – or rather over his signature – during the crucial months. Thus it was Asher who as Secretary *pro tem.* of the United Synagogue wrote to the secretaries of the various constituent synagogues asking them to give him details of seatholders in their congregations, and who had to soothe down Judah Jacob's complaints about being overlooked by his synagogue secretary. But a close analysis of the letter-books is even more revealing. Most of the first 600 letters in the first two books are in Asher's own hand, evidencing that there was not even a clerk to the Council to give help to Asher until 1873 when Ornstein was so appointed. But, even so, Asher continued to sign the letters save on the obviously rare occasions of his absences from town.

The business of the letters is equally revealing. Many of the matters dealt with concern prisons and conditions in them. Arrangements are made for the supplies of matza and other foodstuffs although it was not possible to provide kosher food in general. Letters arrange for remission from labour by prison inmates on Sabbaths and Holydays, and others with the difficulties incurred over visiting; when, for example, Leeds congregations had declined to pay expenses to a minister for visiting a local prison, Asher was very scathing and asked the recipient to let him have details, when he would be paid immediately from London funds. As he wrote about another case to the President of the Birmingham Board of Guardians:

> Your resolution . . . is the more gratifying because it is an indication that your excellent Institution is, in common with this Synagogue, actuated by the principle that our philanthropy and religion are not to

be confined to local objects only, but should be extended to those general communal interests which all Jews have at heart.

There was correspondence with the Chief Rabbi over the Christian nature of prayers on the walls in asylums and prisons, and letters to the Secretary of the Directors of Convict Prisons enclosing the form of approved Jewish prayers. The Secretary of the United Synagogue intervened to stop a prosecution for begging on condition that the boy in question attended a Jewish school regularly. In one letter Asher wrote:

The Executive are extremely anxious that every Jewish boy be properly educated, they will esteem it a great favour if you will kindly inform them through me whenever a Jewish boy is apprehended by an officer of the [London] School Board, and when the case is coming up for trial.

He had complaints over funerals. Funeral attendants had been smoking, to the annoyance of the bereaved, a foetus had been removed by the doctor who had delivered it, a Jewish lunatic pauper had been buried among Christians, there were halachic problems concerning the burial of a Jew who had been cohabiting with a Christian – all these had been referred to Asher and he had to make enquiries and report back.

But there were others too. There were letters arranging meetings of all sorts, making arrangements for women receiving clothing from the Board of Guardians to be measured, informing recipients that they had been balloted for to receive marriage portions. There were several letters in which he wrote 'more officiously than officially' and a few marked 'non-official'. He had too to write to firms such as Charrington's ordering coal to be delivered either to United Synagogue officials or to the poor who had been issued with coal tickets. One firm had been defaulting on deliveries and Asher noted that 'the poor people are clamouring for their coals'. He could be scathing on behalf of the United Synagogue and its officials. On several occasions he wrote to the Hambro' that the Finance Committee 'are strongly of the opinion that it is quite impossible for one of the Ministers of the Congregation to live upon £200 per annum'. He was always at pains to point out that 'the mistake is yours, not mine', but he was always punctilious about his office routines; many letters referred to 'yours of yesterday', 'I was directed at a meeting last evening', and when papers such as synagogue accounts came into the office Asher went through them carefully before they went to the appropriate committees. He queried in advance matters 'which would be likely to engage the attention of the Finance

Committee' and for which they had better have explanations. He was also punctilious about upholding the status and authority of the United Synagogue. A letter to the Secretary of the Board of Deputies reminded him that the correct procedure if the Board wished to contact London synagogues was to write to the Council of the United Synagogue.

> I am sure you take this letter in the friendly spirit in which it is written. The bruit has gone forth that you try to ignore the fact of the Union of the Synagogues having taken place, and I am anxious to weaken and counteract such an unfounded report.

The burden of office was heavy, not of course only for Asher alone but for others as well, although Asher was one of the few who had to appear at each meeting. Thus, for example, in 1876 there was a meeting on Monday 13 June of the Visitation Committee, Tuesday 14 June of the Executive Committee, Thursday 16 June of the Finance Committee, Monday 20 June of the Executive again. All these meetings had to be 'serviced' by Asher, the minutes to be written, and correspondence arising to be dealt with by him. All this was straightforward routine, demanding energy and perseverance but not necessarily much else. What stands out even more is the way in which Asher shaped the United Synagogue and its routines; it was Asher, for example, who managed to have the budgets rearranged in a recognisable and meaningful form, so that the Council could judge for itself the financial strengths and weaknesses of the United Synagogue, and it was thus possible to assess the due balance between the constituent synagogues and the institution as a whole. It was this task of financial reorganisation to which particular attention was drawn after his death, and it was the more remarkable in that he had had no training in book-keeping at all.

These were the main facets of his life so far as London was concerned, but he was by no means restricted to London. When the great waves of migration began from Eastern Europe Asher was one of the leaders of the community deputed to travel to Russia to report on conditions there and to try to set up some sort of reception organisation at the main frontier crossing-points. At other times he was sent to Palestine to investigate the state of Jewish colonies there; when he was sent to America for a similar purpose in 1884 he even managed to find time to make a stop in Montreal and attend meetings there of the annual conference of the British Association for the Advancement of Science. He was, however, a very poor traveller, so that he was always seasick, and these journeys invariably left him physically exhausted. It is small wonder that he too died at an early age – fifty-two – almost certainly worn out by his efforts. He made no fortune in his work. His salary had risen eventually to the total of £800 a year, and even though he may have received various honoraria from private practice his gross estate reached the sum of £8,657. 5s. 6d. His will was drawn up in October 1888, some three months before his death, and the specific bequests say much about his friendships and his interests.

> I bequeath to the said Dr Abraham Cohen [his son-in-law] the watch presented to me by Mr Alfred De Rothschild and the chain and appendages (except the locket containing my parents' portraits) I usually wear with it my microscope and all medical books surgical instruments and applicances and drugs which may belong to me at the time of my death and I bequeath the said locket to my son Philip I bequeath the wines liquors fuel and other consumable stores and provisions of which I shall die possessed to my said wife absolutely I bequeath to my said wife the use and enjoyment of the articles hereinafter specifically bequeathed during her life   And after her decease I bequeath to my daughter Hannah the wife of Dr Abraham Cohen my silver candlesticks large silver waiter and cup and bottle used for Kaddisch   To my son Philip the tea and coffee service presented to me by the Jewish congregation of Glasgow my silver Mohel case my large family bible and all portraits and testimonials belonging to me   And to my son Samuel my typewriter the claret jugs presented to me by Lord Rothschild and the inkstand and candlesticks on my writing table.

There were obviously other members of the staff – Ornstein for example – and there were other members of the Council and committees. All of them and the various experts brought in on occasion – such as architects and surveyors – played their own significant parts in these early years. But it is not necessarily unduly denigrating to suggest that their work was secondary to that which has already been discussed. The same would also be true of the clergy of the United Synagogue. Their salaries were not outstanding, nor were they usually more than the servants of their congregations. Few were of a standard of either personality or scholarship to dominate their communities; rather were they very much dominated by their local congregations. There were honourable exceptions: apart from Nathan Adler himself there was his son Hermann, A. L. Green, and, a little later, Simeon Singer. The general status of the ministry can well be seen from the salary levels; in the majority of cases they were decidedly lower-middle class in an age when the leadership as a whole was equally decidedly very much upper-middle class. Many recognising the problems of the adequacy of the ministry looked to the United Synagogue to find a remedy.[8]

> The general rise of intelligence in the community and the courageous efforts of the few ministers . . . have rendered it impossible today that anyone should be appointed to an important post who does not possess adequate preaching power and general culture . . . The rise in the status of the Jewish Clergy must be a gradual one. It must take some time before a generation of Jewish youths can be trained for the ministry on a sounder system . . . before all English congregations shall have risen above the temptation of preferring a singer to a scholar as their minister. . . . [It is necessary] to organise some machinery which shall render the position of the Jewish ministers at once more independent of their own congregation and yet amenable to some check. . . . Here, as elsewhere, the United Synagogue affords the *via media*. It has often been remarked that the Church of England has better clergymen than any body of dissenters, because the former does not put its pastors under the direct government of their flocks. Similarly, now that the right of dismissal is controlled by the General Council of the United Synagogue, the tone of the Jewish ministry will probably be greatly raised.

There is no evidence, however, of this happening, and certainly the establishment of the United Synagogue in itself set up even stronger lay control over the clergy employed by it. In many cases the minister of the local congregation became the local secretary as well, and was even more regarded as the servant of the congregation at the beck and call of almost anyone who cared to demand his services. His salary reflected this lowly status, and the continued complaints about the lack of recruits to the ministry, shown for example in the report on the future of Jews' College already mentioned, demonstrate the unwillingness of the leading Jewish families to send their children into the ministry. It is after all highly significant that the Cousinhood did not contain ministers in its ranks.

The only exceptions to these generalisations can be found in the Adlers. Their position was exceptional, since the one was Chief Rabbi and the other, for many years, Delegate and then Chief Rabbi. Their deliberate policy was one of assertion of their own authority, over both their ecclesiastical and lay colleagues, achieving both these ends through their close connections with the lay leaders of the United Synagogue itself. In other words, the authority of the Chief Rabbi was best established by the assertion of the authority of the honorary officers of the United Synagogue, a confirmation of the tendency already demonstrated earlier. The corollary of course was that an attempt by any Chief Rabbi to assert his own authority would become associated with attempts at reducing the control of the institution by the small inner circle. Thus also any attempt within the institution to assert 'democratic' control became associated with attempts by the ecclesiastics to assert their own independent authority. At all events there is little evidence of any independent authority being exercised by Nathan Adler, even if the '*succah* story' were to be correct. On occasion he did intervene, either to be very firmly put in his place or else to find that others were already doing what he would have wished on his behalf. Illustrations of this can be found, for example, in the discussions over the laws for the burial society when Adler tried to intervene or in the arguments over opening and closing places of worship; Adler tried to put forward a point of view only to be told that nobody denied that he had to be consulted. The effect was to emphasise the dictatorial position of the men at the top of the organisation, including in this of course the man chiefly responsible for the everyday running of the United Synagogue.

Here then were the architects of the United Synagogue, and here are to be found the foundations of its later work. Certainly whatever the United Synagogue became in the following years was a reflection of the intentions and wishes of these founding fathers, and to a very large extent the second generation of leadership tended to follow up and develop the patterns which their predecessors had established.

PART TWO

EXPANSION AND ADAPTATION
1890–1912

The passing of the first generation of active leadership in the United Synagogue was accompanied by strains of a nature that could never have been foreseen. In the history of any organisation the handover from one generation to the next is always a period of difficulty; there is never the certainty that the original aims and ambitions could be continued, even if they were still practicable. In addition, of course, there is the question whether 'continuation' means the maintenance of the organisation as it stands or a radical change in its structure in order to uphold the original spirit of the founders. These years, then, would have seen the leadership of the United Synagogue put through a severe examination. London was changing; its population was expanding, and new districts were developing, so that in any case it would not have been surprising to find the Jewish population on the move. But these years saw considerable external strains as well, which had profound effects upon London Jewry in general and the United Synagogue in particular. The years after 1880 saw a shift of Jewish population on a large scale; nearly three million Jews left eastern Europe, many passing through Britain en route for America or Africa, but nearly three hundred thousand stayed in this country and raised the size of Anglo-Jewry nearly tenfold. There were precedents for migrations of this size, as in the upsurge of Irish communities in Britain at the time of the great famine, but the problems presented to the London Jewish community and the United Synagogue were none the less outside their normal experience, and affected the development of the United Synagogue in ways that could not have been imagined. It was the more important, therefore, that the community was able to cope; indeed it was to be the very existence of an organisation like the United Synagogue which made the absorption of these newcomers easier.

CHAPTER 5

THE GROWTH OF LONDON JEWRY

Any study of London Jewry in the last stages of the nineteenth century must be related to two major factors – the changing face of London itself and the introduction into a numerically relatively stable Jewish population of a wave of new immigrants, outstanding both in their numbers and in their social differences from the Jews already present. Both these factors had a profound influence particularly in the years between 1890 and the outbreak of the First World War, and both affected fundamentally not only the problems which the United Synagogue had to face and the ways in which they were faced, but also the ways in which the United Synagogue could face the problems of the sixty years following.

London in the middle of the nineteenth century had been comparatively stable; it had expanded slowly from its central core, but the expansion had always been dominated by the need of its citizens to remain in contact with their employment. Gradually, however, a slow trickle from the heart of London into the outlying areas became a virtual torrent, and the transformation of transport inside London made possible what was to all intents and purposes an explosion of both numbers of inhabitants and the area they occupied. Private dwellings in the centre were reduced in number and in quality, and all levels of society – no longer merely the wealthy who could afford to keep up their own carriages – sought new ways of life; 'the shopkeepers and the clerks began to seek villas', and in order to find them moved ever further and further out. There is an obvious correlation between the growth of the railway system round London and housing expansion, so that fewer and fewer lived near their place of work and more and more created that relatively new phenomenon, the 'dormitory suburb'. This expansion was not of an even social mix, and certain suburbs became associated with particular social classes. The large-scale introduction by various railway companies of 'workmen's trains' and workmen's tickets induced the growth of working-class suburbs towards the north-east of London, while restrictive building covenants encouraged the growth of very wealthy suburbs in such areas as St John's Wood. This general process of change in late-Victorian London, not in the least confined to any one minority group, emphasises once more the extent to which the development of London Jewry reflected the patterns of the society into which it was moving, socially and culturally.[1] As the main fashionable centres of London upper- and middle-class life moved, so did the Jewish middle-class centres of population – albeit often after a certain hesitation and delay – and the pattern was repeated too as between the non-Jewish and Jewish working classes. The changes, so far as the Jewish communities were concerned, were also accelerated by the increasing growth of a Jewish middle class, and by a changing social pattern as between upper- and working-class members of the Jewish community. None of this is a feature that is particularly confined to the years after 1890. Indeed, there are clear signs of these developments even before 1870. The growth, for example, of the North London and Dalston Synagogues cannot be dissociated from the opening of the branch railway line from Dalston to Broad Street and the possibility of rapid and cheap transport into the City from this newer area. What, however, does develop after 1890 is the rapid expansion of this process, and the connection between these physical aspects and the need to create on a much larger scale the whole apparatus of synagogue accommodation.

The results of these changes were twofold. The new middle classes began to demand, and even to secure, a greater share in the active work of the United Synagogue and in its leadership. This was not yet in any sense an attempt to overthrow the privileged position of the Grand Dukes, but rather a claim for partnership at the level of the Council and even the Executive Committee, and it showed itself most immediately in the local leadership of the United Synagogue. This was in itself a reflection also of the second result of these changes. The newer classes, moving into fashionable areas, demanded their own local congregations, just as a generation or so earlier their predecessors in Bayswater had done. They had not merely the money to pay for their buildings but also were vocal enough to be able over and over again to get much of what they wanted in other respects as well. The detailed history of the foundation of the Hampstead and Brondesbury Synagogues, the clashes between their local Boards of Management and the honorary officers, and the way in which these honorary officers did not always manage to browbeat the congregations to follow the 'establishment' line, illustrate clearly the restiveness among these newly emerging middle-class Jews. Clearly, these aspects of London Jewish development in themselves would have been enough to strain the organisational resources of the United Synagogue. There were also strains on the financial resources as well. It had always been difficult to persuade the honorary officers to view favourably the establishment of new congregations: before 1890 only six had been admitted as constituent members and two of them had already been in existence. Now five new congregations were admitted within twelve years as full members, and there were four clamouring for some form of status – eventually receiving the new status of associate synagogues. At the same time there was strong pressure on the central capital funds for repairs, alterations, and improvements to the stock of existing buildings. What made the whole position tenable from the Treasurers' point of view was that these new full congregations were, for the most part, able to make substantial contributions to the finances of the United Synagogue as a whole. The deficits of the older, decaying congregations could be more than balanced by the surpluses made available from these newer bodies, and thus the essential aims and hopes of the founding fathers could be upheld, despite the changing circumstances of the times.

In a real sense these developments could well have been foreseen and were inherent in the elements contributing to the original foundation. The spread of London's suburbs and the rise of a Jewish middle class were alike to be envisaged by the contemporary observer of 1870. What could not have been foreseen was the other major change which overtook London Jewry, the major immigrations from Eastern Europe. A historian dealing with any aspect of modern Jewry is bound to point to the major population movements out of Russia and Eastern Europe generally at the end of the nineteenth century as one of the fundamental factors in his studies, but this is particularly true of the historian dealing with Jewish London. No one can tell exactly how many Jews arrived in London and stayed there, but certainly they swamped the existing communities in London as they did in New York, at approximately the same time. Many times more in number than their Jewish hosts, they could hardly fail to make an impact upon the Jews and non-Jews of their time.[2] In London their impact was, in the first instance, confined geographically to a very small part of London, the East End, but their concentration in itself intensified this impact. The East End to which they came was not the same area which had seen the earlier Jewish centres, so that these new arrivals created problems even from the very beginning. They represented an outlook on Judaism and traditional practices which had hardly been seen previously there, and they also represented a social and economic group which had virtually never before existed in the London Jewish communities. Their religious needs, their social needs, and not least their economic needs were to all intents and purposes alien to much of the thinking of the leadership not merely of the United Synagogue but of London, and British, Jewry as a whole, and in some respects, as will be shown, the existing communities found it difficult to understand and meet these needs. It would have been all too easy for the immigrants and the existing communities each to go their own way. The immigrants, for example, for reasons which will be discussed later, tended to create their own religious organisations instead of adhering to the existing congregations, and they resented such schemes put forward by the United Synagogue as 'the East End Scheme'. Their religious and social needs tended to be met by the growth of friendly societies, which were to a large extent tied closely with burial societies, the payment of funeral expenses, and the provision of weekly payments during the period of mourning. But the two sets of communities could not ignore each other. The 'hosts' could not avoid being involved, even if only as a result of a growing agitation against alien immigration. They felt the need, however, not only to protect their own position but to alleviate the distress among their co-religionists. The immigrants, for their part, stranded in an alien land, turned naturally to their co-religionists for help and guidance, and were not disappointed. It was the 'establishment' of London Jewry which gave a lead in the formation of the Federation of Synagogues, while it was Lord Rothschild who was responsible for the foundation of the Four Per Cent Industrial Dwellings Company and who chose Philip Ornstein, the Secretary of the United Synagogue, as its company secretary.

The bases of all the approaches by the host community were fundamentally alike; they sought to anglicise the new immigrants, to teach them English and English habits, and although the immigrants still turned to such eminent foreign preachers as the Kamenetzer Maggid – the very eminent, revered, and highly respected Chaim Maccoby – the process of anglicisation on the whole worked, assisted of course by the impact of such factors as universal, free, and compulsory elementary education. The United Synagogue could make no direct impact upon the East End itself. There the small congregations established by the new arrivals, the Chevras, continued to be more attractive, as did also such other bodies as the Machzike Hadath. But the geographical cohesiveness of the East End proved to be comparatively short-lived. There were many factors tending towards 'dispersion' of the newly arrived immigrants; as they bettered themselves financially they, or their children, moved out of the narrow ghetto-like existence of Whitechapel and followed the paths laid down earlier, into north London and eventually into the north-west, or even went directly into the north-western or north-eastern suburbs, where they came under the umbrella of the United Synagogue and the congregations already established there. Some of them were moved, by a deliberate policy of dispersion, into suburbs that had been less popular among Jews – such as south-east London – but there too the associate synagogue scheme, sponsored by the United Synagogue to provide religious facilities, induced them to participate more actively in the work of the United Synagogue.

It is clear, therefore, that the United Synagogue was to have a direct and important impact upon these immigrants and play an important part in helping them to adapt to the English scene. But they in turn were to have a profound impact upon the United Synagogue itself. The United Synagogue had sought to anglicise them, but they were never assimilated in any religious sense into the non-Jewish society in which they lived, and whereas it might have been possible within the framework of the United Synagogue to see at the end of the century various factors which might have drawn the United Synagogue closer to a vaguely 'reform' type of Judaism, it was to a large extent the presence of this newer element which kept the United Synagogue loyal to that part of its foundation which enjoined the continued observance of the *Minhag* of Germany and Poland. In America the children of the immigrants turned eventually towards a reform-type Judaism, but in England these immigrants – coming from the same milieu, and often closely related to the Jews who had almost by chance gone to the New World – maintained their own orthodoxy and even in many ways upheld and strengthened the orthodoxy of the host community. In itself this represented a constant backwards and forwards movement of ideas and influences. The constant entry into the existing synagogues of the new immigrants kept up – even strengthened – standards of religious observance, while since very often it was only the United Synagogue which could provide synagogues and religious facilities in the areas to which the outflow from the East End moved, there had to be a certain amount of reciprocal give and take by the immigrants in their turn. The result was that by the time the migrations had died away in intensity the newcomers had been virtually absorbed into the very much enlarged host community. Various consequences were still to work themselves out, and indeed some of these were to become increasingly important during the middle of the twentieth century. These were, however, only obvious in retrospect, and what was much more important and vital about these years was the way in which the process of absorption had developed. The organisation of the United Synagogue had been founded on a small scale and had been elaborated in conditions of stability; it had been tested severely not only by various factors which can be envisaged as inherent in the original background of the years of foundation but by strains which could never have been envisaged, and yet it had been able to survive these strains and emerge virtually unchanged.

The parallel with the United States in general and New York in particular is one which cannot be avoided, though it need not be elaborated. New York was affected by a similar wave of immigration, and there too a host community found itself faced with similar problems. However there existed no 'umbrella' organisation comparable to the United Synagogue, and the result was that the fragmentation of small congregations continued unhindered. Nor were there any communal organisations to link the non-Jewish environment, the 'host' communities, and the new immigrants, so that when various patterns of anti-alien or anti-semitic sentiment came to be experienced in New York a form of 'Kehilla' organisation had hastily to be cobbled together. The concept, which seems to have paralleled various aspects of both continental and British experiences, came to nothing, and the whole episode faded away.[3] The reasons for this are complex, and, although for the most part they have no direct relevance to the history of the United Synagogue, they do serve both to portray in higher relief the success in London and to indicate some of the strengths of the United Synagogue's position. It had weaknesses too, and there were many of the immigrants who would not have regarded its standards of orthodoxy, of scholarship, or of religious leadership as being in any way adequate. But it did represent a unity; all classes were combined in it, and its leadership, having been accepted by the body of London Jewry, could be accepted by these newer members as well. The close ties among the Grand Dukes, the leading London Jewish families, and the way in which they almost automatically assumed their responsibilities, meant that in a curious sort of way the newer members of the London community accepted them also as leaders. The Rothschilds, for example, were taken for granted as the heads of all the community, even of the association which the Chevras created, the Federation, so that there was both a tradition of communal service and responsibility on the one hand and a feeling of solidarity on the other that even various social discords and strike actions failed to dislodge. The comparison between New York and London remains, and the failure in the one contrasts very strongly with the success in the other, illustrating most clearly not only the part played by the United Synagogue in these crucial years but the debt owed by the community at large to the United Synagogue for this vital role.

CHAPTER 6

DEVELOPMENT
AND GROWTH

The physical growth of London Jewry in these years brought enormous problems to the United Synagogue. It was not merely that the number of Jews had grown so rapidly. These newly arrived Jews concentrated in the East End, primarily in areas where Jews had not previously been resident, and on the whole they represented classes and social and religious groupings which had not previously been so strongly present in the metropolis. The impact therefore was felt by the United Synagogue in various ways, yet most of these can be traced back to certain basic factors. These immigrants tended to be poor, they were unused to the laws, customs, and conventions of their host society, and they attempted to continue in the West the habits of Eastern Europe.

The first problem was that of the provision of synagogues. These immigrants did not, of course, wait for the United Synagogue to provide synagogues for them, but developed a large number of small societies, the Chevras. These societies were not all the result of the 1880–90 immigration, since some dated back to the eighteenth century, but the vast majority sprang up in the 1880s, often in unsuitable and unhygienic premises. They often combined the provision of accommodation for prayers with benefit societies, but they also fulfilled a social function, for many of them were virtually *Landsmannschaften*, bringing together individuals from particular districts or towns, in ways the existing synagogues could not have done, so that the Great, the Hambro', and the New continued to have vacancies.

The plea was often made that these new dwellers in the East End could not afford the fees that membership of a constituent synagogue involved, but even if there had been no problem of fees there would still have existed an enormous gulf between the two worlds. The newcomers felt that neither in religious customs nor in outward appearances did the Anglo-Jewish establishment and the East End have anything in common. They had weighed up the orthodoxy of the United Synagogue and found it wanting. Deriving little from the United Synagogue, they at first resented the attitudes of its leaders and wanted only to be left on their own. For their part the leaders of the United Synagogue were subject to two sorts of pressure. They objected to the uncouth appearance of these immigrants and wished only for their outward anglicisation, fearing that the host community might transfer a distaste for foreigners and newcomers into a dislike for Jews already socially assimilated. In addition these immigrants did not always understand the secular laws of the country and in many respects, such as the laws of marriage, found that their imported customs could run counter to established practice.

So far as the United Synagogue was concerned the feelings over these immigrants crystallised into a dislike of the Chevras and into a belief that these institutions should not be encouraged. These attitudes had been foreshadowed during 1870 in disagreements with the Sandys Row Synagogue when Lionel Louis Cohen, arguing against the growth of small synagogues, was opposed by his friend and colleague N. S. Joseph, who was strongly in favour of them.[1] It was in 1887, however, that Samuel Montagu took the initiative in the foundation of the Federation of Minor Synagogues,[2] through which he hoped to bring the Chevras into one umbrella organisation. At the outset, at least, there was no intention of setting up a rival to the United Synagogue. Many of the leading lights of the Federation, including Samuel Montagu himself, were conspicuous members of the United Synagogue; the Federation went out of its way to make it easy for Lord Rothschild to accept office as Honorary President; and indeed it was disclosed by Samuel Montagu, after the death of Asher Asher, that although, as Secretary of the United Synagogue, he had been opposed to the establishment of the Federation he had given every assistance in the drafting of its rules. Moreover there could be little suggestion that the Federation would attract members of the United Synagogue, and the idea of a gathering of small synagogues fitted in well with much of what Montagu had been saying for many years within the United Synagogue on the subject of 'big' synagogues. On the other hand, there were many who pointed out that it was only through the foundation of an alternative group of synagogues that Samuel Montagu could achieve a position in the community in any way rivalling that of his cousin, Lord Rothschild. Certainly it would seem to be more than merely a coincidence that the foundation meeting of the Federation came very shortly after the highly publicised row between the two men on the financial reorganisation of the United Synagogue in 1886. The *Jewish Chronicle* had regretted the tone in which the debates in the United Synagogue Council had been conducted, certainly as between the two principals. The personal breach between them was covered over, but even when Rothschild was brought into the Federation it was clear that he would be able to do even less for the Federation than he was able to do as President of the United Synagogue, and that Montagu would be the more firmly in the saddle.

At all events, by 1889 there was open war between the two organisations. The United Synagogue refused to allow the Federation either representation on the Board of Shechita or a share in whatever profits might accrue. A report on this from the Executive Committee of the United Synagogue bitterly attacked the Federation for its alleged poaching of individual orthodox synagogues, which might otherwise have become members of the United Synagogue, and for its apparent disinclination to bear a full proportion of communal burdens. On its side the Federation was equally bitter in its comments; Samuel Montagu announced ostentatiously that he had arranged for the acquisition of a separate burial ground for the Federation and that he had reserved in it a double plot for his wife and himself, declaiming that he would never be separated from the Federation even in death. None the less, despite the growth of the Federation, opinion as expressed in the *Jewish Chronicle* turned towards the United Synagogue as representing the sole body able to deal with the problems developing in the East End. The Federation had neither the money nor the organisational machinery for any large-scale plans, while in any case there was still universal agreement in both the United Synagogue and the Federation that any solution could only come through the activities of the Chief Rabbi and the Beth Din, and through the religious habits of the immigrants.

The first major investigation into the problems of the East End as they affected the United Synagogue was made in 1889. The Executive Committee was asked to prepare and submit a plan for synagogue accommodation in the East End, an adaptation of the conditions of membership of the United Synagogue to suit the circumstances of the majority of the Jewish resident population, and for the setting up of benefit and provident societies in connection with places of worship. The very full report of the Committee[3] discussed in detail the 'conditions of the Jews in East London', both their problems and the attempted solutions, covering such points as the foundation of a synagogue at

Stepney Green, the reduction of marriage fees and the cost of funerals, the establishment of the Four Per Cent Industrial Dwellings Company, and the annual free services in the East End. The problems, as the United Synagogue saw it, arose from the concentration of foreign Jews in the East End, composed of 'the vast majority . . . closely attached to the ceremonies and forms of their religion, as they have been taught to practice them in the land of their birth; and the other, perhaps more difficult of treatment, though far less numerous, who respect few of the observances of their faith, and who are Jews by birth rather than by practice'. The Committee diagnosed new aspects of the problem, particularly resulting from the growing division between rich and poor, and the concurrent removal of the residence and sphere of action of many of the Jewish clergy:

> It must also be remembered that the qualifications which have been required in selecting Ministers attached to Congregations consisting almost entirely of English Jews, have not been those which would render them specially acceptable to, or influential with, the number of foreign Jews in the East of London.

The plans were in two parts, designed 'to establish organisations designed especially to suit the requirements of the Jews in the East of London, to provide Ministers whose whole time shall be devoted to their service, and to found a Place of Worship absolutely in harmony with their wishes and requirements'. A new 'properly conducted Synagogue' would replace the many 'unsuitable and unsanitary places where they now resort for Divine Worship', and this would be linked with a provident society to pay for funerals and for financial support during the week of mourning. The scheme also provided for a large hall for the Beth Din for public meetings, and other general purposes. The Beth Hamedrash, taken over in 1875, would also be absorbed into the scheme. A further feature would be the appointment of a chief official:

> a gentleman who, through his intimate knowledge of the habits and customs of Polish and other Foreign Jews, will possess the necessary qualifications for the combined office of Dayan and Preacher, and whose character will, it is hoped, secure for him the esteem and respect of those to whose requirements he will minister. The want of such an official has been sadly felt. There is an immense field for such a minister in the East of London, and the Executive Committee earnestly hope that they may succeed in recruiting the services of a gentleman who, while studying the necessities of the poor, will elevate their social

condition by inculcating lessons of morality, health and cleanliness, and will at the same time minister to their spiritual wants in times of distress and affliction.

As was usual with new synagogues, the report attempted to place the building on a sound financial basis. There would be 1,000 seats, 200 of which would be free and 800 let at rentals ranging from 3*d*. per week upwards. A certain number of dearer seats (5 guineas a year) would be taken by prominent members of the community.

It is likely that these seats will rarely be occupied by their owners, most of whom will probably reside at a distance, so that they will form a considerable addition to the number of free seats available, while the rental derived will be a material contribution to the accomplishment of the Scheme, which . . . must inevitably impose a serious annual burden upon the already straitened resources of the United Synagogue.

The capital cost was estimated at £20,000, and in order to raise this sum the Committee recommended that rather than using its own capital the United Synagogue should appeal to the community as a whole, specifically calling upon 'important bodies and influential gentlemen outside the United Synagogue . . . to co-operate in any measure which will tend to raise the religious, moral, and social status of the Jews of the Metropolis'. The Committee also reported on details of the provident society, a savings bank, and 'the desirability of establishing a Mikveh. It is known that great importance is attached to such an institution by the class of persons for whose wants it is proposed to provide.' The report concluded:

It is not pretended that the labours of a minister, however zealous and respected, nor that the erection of a synagogue, even of the capacity of the one proposed, will supply all that is required, but if the Community will rally to the support of the Council . . . at least an important beginning will have been made in grappling with one of the most pressing questions of the day. . . . The main problem . . . is to attract the Jews of all classes in the East of London, whether foreign or native, within the fold of the body politic; to give them membership in the representative institutions of the community; and thus to afford them . . . that share in the government and administration of the great communal establishments.

A year after the publication of the scheme a meeting was held 'of gentlemen by themselves or representing institutions outside the United Synagogue, willing to co-operate in the measures to be taken to give effect to the scheme'. Thirty-two attended, among them representatives from the Federation as well as the West London Synagogue. Lord Rothschild, in convening the meeting, expressed his disappointment at the 'little or no enthusiasm for the present scheme'. Even at that meeting, however, the divisions in the community were evident; one person openly attacked the Federation, while once again Samuel Montagu defended his attitude. 'For the last quarter of a century or more I have always been in favour of the establishment of local synagogues of moderate size.'[4] The meeting did not achieve agreement, and the scheme was for the moment dropped. The opposition to the idea of a large synagogue derived from many different sources, ranging from the claim that there were many seats available in the vicinity of the proposed synagogue to the unwillingness of members of the Chevras to surrender the opportunity of holding office among their own communities.

Having adopted the scheme in principle, however, the United Synagogue did not lightly abandon the hope of implementing it. It was difficult for the honorary officers to ignore the needs of the situation. As they pointed out in 1895:

> the repeated complaints of County Court Judges and of Magistrates (whether well founded or not) should be taken as a serious warning to those who have at heart the well-being and good sense of the Community. . . . The responsibility for instance is too serious: that responsibility they decline to bear, and the Council is therefore asked to authorise an immediate appeal to be made to the public for carrying out the East End Scheme.

The scheme was revived several times over, at times in association with a scheme to rebuild the Hambro' Synagogue in the Spitalfields district, at others with the intention of fully using a site in the Commercial Road, and again Samuel Montagu opposed the idea. Reports were presented to the Council in 1893, 1894, 1896, and 1898, and each of these, save that of 1898, concentrated on the provision of a large place of worship and of one minister at least for full-time service in the East End, and various other facilities designed to ameliorate specific conditions in the area.

The scheme outlined in 1898 abandoned the 'large synagogue'; it was clear that the public was uninterested in such a project, and the Council was far too sensible of the financial position of the United Synagogue to commit itself to such a vast capital outlay without the promise of substantial support from the community at large. There was the clear realisation that to undertake such a project would probably cripple the United Synagogue in many other fields; if there was no great enthusiasm for the scheme the United Synagogue would be well advised to take no further steps in promoting it. As a consequence the report spread itself over a wide variety of other possible activities and is an invaluable source of information about conditions in the East End at the end of the century. The principle underlying the report was that

> the poor but honest, hardworking foreign Jew may realise that his Brother in faith in this country, while respecting his religious feelings, desires to extend to him the helping hand of fellowship to enable him to raise his social position and establish himself and his family as worthy citizens of the country in which he has found shelter.

The Committee's report contained a variety of recommendations. Its members urged the building of a large social centre, the registration of official interpreters for the police and county courts, the establishment of panels of arbitrators, the sponsorship of a provident society and persuading various friendly societies to make the proposed United Synagogue building their headquarters, the formation of a Visiting Committee 'for the sole purpose of elevating the poorer classes', the extension of mothers' meetings and circles, the improvement of education classes in English and other instructive subjects, all these to be supervised by a governing body free from the control of any extraneous body 'both lay and clerical'.

Some parts of this scheme were implemented, and some other parts developed almost naturally during the next few years. But if the idea of a 'large synagogue' never got off the ground, and if this failure entailed also the failure of much else about which the United Synagogue concerned itself, it exemplified the basic feeling in the United Synagogue that something ought to be done to help the masses of London Jewry. When in 1889 the honorary officers had originally suggested the first committee to investigate the situation in the East End, they had pointed out how large a part the United Synagogue ought to play and how important it was that the United Synagogue should demonstrate a moral purpose.

> The advantages of the Union will be made more apparent when it is seen that the Council are engaged in formulating important measures for the amelioration of the condition of the poorer Jews throughout the Metropolis.

The editor of the *Jewish Chronicle* hailed the project. 'The United Synagogue is not a financial machine only,' he declared on 8 February 1889. 'It is an institution charged with the high and responsible mission of promoting the religious progress of the Metropolitan Jews.' The failure of the wider non-building aspects of the East End scheme represented a great potential weakness in the United Synagogue structure. That it did not mark a long-term deterioration in the future of the United Synagogue resulted from the way in which the second generation of the inhabitants of the East End tended to move away from childhood districts into newer London suburbs and into renewed contact with those synagogues which the United Synagogue was constructing, as if to meet them.

This new synagogue building was certainly on a large scale. Five new constituent synagogues were opened between 1890 and 1912, while two of the original five synagogues forming the United Synagogue in 1870 were rebuilt on new sites; the Hambro' was rebuilt in comparatively close vicinity to the East End, but the New was rebuilt in Stamford Hill to serve a much enlarged Jewish population there and in all but name represented a new foundation. The areas of this development represented too a wide dispersion of the Jewish population and a polarisation of the different classes of membership. Hammersmith, Hampstead, and Brondesbury were far removed geographically from Hackney and Stoke Newington (or even Stamford Hill) and presented enormous problems of community organisation. On the other hand it must be pointed out that the Federation did not remain content to be concentrated into what was already becoming a decaying area, so far as Jewish settlement was concerned, so that it too was already beginning to be interested in geographical expansion. The process of becoming accepted as a constituent synagogue of the United Synagogue was a long-drawn-out and rather expensive one. The honorary officers were consistently concerned to make sure not only that any new applicants could stand on their own feet but that they could make a full contribution to the financial needs of the whole organisation, and where they were unconvinced of the viability of a potential member the application was turned down or, at best, deferred for several years. Small congregations therefore could have been in existence for several years before being able to come to the United Synagogue for help, and as likely as not the greater need for assistance the less likely they were to receive it. These very same congregations were very likely to receive financial help and advice from the Federation, so that it is not to be wondered at that the Federation grew so enormously during these years, having at its virtual disposal the purse of Samuel Montagu. It was presumably as a response to this, though no evidence is forthcoming, that two very prominent members of the United Synagogue Council, Nathaniel Louis Cohen and Charles Samuel, wrote to the Treasurer offering £500 each to act as the nucleus of a fund 'to enable the Council to assist, on some footing less reciprocally onerous than that of full constituent membership, the establishment of self-supporting Metropolitan Synagogues, distant at least two miles from Whitechapel'.[5]

The scheme as outlined by its authors was accepted enthusiastically by the United Synagogue, and even though it did not finally include the formal provision that synagogues should be well away from Whitechapel, in fact the overwhelming majority of the synagogues which benefited from this scheme were in the outlying parts of London, contributing therefore to the dispersion of the East End Jewry. The Executive reported to the Council:

> While it is the primary duty of the United Synagogue to assist in the erection of places of worship, it is difficult for Synagogues whose members are nearly all of the industrial class, to become 'self-supporting', as that phrase is understood of constituent Synagogues, and . . . it is desirable, if possible, to encourage in new Synagogues a sentiment of independence, which perhaps can hardly be evoked in a young congregation which depends for its maintenance upon the more affluent constituents. . . .
>
> It will . . . be noted that the Associate Synagogues are to be self-supporting, and practically under the control of their local Managers. No tax is sought to be levied upon them for the many important Communal burdens which are maintained by the United Synagogue, the only stipulation is that a small annual contribution shall be made to the Chief Rabbi's Fund.

Reference was also made to the possibility of the new synagogues' inclusion into the union, but it was emphasised that this could be only at the express desire of the members themselves. On the other hand it was also made clear in the scheme that the committee would first have to decide whether associate or constituent membership was the more appropriate.

Almost immediately the South-East London Synagogue, which had been rejected for full membership, applied for a grant from the new body, urging strongly that 'a new Synagogue would be the means of attracting to South-East London residents from the congested districts of the East End, and would thus serve to disperse the Jewish working classes from those districts where they are at present concentrated'. By 1907 four synagogues were members of the scheme, South-East London, East Ham and Manor Park, West Ham, and Poplar. The scheme, however, continued to be limited in its application, and by 1927 was recognised as having been overtaken by circumstances. The jump from associate status to constituent status was too great, and it was also felt that these synagogues were contributing too little to the basic needs and finances of the United Synagogue itself. The scheme was eventually brought to an end by the introduction of the district synagogues scheme, itself to be supplemented eventually by the affiliated synagogues scheme. While it lasted, however, the scheme did good work in maintaining religious life in outlying parts, and in assisting the dispersion of East End Jewry. It might perhaps also be added that none of the fourteen congregations eventually admitted under this scheme ever qualified as a full constituent member, and that although most transferred at some time to district status, others continued for a long time to struggle against economic problems. Yet the scheme was not a failure; it emphasised how important a role the United Synagogue played in providing the physical framework within which metropolitan Jewry could maintain a religious life.

CHAPTER 7

THE ROUTINE OF THE
UNITED SYNAGOGUE

The United Synagogue increased in size quite markedly between 1890 and 1912, both in the number of members and in the number of synagogues associated with it in various forms, and the scope of its activities also tended to widen. None the less, these years are basically years of consolidation. The second generation of leaders were rather more mundane than their predecessors had been; Ornstein, for example, gives the impression of having been more of a routine administrator than Asher had been, possessing little of Asher's flair and personality. Undoubtedly he had a larger organisation to deal with and certainly too the office shows much more evidence of regular and routine administration than Asher's had. Yet even so the evidence of the minute books shows that less thought was given to the presentation of reports and papers to the various committees and less attention given to the minutiae of recording discussions and details, while no contemporary describes Ornstein's activities as Secretary, or in any other capacity, as being influential in the way that Asher's activities played such a leading role in the London Jewish scene of his time. His obituary, in the *Jewish Chronicle* of 9 January 1920, went far towards implying this. He had been appointed as clerk to Asher at the age of sixteen, and had served the United Synagogue for forty-seven years. 'He was a veritable Encyclopaedic authority on the complexities of the United Synagogue Act and on the intricacies of the Standing Orders of Procedure and the Laws and Bye-laws of the United Synagogue.' His correspondence with the honorary officers certainly demonstrates his role as an office head rather than as an initiator of policy. Had the honorary officers been men of strong character and domineering personality, such a change as between the first and second secretaries might have been of less importance. But during these years Lord Rothschild was progressively of less importance − his growing deafness made him increasingly a figurehead except on such issues as he chose to exert himself − and the Chairmen after Lionel Louis Cohen did not command the immediate respect in the broader community which he had inspired.

The result of this was, as one of its honorary officers wrote in 1913, that 'the Council is not so easily led (or driven) by the Honorary Officers as was the case when I was first elected on it twenty-four years ago'.[1] The result almost inevitably was that described by Lord Rothschild to Lord Swaythling during their interview of July 1910, when he complained that there was 'a large system of log-rolling' and that when he used to attend the business meetings and ever 'put his foot down, there was a large outcry, larger from the Jewish Press than from anybody else'.[2]

At the same time, however, the United Synagogue had developed a sense of mission, and these same honorary officers were not deaf to the various calls made upon them, much to the disgust of some of the vociferous members of the United Synagogue itself. As one anonymous writer to the *Jewish Chronicle* commented on 16 March 1906 on the subject of the Treasurers' Annual Report:

> I take it that the first object of a Synagogue is to provide for public worship. Far be it from me to undervalue the philanthropic work which the United Synagogue does, and does well and thoroughly. But these are communal and general duties, and while you, as Treasurers, complain that the various communities are wanting in duty, the constituent synagogues have the right to complain that you are using the funds set aside and collected for the specific working of the Synagogue for a purpose which, however good, is a general communal charge.

These indeed are the two charges levelled against the United Synagogue in those years. It was too narrowly a financial body, looking only at its balance sheets and not unduly concerned with the wider needs of the London Jewish community. Israel Zangwill's well-known comments in his novel *Children of the Ghetto*[3] − 'the United Synagogue could be run as a joint-stock company for the sake of a dividend, and . . . there wouldn't be an atom of difference in the discussions if the councillors were directors. . . . Finance fascinates them. Long after Judaism has ceased to exist, excellent gentlemen will be found regulating its finances' − can be matched by the attacks by the *Jewish Review* in 1910 when Ernest Lesser attacked the 'persistent propensity of the United Synagogue for assuming fresh duties and responsibilities alien to its main purposes, and on its ingrained and unfortunate habit of measuring the success of its work by the state of its balance sheet'. Lesser managed thus to combine the attack on the purely financial aspects of the United Synagogue with the charge that it was disbursing its funds on purposes which should have fallen on the wider community. Perhaps the only possible rejoinder would have been that there was no body, save perhaps the Board of Deputies, which could have undertaken that wider responsibility, and that in these years the Board of Deputies seems to have been in worse condition than the United Synagogue, having even less money available.

The annual reports during this period contain much valuable information, particularly the reports covering the 25th, 30th, and 40th years of the institution. The Treasurers and honorary officers generally seem to have treated these as anniversary years, and to have taken the opportunity of surveying the work of the United Synagogue at greater length than they normally did. In their 25th Annual Report the Treasurers discussed the growth of membership of the United Synagogue:

> But the policy of the Council has not alone been directed to the multiplication of synagogues in the metropolis. . . . The purpose of the Synagogue itself has been enlarged and extended. It is no longer a meeting house for prayer only. It has been made a rallying point and a centre for Communal work, where men and women of all shades of thought and opinion may meet to promote the welfare of the Community in general. The jealous feelings of bygone days, when 'Shoolism' in its narrowest form reigned supreme, and prevented freedom of choice in selecting one's own place of worship, have been obliterated. The narrow policy which confined itself to the four walls of one particular edifice has given way to a more enlightened and liberal policy of progress, inculcating the lesson that the Jewish Community in London should be regarded as a whole, and not be disunited by geographical divisions or its growth stunted by infinitesimal differences in ritualistic practices.

One short paragraph, however, sufficed for the social welfare work of the institution.

> New Cemeteries have been acquired both in the western and eastern parts of London. The Beth Hamedrash has also been affiliated with the United Synagogue, and among the many important Communal duties

which the Council have undertaken is the visitation of Jewish inmates of prisons, asylums, hospitals, etc., and the formation of a Relief Fund to assist them on their discharge. The Visitation work alone has grown into the dimensions of an institution.

The 30th Report for 1899 to some extent repeated the self-satisfaction of the earlier one, but certainly a new element began to appear. In their discussion of the growth of the United Synagogue, and of the building and rebuilding of synagogues, the Treasurers commented:

A new and important feature has been established by the provision, in many instances, of Class-rooms for religious instruction. The Council have also assumed the duty of providing means for religious instruction of the poorer members of the Community, for which a special rate of 5 per cent on the seat rentals has been levied.

They pointed out too, with the extension of the United Synagogue 'ramifications', that

nearly every want of the Community may be said to be filled by its working, and nearly every interest safeguarded. Religious, educational, and domestic interests are looked after by the Managers of the United Synagogue, with equal zest, and the welfare and amelioration of the poor foreigner of the East End are regarded with the same consideration as the requirements of the rich seatholder in the West End. This extension of self-imposed duties is shown in various Committees of the United Synagogue, which were not in existence at the inception of the United Synagogue, and which have become established as the exigencies of the continually increasing Community have demanded.

The 40th Report, for the year 1909, was much more complacent, and the catalogue of activities which the Treasurers adduced in reply to the question which they themselves put – What does the United Synagogue do outside the control of the management of synagogues? – was largely elaborated by them in financial terms, at the head of the list being the 'management of Bequests for charitable purposes'. Visitation, burial, education, High Holyday services, were all discussed alike in terms of the subventions voted from United Synagogue funds, and even when they claimed – 'the policy of the Council has never been prompted by selfish motives for the interests of the members of the United Synagogue alone. In their every act, the interests of our poorer brethren have been paramount, and the well-being of the Community as a whole has been the guiding fact – they went on to substantiate this in purely financial terms. One of the last reports to be published in this form by the Treasurers was the 44th issued in 1914 and covering the year 1913. This is of particular interest, foreshadowing as it does much of the work of the next generation of honorary officers – it was at this time that Robert Waley Cohen appeared as Treasurer. The Treasurers referred to the growth of suburban Jewry and commented:

> The paucity of numbers in each locality does not justify the erection of separate Synagogues, with all the necessary expense appertaining to their upkeep, but the provision of Meeting Rooms for prayers and religious instruction to the children is a matter which local effort could and should supply.

They also drew attention to the setting up of a 'Committee for the Welfare of Jewish Residents in East London', with two Assistant Visitors, normally ex-students of Jews' College, who would tend to regard these appointments as 'a stepping-stone to higher positions in the Jewish Ministry'. They continued:

> The whole system of East End visitation is being developed on a systematic basis, the 'Welfare' Committee exercising supervision and control over the entire work, including the administration of the activities of the Committee of Workers among the Jewish Poor and Visitors to Houses of Mourning.

If the Treasurers' reports dealt largely with the financial side of the activities of the United Synagogue, or even measured the extent of the United Synagogue's involvement in terms of the money spent, they at least had the justification that it was the money for whose disbursement they were responsible that made all the social work of the institution possible. The report on the accounts for 1902, in commenting on the working of 'so far-reaching an organisation as that of the United Synagogue, with its varied, general as well as local, interests', put the matter succinctly:

> The economic side of the Institution cannot be ignored and its finances allowed to run wild to their own self-destruction. It is only by a careful nursing of the resources of the Institution as a whole, that the many and varied obligations assumed by the Council can be successfully accomplished.

It was not that the United Synagogue's activities were as yet vastly different from what those of the individual synagogues had been, or

PLATE 1
United Synagogues Act of Parliament—1870

[33 & 34 Vict.]   *Jewish United Synagogues.*   **[Ch. cxvi.]**

CHAP. cxvi.

An Act for confirming a Scheme of the Charity Commissioners for the Jewish United Synagogues.   [14th July 1870.]

1870.

WHEREAS the Charity Commissioners for England and Wales, in their report to Her Majesty of their proceedings during the year one thousand eight hundred and sixty-nine, have reported that they have provisionally approved and certified (among other schemes for the application and management of charities) a scheme for the Jewish United Synagogues, and such scheme is set out in the appendix to their said report :

17th Report, dated 26th February 1870.

And whereas it is expedient that the said scheme, as the same is set out in the schedule to this Act, should be confirmed :

Be it enacted by the Queen's most Excellent Majesty, by and with the advice and consent of the Lords Spiritual and Temporal, and Commons, in this present Parliament assembled, and by the authority of the same, as follows :

1. The said scheme shall be confirmed and take effect.

Scheme confirmed.

PLATE 2

Lionel L. Cohen,
Vice-President, United Synagogue,
1870–1887

Sir Robert Waley Cohen,
K.B.E., President,
United Synagogue,
1942–1952

PLATE 3

The Hon. Ewen E. S. Montagu,
C.B.E., Q.C.,
President, United Synagogue,
1954–1962

Sir Isaac Wolfson, Bt., F.R.S.,
President, United Synagogue,
1962–1973

PLATE 4 Honorary Officers of the United Synagogue—1970

Alfred Woolf, J.P.,
Vice-President

Salmond S. Levin,
Vice-President

F. M. Landau,
Joint-Treasurer

George M. Gee, J.P.,
Joint-Treasurer

PLATE 5   Honorary Officers of the United Synagogue—1970

Raymond Goldwater,
Joint-Treasurer,
Bequests & Trusts Funds

Victor Lucas,
Joint-Treasurer,
Bequests & Trusts Funds

Mark Kleiner,
Joint-Treasurer, Burial Society

Reuben Kandler,
Joint-Treasurer, Burial Society

PLATE 6   Chief Rabbis—1870-1970

The Rev. Dr Nathan Marcus Adler, Chief Rabbi, 1845–1890

The Very Rev. Dr Hermann Adler, C.V.O., Chief Rabbi, 1891–1911

The Very Rev. Dr Joseph H. Hertz, C.H., Chief Rabbi, 1913–1946

PLATE 7   Chief Rabbis—1870-1970

The Very Rev. Dr Sir Israel Brodie, K.B.E.,
Chief Rabbi, 1948–1965

Rabbi Dr Immanuel Jakobovits,
Chief Rabbi, appointed 1967

PLATE 8

Dr Asher Asher,
Secretary, United Synagogue,
1870–1889

Nathan Rubin,
Secretary, United Synagogue,
Appointed 1968

would have been; it was principally that only the United Synagogue had the organisational resources to begin to cope with the volume of work which now had to be undertaken.

One good example of this work was that represented by the Visitation Committee. This committee had gradually expanded its activities until it had become largely an institution in its own right, with a volume of work and range of activities comparable to those of the Board of Guardians.[4] This committee arose out of the activities of the Jewish ministers in London before the United Synagogue had been first established. One of the first actions of the new United Synagogue had been to request them to continue 'the visitation and religious Supervision of Jewish inmates of Workhouses, Asylums, Hospitals, Reformatories, Prisons etc. . . . on an organised system'. The suggestion for this had come from the ministers themselves who having met together placed their services at the disposal of the United Synagogue for this purpose. A formal committee was set up in 1872 and the secretaryship devolved almost naturally upon Asher Asher and thence on to his successors in that office. The committee was almost unique; as Philip Goldberg, the then secretary, wrote to the committee's chairman, Charles Myers, on 19 October 1922,

> The Visitation Committee has always been a force of its own and somewhat distinct from the general Committees of the United Synagogue, for in 1875 the Council decided that henceforth all members of the various Committees of the Council should be elected from the Council except the Visitation Committee – a distinction it has since enjoyed.

By the end of the nineteenth century the Visitation Committee had extended its activities to such fields as sponsoring and generally backing the foundation of a 'Certified Industrial School' for Jewish boys who had come before the magistrates' courts, so that in 1900 the Hayes Industrial School for Jewish Boys became part of the general Jewish scene. In 1902 the Visitation Committee decided 'to extend the present system for the after-care of prisoners, and prisoners who have been charged with offences' and set up a sub-committee which was given official recognition as a Discharged Prisoners' Aid Society; the reports of the Visitation Committee as incorporated into the annual reports of the United Synagogue show how necessary both the visitation and the after-care were to the Jewish community of London.

These were, however, not the only welfare activities of the United Synagogue in those years, for, in addition to those welfare activities which the Board of Guardians had taken over from the various London synagogues, *ad hoc* special committees had very often to be set up to deal with new and unusual problems. The most important of these was undoubtedly the special committee of enquiry which was set up by the United Synagogue in 1896 to consider what could be done towards 'ameliorating the social, spiritual and intellectual condition of the poorer Jews in the East End of London'. It was as a part of this scheme for example that the Beth Hamedrash was refounded, that a centre was established in Whitechapel for the provision of classes and reading rooms, and that assistance was given in such fields as the provision of interpreters in the police courts. It was a result too of enquiries instituted by the United Synagogue that the 'Four Per Cent Dwellings' company was set up, and that other plans of social amelioration were begun. 'Ever since the establishment of the United Synagogue one of the main objects of its legislation has been to improve the religious, moral, and social status of the poorer classes' declared a Report of the Executive Committee of 7 January 1890; 'the solicitude of the Council for the spiritual welfare of the Jewish poor has been manifested year by year in the provision, at its sole cost, of religious services'. By 1903 the Committee of Workers for the Jewish Poor was established, and in 1913 this committee in its turn was replaced by the Committee for the Welfare of Jewish Residents in East London. This was in part a social work committee, since it had from the start a certain amount of religious and social 'visiting', but its terms of reference were very much wider:

> The Visitors in visiting . . . shall have the following main objects in view:
>
> (a) To encourage the children to attend such Hebrew and Religion Classes as are attached to the above Schools.
>
> (b) To encourage the children to attend the Sabbath Classes and Children's Services at the East London Synagogue.
>
> (c) To encourage the young men and women to attend the Special Services at the East London Synagogue on Sabbath, designed to meet their special needs.
>
> (d) To participate in the after-care of children on leaving school, with a view of placing them in the way of learning a suitable trade or occupation by which they may become efficient workers and adequate wage-earners.
>
> (e) To introduce eligible young people to girls' and lads' clubs, so that their hours of recreation and leisure may be spent under safe, healthy and moral conditions.

(f) Generally to keep in touch with the families, so that they may realise that they are always in a position to have recourse to a friend in any emergency affecting their religious, moral and social welfare.

There was obviously still a great deal of overlapping of function, and by 1918 this committee too was replaced by the Jewish Welfare Committee which had the task of taking over and co-ordinating a great deal which previously had been supervised by several *ad hoc* committees.

It would be true to say of these years that there was no call for help which was not looked at carefully by the officers and Council of the United Synagogue; the result was almost invariably that either the United Synagogue took the matter itself under its own wing or else that prominent members took up the challenge as part of their own personal contribution to their co-religionists. This was, however, only to be expected. Brought up as they were within the milieu of the Grand Dukes, and having a tradition of quasi-paternalism, the leaders of Anglo-Jewry continued to assume the burdens that that position in society demanded of them. The Rothschilds took it for granted, for example, that appeals for help would be made to them, and so charity after charity, in London or in the provinces, found support both in cash and in advice from the family and the firm. Similarly of course Samuel Montagu, equally a member of the Cousinhood, found himself as deeply involved in the affairs of the Federation of Synagogues for which he was largely responsible.

Given all this, however, the truth still remained that the United Synagogue was the only possible administrative framework for the operation of various developments, and this is seen in nothing so clearly as in the field of education, primarily Jewish education. In the past the education of the London Jewish community had never been regarded as being specifically within the province of synagogue organisation. Even where there were schools, elementary or secondary, associated with synagogues (such as the Bayswater or Borough schools), this was much more a reflection of the place of these synagogues as centres of strong communal life, and as communities having increasing numbers of children. With the introduction of a satisfactory system of secular schools after the 1870 Education Act, much of the impetus for such a system of voluntary schools died away, and the bulk of whatever Jewish education existed for the majority came through the Association for the Diffusion of Jewish Knowledge or through the growth of Chedarim and the Talmud Torah movement. None of this was really adequate, and there were many who felt that some change was needed, Hermann Adler for example calling for a body 'that shall do for the educational organisation of the community, what the United Synagogue was doing for its religious constitution'. Although there were undoubtedly many among the leading lights of the United Synagogue who felt that it was not the task of that organisation to enter the field of Jewish education, it was none the less from among the United Synagogue leaders, such as Henry Lucas, one of the Vice-Presidents of the United Synagogue and President of the Association, that important support for an extension of that work was gained. The debts of the Association had actually reached the total of £380, and it had proved impossible for the body to pay any heed to the extension of religious education to any other Jewish children 'attending Metropolitan Board Schools'. A conference of representatives of the various synagogues in London agreed 'that this conference is of opinion that the Synagogues should help to provide the funds necessary for instruction in Religion and Hebrew of Jewish children attending Metropolitan Board Schools'.[5] The result of the conference was the creation of the Board for Jewish Religious Education, into which the Association was merged, and the sponsors, who included leading members of London Jewry, made it quite plain that the Board's needs were urgent. It was as a result of the representations that were made that it was accepted, almost immediately, that 'the Synagogues should help to provide the funds necessary for imparting instruction in Religion and Hebrew', and that this was part of the general communal responsibility. Each of the leading synagogue groups accepted a share based on its own financial situation, and the United Synagogue resolved that all constituent synagogues should levy a tax of 5 per cent on seat rentals.

This was of course largely education in school premises of the children of the poorer members of London Jewry. There existed more or less parallel with that system a group of classes held on synagogue premises and paid for, unofficially, by congregations out of their local surpluses, where these existed, or 'from collections from private individuals'. The Annual Report by the Treasurers for 1907 pointed out:

> The Council has no control whatever over these classes, which are managed by Committees co-opted by the Local Boards, and have no statutory existence. The majority of pupils attending the classes are the children of non-members. The Treasurers do not in any way desire to belittle the good work effected by the classes: in fact, they believe excellent work is accomplished in many instances, but it will be a matter of serious concern to the United Synagogue, if the cost of these classes is to be made a charge on the Budgets of the Synagogues. An

important principle is involved, and if the grant is made to the Bayswater Synagogue, the Treasurers feel it cannot be withheld from other Synagogues. . . . It . . . involves a new departure, which may have such far-reaching effects on the future prosperity of the Institution, that the Treasurers consider it incumbent upon themselves to direct special attention to the matter.

The occasion for the special detail in the report was that Bayswater had asked for £60 for the Bayswater Synagogue classes, and that in the two preceding years Hampstead and another, unnamed synagogue had asked for money for a similar purpose. In 1907 these various synagogue classes were brought together into the Union of Hebrew and Religion Classes. The motive for this further creation was the desire of those families which had moved out into the north and north-west of London for some sort of Jewish religious education. As was claimed by the first President of the Union, Frank Lyons, a warden of the Hampstead Synagogue, 'the poor were sufficiently well attended for religious education. The principal aim and care was that middle-class and well-to-do people should have provision made for them.'[6] A request was made for a grant from the United Synagogue, but the response initially was that 'the present circumstances of the finances of the United Synagogue made a grant impossible'. This came from Henry Lucas, active with the Board of Jewish Religious Education, probably fearing that sponsorship for the Union might well make his own organisation's finances even more precarious, but a grant of £100 was made in 1909, and thereafter there was an annual subvention. At first the grant specified that awards should be made only to the classes held by constituent synagogues and should exclude the associate synagogues from all share, but that restriction was soon dropped.

Almost inevitably there were complaints of duplication and overlap. The annual reports of the United Synagogue, of the Union, and of the Board show this as well as a considerable growth in the numbers of children attending classes of some sort or other; in 1913 for instance the Treasurers commented:

> The Treasurers venture to think that the time is ripe for a co-ordination of the different educational agencies in the Community and for the introduction of a systematic plan of Religious Education based upon an authorised curriculum.

The annual reports of the Union show also the different ways in which the inadequate finances were given additional help. Synagogue premises were made available, extra sums were found locally, and often enough there is the comment 'Minister takes a class'. The very inclusion of such comments serves as a reminder that such duties were not necessarily part of a minister's duties.

Another indication of the way in which the individual synagogues were increasingly concerned with education came in the number of congregations which requested permission to build or extend classrooms during the 1890s. The Executive Committee was prepared to agree to these requests where these synagogues showed themselves reasonably sound financially, but these demands came at a time when the constituent synagogues were beginning also to need quite extensive repairs to their buildings. Repairs and redecorations began to represent a sizeable drain on the building rate and thus a further strain on the structure of the United Synagogue itself. Obviously all these activities depended a great deal on the relations between the Council and honorary officers of the United Synagogue on the one hand and the individual synagogues on the other. Each synagogue merits a history of its own, since there can be no general pattern covering them all, but certain features do emerge. Save in the obvious cases where honorary officers had particularly strong connections with individual congregations, there was a marked divergence between the central organisation and the local community. So long as the local community remained solvent and not only repaid the advances made to it in the first place but also bore its share of communal burdens, the honorary officers could have very little control over it. Time and time again the reports of the Treasurers assailed what seemed to be the enormous waste involved in the payments for *minyan* men, by which one group of paid officials attended synagogue in order to hear prayers read by other paid officials. But whenever they drew attention to this expense and tried to reduce it they were faced with opposition, not only from the synagogue in question but by a united front of others likely to find themselves in the same boat. Similarly there was pressure for the replacement of paid choirs by voluntary choirs, and here too the honorary officers met with opposition. In at least one synagogue the entire Board of Management resigned office and refused to resume their duties until the Treasurers restored the funds necessary for this feature of the services, claiming that many who had promised to join the congregation would not do so until there was a permanent choir. So that in consequence the only issues on which there was any disagreement were financial matters. On the other hand the honorary officers had a certain amount of control over the synagogues through the necessity for securing the approval of the Council before making appointments to vacancies and incurring any additional expenditure. On the whole, however, Lord Rothschild was right when he commented that the control exercised by the honorary officers and Council was a very light one, and even that degree of control could be overturned if representatives on the Council ever made common cause.

The system worked because, for the most part, the essential links in the organisation were not those between honorary officers and local boards of management but between Philip Ornstein and the local secretaries. Almost invariably it was the local minister who doubled as secretary, and it was he who virtually ran the local synagogue. As one contemporary commented, the average minister was expected[7]

> to preach simply, decently and in good English and not above the heads of the congregants, to read the Law correctly, to assist in the reading of prayers, to engage in charitable work, to keep [account] books, render synagogue bills, and to be all things to all men.

Solomon Schechter criticised the system whereby he was expected to divide his time 'between the offices of cantor, prayer, preacher, bookkeeper, debt-collector, almoner and social agitator . . . a sort of superior clerk in whom business-like capacity is more in demand than any other virtues they may possess'. It may well be argued that much light can be thrown on the relative status of the United Synagogue ministers by examining their salaries and the conditions of their training at Jews' College; at all events in these years the vast bulk of the United Synagogue ministers had received their training at Jews' College, and it was precisely in this period that the United Synagogue once again put the organisation of the college under close examination. The salaries of the ministers, it was generally accepted, were too low, and were related less to the capacities of the ministers than to those of the individual congregations' budgets; there had therefore been for some time a fund for augmenting these salaries which was eventually replaced by a scheme for a unified salary scale, the balances being found eventually from the general funds of the United Synagogue. It took many years for the full scheme to come into effect, but in the years before the First World War the salaries and perquisites offered by the majority of London Synagogues were around the category of £200–£250, with a figure of £600 representing virtually the top possible. Even if it is accepted that the salary of the Chief Rabbi – £2,000 – represented an exceptional case the gap was very great indeed and emphasised once again the lack of respect felt for the majority of Anglo-Jewish ministers. The particular importance of the part played by the Chief Rabbi is given further significance by the difference of opinion at this stage over whether the United Synagogue's or indeed any of the Anglo-Jewish ministers should be encouraged to earn the title of Rabbi. So long as they did not hold that title they would gain no influence over the recent immigrants, but there was no encouragement, financial or other, for them to gain it. An investigation in 1910 into the affairs of Jews' College was equally unrewarding in so far as resolving the question of the status of the ministry was concerned, save that once there were echoes of the idea that the middle-class London Jew had no intention of allowing his sons to enter such a profession.

A parallel situation existed at the head office, where there was an enormous gap between the salaries of the Secretary – Ornstein received £700 a year – and those of his various clerks and assistants. The maximum for the leading clerks in 1910 ranged from £215 to £104; these were now to be raised to £275 to £150 respectively, by annual increments of £5, so that it would have taken until 1922 before they reached the top. In addition, of course, Ornstein received various additional salaries for such appointments as Secretary to the Four Per Cent Industrial Dwellings Company, but even so, in the age of Edwardian affluence, these officials and ministers were hardly to be accounted as having a great influence as compared with the lay leadership.

CHAPTER 8

RELATIONS WITH SOME OTHER BODIES

There were many occasions for close contact between the United Synagogue and the other communal organisations of London, especially the Federation of Synagogues during the years after 1887, and some of these represent aspects of the work of the United Synagogue which no historian could omit without distorting that work. The question of marriages and funerals, the operation of Shechita, and the development of education – all these show the major bodies in contact and sometimes in conflict. But there was one particular series of contacts which was absolutely central, for this particular issue demonstrates most emphatically the problem of relationships between the United Synagogue and all the rest of Anglo-Jewry, in a way which continues even now to play a part in communal relationships. This was the issue of the Chief Rabbinate. The office of Chief Rabbi antedates the foundation of the United Synagogue, and in a very real sense was never formally created, the office and duties gradually being evolved from the responsibilities which accrued to the rabbi of the Great Synagogue.[1] As has also been pointed out, the 'Scheme scheduled to the United Synagogue Act' of 1870 never specified the office, and the only references to it are to be found in the Deed of Foundation and Trust entered into by the officers of the United Synagogue in January 1871. Much of the routine detail of its work and the division of responsibilities derived from the personal relationships between individual Chief Rabbis and particular honorary officers of the United Synagogue. As again will be shown, there could be deep divisions between them, and on occasion the splits went far towards becoming an open scandal in Anglo-Jewry. On none of these occasions, however, was there any real opportunity for any thorough examination of the principles underlying the office, so that there could only be any public discussion of these at a period of vacancy. On the other hand, even on such occasions there were always complications inhibiting a full discussion, such as rivalries between favoured candidates or more especially arguments over voting rights between various congregations and the extent to which the United Synagogue could legitimately dominate the choice. It was to be on these occasions, in 1879, 1890, 1911–13, 1947–8, and 1964–6, that the fullest discussions took place on the nature of the office.

These occasions, with, of course, the exception of the first, also demonstrated the nature of the relationships between the United Synagogue and the other communal bodies in Anglo-Jewry, and specifically London Jewry, and in this connection the elections of Chief Rabbis in 1890 and 1911–13 are of outstanding importance. In 1879 there was no suggestion that there should be a new Chief Rabbi. Dr Nathan Marcus Adler was still Chief, there was no age limit, and there could be no suggestion of an enforced retirement. On the other hand he was far from well, and so permission was given to him to 'relegate' some of his duties to his son, Hermann. Various conditions were laid down, however, by the honorary officers of the United Synagogue. The Chief Rabbi had expressed a desire to move from Finsbury Square to the 'extreme West or North-West of London'; the honorary officers pointed out that the removal of the office of the Chief Rabbi

> would be not only a personal loss, but a grievance. The Communal life of the Congregation is intimately bound up with the personality of the Chief Rabbi, who must be readily accessible to every member of his flock. . . . If, acting under medical advice, Dr Adler should be obliged to remove from the City, it is imperative that the Office should still be within, or immediately contiguous to, the City, and that his Delegate shall be in regular attendance thereat.

Nor did the honorary officers intend to permit the Chief to 'relegate' a full range of duties, laying down the five functions which they would permit him to pass on:[2]

> To attend at his office in his behalf; to issue authorisations of marriage; to represent him at the court of the Beth Hamedrash, and at meetings of the Board of Shechita; and generally to take charge of matters of detail requiring attention in his absence.

Certainly the Chief Rabbi himself insisted on keeping as tight a hold as he could on the duties of his office; in his later years he lived in Brighton but insisted on being consulted by his son on a wide range of matters, including possible changes in *Minhag*. None the less, for the bulk of London Jewry Dr Hermann Adler, the now Delegate Chief Rabbi, was in practice the full equivalent to his father, so that, on the death of Nathan Adler on 21 January 1890, it was taken almost for granted that Hermann would be appointed in his stead. Since the choice was not in question, however, there arose arguments about the manner of choice and about the range of the new Chief Rabbi's duties, powers, and responsibilities. In fact, as a result, it was not until 1891 that the formal announcement of the appointment of Dr Hermann Adler as Chief Rabbi could be made. The first issue was that of the extent to which the Chief Rabbinate could be widened to cover the whole of Anglo-Jewry. In April 1890 six prominent London Jews sent a joint letter to Lord Rothschild, suggesting that the time was perhaps ripe for a meeting representative of the Spanish and Portuguese Synagogue, the Federation, and the West London Synagogue of British Jews, together with the other metropolitan and provincial synagogues and the United Synagogue. It was suggested that at this meeting some arrangements could be made to bring all the various congregations together under the nominal headship of the new Chief Rabbi. There should be limitations on his authority; the Sephardi and Reform congregations would accept the Chief Rabbi's authority 'in a consultative capacity only, such congregations respectively retaining their autonomy', and changes in ritual would only be decided by the Chief 'with the assistance of a council'. The signatures included not only members of the Sephardi and Reform congregations but also one of the honorary officers of the United Synagogue and Samuel Montagu. This letter was backed by a memorial signed by 472 members of the United Synagogue calling for changes in the powers of the Chief Rabbi as a person over the control and regulation of public worship, these powers being transferred to a representative board, and for changes in the Constitution of the United Synagogue to enable the Reform Synagogue being included in it. To counter these, however, the Bayswater Synagogue sent in a memorial calling for no changes at all in the mode of election, no alteration in the status of the Chief Rabbinate, and no concession to Reform.

The attempt at reunification was short-lived. Hermann Adler was very much opposed to certain features of the scheme proposed, especially the idea of a rabbinical advisory council, but other objections were also taken. Lord Rothschild came under strong pressure from some of his honorary officers who had schemes of their own and who saw in this a 'union of shadows, without substantial benefit to anyone except

Montagu and the Federation'. Surprisingly enough, they also saw in it a strengthening of the rabbinate at the expense of the lay element of the United Synagogue. Rothschild, however, did not give way to these pressures, and insisted on extending an invitation to both the Sephardi and Reform congregations to attend a conference of all congregations in the United Kingdom and discuss various issues concerning the Chief Rabbinate. As he declared,[3]

> the idea of this conference was chiefly my own, and I was emboldened to summon you . . . because I became aware that there was a wide-spread and deep-rooted feeling in the Community that the time had come when even the humblest portion of the Community . . . and certainly the most orthodox, should invite the other branches of the Community to join with us in attempting to unite us all. I will not say under one head, but under one spiritual Chief.

By the time the conference met, the Sephardi and Reform congregations had declined their invitations. On the other hand, the Federation of Synagogues was quick to seize the opportunity of participation. On 2 March 1890 the Federation voted the sum of £10 as a contribution to the Chief Rabbi's fund, and the receipt of this money was held to entitle the Federation to be included among those which had 'contributed money to the maintenance of the office of Chief Rabbi', even though 'there was no Chief Rabbi at the time that they made their contribution'. It was in fact clear that the officers of the Federation had in mind not so much the choice of Dr Nathan's successor as Dr Hermann's; the officers of the United Synagogue noted 'it appears desirable that in future no contribution towards the maintenance of the office of Chief Rabbi be received otherwise than by way of annual contribution'.

At all events Lord Rothschild invited all the synagogues contributing to the Chief Rabbi's fund and all the other synagogues with fifty seatholders and above to attend a conference to discuss the whole question of the Chief Rabbinate. Lord Rothschild presided and pushed forward certain of his own ideas, such as the payment of the Chief Rabbi on a fixed basis independent of any fees and the desirability of the Chief's residing in the East End. He also went out of his way to emphasise that the United Synagogue did not rule its various constituents with 'a rod of iron', and that there was no control exercised over forms of ritual, so that it was up to each individual group to persuade the Chief Rabbi to sanction change if any change in *Minhag* was desired. The discussion, which lasted two hours, showed a certain amount of divergency of views over such issues as to whether the Chief Rabbi should live in the East End or merely work there – as one speaker put it – but there was difference over a resolution that the President of the United Synagogue should take the necessary steps preliminary to the 'election or appointment' of a Chief Rabbi.

The basic issue was whether the United Synagogue, which paid the bulk of the Chief Rabbi's salary, should also dominate the body which selected the Chief. The honorary officers of the United Synagogue invited the attendance of delegates on the same basis as had operated in 1844. That is, each congregation was allocated a number of delegates in proportion to the amount it contributed to the Chief Rabbi's salary, and the United Synagogue's total contribution was nominally divided among its constituent synagogues, so that there was a total of 218 votes exercised by the United Synagogue as against a total of 47 from all the others. The Federation were permitted two votes, in virtue of their £10 contribution. On this occasion, since there was no question of any competition or even advertisement, the Federation accepted the regulations as laid down, but made it clear that they did so only under protest. There was certainly less argument about the conditions laid down for acceptance by the new Chief Rabbi. He was to maintain an office on the east side of the City and he was to visit the provincial synagogues in his official capacity. It was reaffirmed that the Chief was to have control over all marrriages and that he would not be allowed to excommunicate. Both sides reasserted the terms of the Trust Deed of 1871. What is of as great an interest is what was not stated. Dr Adler, for example, was much annoyed at the interest taken in his place of residence. In a letter to the Secretary, written about 23 November 1890, Hermann Adler insisted that he had accepted an informal offer of the appointment on the clear understanding that, in Lord Rothschild's words, 'You are to have a residence in the city, but you may sleep and live wherever you like.' He was prepared to accept the appointment only on those terms. He also made it clear that he was not prepared to accept any limitation on the powers of the Chief Rabbi. There had been a great deal of argument about the appointment of an advisory committee of ministers or ministers and laymen; to Hermann Adler any attempt to create such a council or to insist that the Chief Rabbi should even be bound to consult the Beth Din was completely unacceptable, and the Executive bowed to his wishes in this matter, declaring that any relegation of the Chief Rabbi's duties or responsibilities would be contrary to the Deed of Foundation and Trust. Adler laid down clearly the duties of the Chief Rabbi as he saw them, and in a phrase which was adopted by the sub-committee charged with reporting on this issue, denied to the Beth Din even the powers of supervising provincial synagogues and schools: 'The visitation of Provincial Synagogues and Schools is exclusively the function and duty of the Chief Rabbi, as is the visitation of a diocese by its Bishop.' The parallel would not have commended itself to those urging a change in the procedures of the United Synagogue, and certainly not to the members of the Federation who would have disputed with Dr Adler his views on the origins of the office of Chief Rabbi. It does sum up a great deal of Dr Adler's own interpretation of his role in the Anglo-Jewish community; it is after all true that he wore episcopal-type clothing and he is said on at least one occasion to have worn bishop's gaiters.

The Executive Committee, making these recommendations, was clear about what it intended for the Chief Rabbinate. It expected that the presence in the midst of the East End Jews, 'the class which require the Chief Rabbi's service and advice in almost every conceivable circumstance of their lives', of 'an enlightened *Rav*, of a highly cultured and educated gentleman, one who understands and will study their peculiarities, one who will sympathise with them in their daily wants, and will satisfy their spiritual requirements, will tend to raise their moral and social status, and to make them loyal citizens as well as to keep them steadfast Jews'. Elsewhere the Committee declared the importance of effecting changes in the habits and customs of the new immigrants:

They must be urged to educate themselves and their children, so that ignorance and superstition may be replaced by enlightenment and true religion, accompanied by those traditional observances which have been handed down from generation to generation, and have helped to make the Jewish religion dear to Jews. The influence for good of a Chief Rabbi may be very great. It is the more important that the office should be filled by one who will not only himself do his duty, but who can and will exercise an influence over others to induce them to do theirs, who will act with tact and consideration for the susceptibilities of the members of the Community, and who will work in harmony with the various persons, both in and out of the community, with whom in his official capacity he may be brought into contact.

This is certainly not the place to discuss the Chief Rabbinate of Dr Adler. The arguments over the Kashruth of the Machzike Hadath, for example, did not redound to the credit of either side, but in any case this was not directly the responsibility of the United Synagogue. The other controversy of importance in these years was the question of 'cheap marriages' and the *Stille hasnas*, marriages which might have been perfectly valid by Jewish law but were illegal by the law of the land, having been conducted by persons not certified by the Chief Rabbi in places not licensed by the Board of Deputies. On this latter point no difference of opinion existed, all being adamant that such marriages should not be allowed, and in any case many of those being married would not have been willing to undergo the personal scrutiny involved in securing the Chief Rabbi's authorisation. The only real issue was the extent to which the cost of getting married could be reduced by the lowering of various synagogue and community fees. Earlier reductions of fees had been agreed to by the honorary officers in 1871 and 1877, when it had been made clear that all concerned were anxious to avoid any undue distinction between 'normal' and 'cheap' marriages, the Committee feeling strongly that restrictions as to time or place of marriage would 'establish a difference in the Jewish Community between the marriages of rich and poor'. It was in recognition of this that in 1897 and 1898 negotiations were reopened between the Chief Rabbi, the United Synagogue, and the Federation over the payment by the various synagogues in the Federation of the fee for the Chief Rabbi's authorisation. The Federation sought to secure a reduction of this, and the Chief Rabbi showed himself very willing to urge such a course on his honorary officers. Certainly he could now do so without any financial penalty falling on himself. One of the changes made in 1890 had been to substitute for the former practice of including these fees in the Chief Rabbi revenues the new idea that he receive a fixed sum; the fees would instead be paid into the Chief Rabbinate fund, and any shortfall would be made up by the United Synagogue itself. The negotiations did display a certain amount of touchiness on the part of the Federation and the United Synagogue, their respective secretaries, Joseph Blank and Philip Ornstein, standing very much on their dignity, neither of them prepared to concede anything, even of the most formal nature, in the interests of a more cordial understanding between the two bodies. At last agreement was reached, the synagogues in question paying a reduced fee and the Federation contributing an increased payment – £20 – to the Chief Rabbinate maintenance fund.

The same attitudes became even more explicit in 1910 when negotiations were opened between the honorary officers of both organisations with a view to establishing some sort of unity between them.[4] The particular occasion for the conference was never explicitly stated, but it soon became clear that both sides had in mind, in Samuel Montagu's words at that meeting, a wish 'to prevent friction in the election of an eventual Chief Rabbi, when our respected Chief, who is over 70, is not able to work any longer at his post'. The minutes of the discussion throw a great deal of light not only on the circumstances of the relations between the two organisations but also on various relations within the United Synagogue itself. The Federation had suggested a scheme by which they could secure representation on the council of the United Synagogue, 'a minimum of one for each Synagogue and one extra for every 200 adult seatholders'. As Rothschild pointed out, 'if that was to be the foundation of the scheme the Federation would completely outvote the United Synagogue. The funds of the United Synagogue would be bankrupt and there would be no advantage except the small advantage of unanimity on the Chief Rabbi matter'. Although Lord Swaythling maintained that there would be no financial obligations whatsoever Lord Rothschild stuck to his point.

> What I have noticed . . . is that when salaries come up at the Council of the United Synagogue, a large amount of log-rolling goes on. If A.B. wants something they say to E.F. and G. 'if you vote for us, we will vote for you' and in that way we shall go bankrupt.

Something of the way in which Lord Rothschild stuck to his opinions is clear also from some remarks he made about Dr Adler, twenty years after the original disagreements.

> He is an excellent Chief Rabbi. He has done Judaism and the Jews of England a great deal of good. He is looked up to by Christians and is a thorough gentleman. I tell you candidly and tell you all, it will be a difficult, if not impossible, task to find some man to fill his place properly. But I do think Dr Adler made an initial mistake in determining that his chief place of abode should be the West End.

The whole tenor of the discussions show clearly the extent to which his honorary officers left Lord Rothschild to make all the running on behalf of the United Synagogue – save at the very end the minutes show no sign of any discussion other than that between the two leading figures – and the extent to which the two bodies distrusted each other. The Federation had also sought to secure the agreement of the United Synagogue for the appointment of a First Minister for the Federation who could be appointed 'delegate Chief Rabbi and eventually Chief Rabbi'.

Both these points were unacceptable to the honorary officers. They turned down flat the representation of the Federation in the United Synagogue, and saw no advantage from the offer, in return, of representation of the United Synagogue on the Federation's Council.

They were equally decided upon the issue of the Chief Rabbinate. The time was inexpedient to discuss that question, there were rules laid down to determine how the Chief Rabbi was to be elected, and it would be unlikely 'that anyone competent to fill the office of Chief Rabbi would be found who would accept the office of Minister and Delegate Chief Rabbi at the proposed stipend'.

Within a year both Samuel Montagu and Dr Adler were dead, and immediately the jockeying and manoeuvring for position began. The Federation had in the meantime appointed Avigdor Chaikin as First Minister, and during the vacancy in the Chief Rabbi's office negotiations were opened between the United Synagogue and Louis Montagu, Samuel's son and successor, for Chaikin's appointment as a member of the Beth Din. Once again there was a petty insistence on minor points of detail on both sides, and once again there was a failure to appreciate the ways in which they could properly co-operate. In addition, however, Louis Montagu was by no means equal to his father. As Cecil Roth, not unjustly, commented:[5]

> He lacked his father's generosity, his devotion, and, above all, his deep feeling of interest and sympathy with the orthodox East End masses. He relied implicitly, moreover, on the Secretary of the organisation the Federation, Joseph Blank, who had served it from its very inception, but had now begun to treat it almost as his private preserve.

The animosity which these two engendered in the honorary officers of the United Synagogue over such minor points as to whether correspondence should be directed to, or received by, the 'Acting President' or the Secretary of the Federation, all of them standing on their dignity and returning to Ornstein letters which they felt were incorrectly addressed, was not surprising, and it culminated in a marginal comment to Ornstein by the Chairman of the Executive Committee of the United Synagogue, Albert Jessel, on one particularly irksome exchange of correspondence, 'What charming people we have to deal with.'

It was against this background that the United Synagogue had to choose a successor to Hermann Adler. As an interim measure the Dayanim were invited to carry on between them the duties of the Chief Rabbi; it was at this stage that Chaikin was asked to participate in this work. But in November 1912 the executive committee of the United Synagogue began the process by which the new Chief Rabbi was to be elected, asking the presidents of all those congregations contributing to the Chief Rabbi's maintenance fund to nominate a delegate for a conference 'as to the duties and emoluments . . . the mode of election, and all other details connected therewith'. The conference was held on 14 January 1912, and for it a memorandum was prepared outlining and commenting on the arrangements of 1890 and 1891, and suggesting what the delegates ought to discuss – the amount of work which ought properly to fall on the Chief Rabbi, an increase of contributions to the Chief Rabbi's maintenance fund from bodies outside the United Synagogue, and the mode of election of the new Chief Rabbi. A sub-committee was set up to discuss these various points, but almost immediately the Federation declared its intentions of withdrawing from the conference, objecting to the idea that the number of delegates to the selection committee should once again be allocated, as in 1890, on the basis of contributions to the Chief Rabbi's fund and claiming instead that they should be allocated on the basis of numbers of congregants. As the Secretary of the Federation wrote on 30 May 1912, reiterating earlier arguments,

> The Board cannot give its adhesion to a scheme which practically secures to the United Synagogue, representing as it does only about one-sixteenth of the Jews of the United Kingdom, the election or dismissal of the Chief Rabbi.

There was a further, potential element of discord from the Conference of Jewish Ministers and from the Association for furthering Traditional Judaism in Great Britain. The former body dismissed as useless the existing Committee of Ministers so far as being an effective 'Council of the Chief Rabbi', called for a wider delegation of the Chief Rabbi's powers of visitation of the smaller provincial communities, and was determined that there should exist an effective advisory committee to help and assist the Chief Rabbi. The Association were much more extreme, stating that 'there was no room for a Chief Rabbi' who could be the ecclesiastical chief of all the other rabbis in the kingdom. Their experience of other countries showed that where a Chief Rabbi existed Orthodox Judaism completely disappeared.

> They were entirely opposed to the appointment of a Chief Rabbi, but would withhold their objections for the sake of peace in the community, only on the conditions that the proposed Chief Rabbi should be a man of great piety, strict orthodoxy, a rigid observant of the Shulchan Aruch, and a great Talmudist.

The sub-committee responded, however, that it was the intention to appoint a Chief Rabbi acceptable to all, who would be pious and a Talmudical scholar. None the less, the Committee urged,

it was absolutely necessary for the welfare of the Jews in this country that the Chief Rabbi should be a man of the enlightenment and social standing of the late Dr Adler, who would be able to represent the community in important national questions, such as for instance the Aliens Bill, or on matters affecting the general community at large, and if the Rabbis opposed the appointment of such an Ecclesiastical Chief they were assuming a great responsibility which could only be to the immense disadvantage of the poor Jews throughout the country.

The conference was unable to make any clear statement about the extent of the duties of the Chief Rabbi, contenting itself with a repetition of the statement of 1890, but adding also a further emphasis on the need to have a formalised and regular system of provincial visitation and using that as an opportunity of urging the need for the provincial communities to increase their contributions to the Chief Rabbinate fund. The Committee also authorised the advertisement of the vacancy, in order to attract formal applications; it was to be laid down, however,

That candidates must have the highest Rabbinical Diplomas, so as to be competent to decide all religious questions, that they must have a University degree, be able to speak and preach fluently in English, and be imbued with strong piety, deep learning, and strictly Orthodox principles.

There were already various candidates in the field. One, Rabbi Dr Hertz, had already arrived in England from the United States in order to preach at various constituents of the United Synagogue, while others also made themselves available. In all, six candidates were put forward by themselves – Rabbi J. Abrahams, Rabbi Samuel Daiches, Rabbi B. Drachman, Rabbi Hermann Gollancz, Rabbi Hertz, and Rabbi M. Hyamson – but only three were seriously considered; in the words of the formal resolution,

That the names of Rabbi Dr J. H. Hertz and Rabbi Dr M. Hyamson be submitted to the elective body; that no meeting of that body be convened until an opportunity has been given to Rabbi Dr B. Drachman to come to England and to preach in various Synagogues; that if he fails to respond to that invitation, these names be submitted without any further meeting of the Committee, and if he accepts it, that the Committee hold a further meeting at the conclusion of his visit.

Although Drachman did arrive in England and considered his being Chief Rabbi, he was opposed to a formal contest, suggesting that a 'straw-vote' might be tried. The Conference was opposed to this suggestion, and resolved.

> That having regard to the widely expressed desire of the Community that one name only should be submitted to the Elective Body, the Committee declares its opinion that of the two candidates mentioned in the resolution of 22nd June last Dr Hertz should be specially recommended to the Elective Body for Election.
>
> That in the event of a contest the Selection Committee hope that the Delegates would be at liberty to come to the Election Meeting unfettered by any pledge to their Congregations as to how they should vote.

So much for the official record, and the semi-official gloss from the archives of the United Synagogue. Another view of the contest was set down in his diary, however, by one of the appointing sub-committee, Saemy Japhet.[6]

> In 1912 the late Chief Rabbi, Dr Adler, died. His death was unexpected. The question of a successor revealed great difficulties. An English personality was out of the question. There was nobody suitable. Dr Hyamson, the Dayan, was rejected on personal grounds. A fierce election campaign and fight started. Many candidates came forward. Dr Abrahams from Australia, born in London, was believed to have a claim as an English-born Rabbi. But his sermon displeased the majority. Dr Drachmann met with the same fate, and so did several others. Then it happened that Lord Milner, in the course of a conversation, mentioned to Lord Rothschild that Dr Hertz, also an aspirant, was a most desirable candidate. Lord Milner reported that during the Boer War Dr Hertz, then at Johannesburg, was openly pro-British. He had suffered for his convictions. This was sufficient for Lord Rothschild. He declared the campaign at an end, and proclaimed Dr Hertz as the sole candidate of the United Synagogue. There was, however, a strong opposition. Sir Adolph Tuck was at the head of a committee of men who believed that there were others who would be fit to take up the position of Chief Rabbi, and they tried to postpone the election. The whole committee, on the strength of a published protest, saw Lord Rothschild. Sir Adolph Tuck acted as spokesman,

but he was never an eloquent speaker, so he read his statement, which was very lengthy. Lord Rothschild, being rather deaf, did not understand a word. He was nervous and impatient. After a few minutes he lost his temper and shouted 'Stop! I know all you have to say, but I have made up my mind. The election will take place and unless Dr Hertz is elected I shall resign the chairmanship of the United Synagogue, and shall as the head of my house, prevent any of my family from holding office there. I have before me heaps of letters strongly approving the choice which the Executive of the United Synagogue have made, and I will just read you one from a lady who has known Dr Hertz in South Africa during all the years of his appointment out there.' She described him as a scholar of the first rank, and a splendid acquisition for any orthodox community. 'And do you know,' he shouted, 'who the lady is? It is Mrs Elsa Cohen, the wife of Harry Cohen.' I was nonplussed. Elsa Cohen! our dear sweet little Elsa, without the faintest conception of anything Jewish an expert on the qualifications of an orthodox Rabbi! But Lord Rothschild did not stop there. With increasing excitement he ordered us to leave the room: 'Go away; leave me alone, I am sick and tired of you all! Out you go!' And we went, some of us disgusted, some furious, and some inwardly amused. Sir Adolph asked us to come to his office. It was proposed to lodge a strong protest with the noble Lord, repudiating the offensive treatment to which we had had to submit, and Lucien Wolf drafted a very strong and rather aggressive letter. I rose and said I wanted to make a statement. I asked those present 'Have you never been chastised by your father on an occasion when he thought you guilty of mischief, whereas in fact you were quite innocent? You see, we may consider Lord Rothschild as the father of the community and neither our honour nor our feeling should be harmed if we are punished by him, and though he certainly is in the wrong, his bona fide is beyond doubt, and I declare emphatically that I shall adhere to the result of the forthcoming election. Should Dr Hertz be elected, I shall be the first to acknowledge him and do so loyally, because it will then be the community which has spoken and "achare rabbim lehattaus", i.e. the majority must decide.' Having said this, I left the room, and so did Sir Stuart Samuel, who assured me that he would endorse every word I had said. And Dr Hertz was elected –

At the formal meeting on 16 February 1913 Rabbi Hertz secured 298 votes and Dr Hyamson secured 39. Hertz was thus elected as the new Chief Rabbi, and was formally installed on 14 April 1913. A new era for the United Synagogue had opened, but it was accompanied also by the further worsening of relations with such bodies as the Federation, which now formally declared that it would no longer contribute to the fund for the maintenance of the Chief Rabbi.

PART THREE

ABSORPTION AND CONSOLIDATION

1912–1945

The years from 1912 to 1945 saw changes taking place in the United Synagogue that were as fundamental as any that had been seen earlier. Though there was not the same mass immigration of the preceding generation – although the wave of refugees fleeing from Hitler did produce problems – the problems of the physical expansion of London and the growth of its population continued to strain the resources of the United Synagogue. The thirty or more synagogues that joined the United Synagogue or were created under its auspices were dispersed across wide areas of the growing suburbs, and their varying size and economic potentials meant that new schemes of membership had to be framed to meet their differing circumstances. Above all, however, this was a period which virtually opened with one world war and closed with another; each of these placed its own strains upon the United Synagogue, but those of the Second World War were almost overwhelming, and at times the very existence of the institution must have been at stake. The physical destruction and devastation were in some ways thrown into the shade by the religious difficulties; it was a mark of the resilience of the institution and the determination of its religious and lay leaders that it successfully mastered these challenges.

CHAPTER 9

LONDON JEWRY
1912–1945

The generation which saw the two world wars also saw dramatic changes in almost every aspect of life. There were social and economic changes at a rate which had probably no precedent, and even though it could well be argued that each had its origins in the more spacious period before the First World War it was their cumulative effect which might well be described as 'revolutionary'. The causes of this process have already been discussed; the improvements made in the internal transport system had channelled a population drift along certain paths, and in themselves these improvements – such as the extensions of the Underground in the north-west of London – once again quickened the drift into a flood. This movement of Londoners was by no means solely a Jewish phenomenon, and the nature of Jewish religious needs – and the extent of religious observance – meant that the Jewish population tended to lag a little behind the bulk of Londoners. None the less it was a feature of Jewish life to which many commentators within the Jewish community drew attention, not least the honorary officers of the United Synagogue, who had to face the problems which this move created. The extent of the problem is illustrated only too well from maps and tables of synagogue expansion and from the annual reports of the Treasurers. What was marked, however, about the expansion – and made it different from that of an earlier generation – was the character of the population from which it arose. The earlier movements have been mentioned, and the way in which the demand for new synagogues was largely self-regulating. The earlier new foundations had been built upon a healthy substructure of buildings free from initial debt and supported by a congregation which could normally hope to provide a financial surplus for the general purposes of the community as a whole. A factor mentioned already in the Treasurers' reports, and one which was to assume even more importance as time went on, was that these newer congregations were not necessarily as wealthy as their predecessors had been. Where the earlier moves to the suburbs had been the result of an improvement of financial status, this no longer applied. Over and over again the outer suburbs were being developed by 'spec. builders', and the bait offered was cheap housing combined with quick, cheap, and ample transport into the City and West End. This was the age of the dormitory suburbs, without even as yet the cheap motor car, so that the populations inhabiting them had even less of a social mix than in the immediately preceding period. They expected a full range of religious services, and complained if they were not forthcoming. Not all of these 'suburbanites' were members of the United Synagogue; many of those who were moving came out of the East End, often bypassing the 'staging post' of north London and moving straight from the Chevras of the Federation to the United Synagogue. Sometimes the Federation did try to follow these congregations and build synagogues for them, but the infrastructure of the Federation was not big enough for it to match the financial problems, so that twice, in Willesden and Dollis Hill, the United Synagogue had to take over the incompleted buildings and the debts – creating even more difficulties for itself in the process.

The move created a different set of problems for the United Synagogue, arising out of the way in which the Jewish population tended to follow the trends of the host country. This was no longer the age of the large family: the average number of children per family was declining, and the same pattern was true of Jewish families as well. The transition was the more marked because it was a change not from the domestic norm of the 1890s to that of the 1920s, but from the patterns of Eastern Europe to those of a Western culture. As children grew up and moved away into the suburbs, the numbers left behind became fewer and represented largely an ageing population. In consequence there was to be seen much more clearly a situation where the older synagogues were unable to maintain their former position, precisely at a time when such factors as repair of the fabric of their buildings became the more pressing. Some attempts had to be made, of course, to create categories of membership which would tap whatever sources of revenue might be discovered, but the essential problems continued to perplex the leaders of the United Synagogue. There was no mass immigration after 1914 to offset this decline in the rate of increase in the Jewish population. The restrictions on alien immigration introduced by the Aliens Act of 1905 were made more effective by the restrictions imposed by the war and above all by the changed political structure of Eastern Europe, so that there was no increase from outside Britain as there had been earlier. Not until the beginnings of the Nazi persecutions in Germany was there another wave of immigration, but that was on a very much smaller scale. It created its own problems, but not the problems of mass movement. The impact of the German refugees upon London Jewry was qualitative rather than quantitative, but in the summer of 1939 the difficulties caused by the attempt to assist their absorption into London led to a clash between the honorary officers and the 'rank-and-file' members of the Council. It was not only the issue of special services in St John's Wood which had created these difficulties but the episode brought out into the open growing organisational difficulties within the institution as a whole. These refugees represented, on the whole, two major streams of Jewish religious practice. There were those whose services approached the Reform congregations, and who either found a spiritual home there, or who were willing to come some way towards a United Synagogue service with certain emendations; and there were also those for whom the standards of the United Synagogue were insufficiently orthodox and who therefore turned towards such elements as the Union of Orthodox Congregations. The influence of those wishing to intensify orthodoxy was felt within the United Synagogue as well, and played a part among the various factors within that organisation at this time which seemed to point towards dissension. A cry commonly heard was that the Chief Rabbi and the Beth Din had fallen into the hands of the 'Ultras' who were exerting in consequence an influence that their numbers alone did not warrant. In some respects, of course, this was true. One of the basic difficulties which had always faced the United Synagogue was that of recruitment to the ministry. Many of those who had been able to secure entry visas into Great Britain had been rabbis, and in the absence of a sufficient number of 'native-born' recruits to the ministry and to Jewish religious teaching these refugees filled a vital need. This was particularly true of the Beth Din, where the problems of finding scholars with the requisite experience had always been manifest. On the other hand, it was precisely in this field that much discontent was expressed, and it was here that various elements in the United Synagogue tried to exercise some sort of control. Even their attempts to ensure that members of the Beth Din could speak and preach in English were not entirely successful, and this emphasised even more strongly difficulties which arose in other directions.

The major difficulties within the organisation were in essence problems of leadership. The absorption within the United Synagogue of the immigrants of an earlier generation, and their impact upon the standards of religious observance within the United Synagogue as a whole, had to some extent emphasised the gap already mentioned between the 'rank-and-file' leadership and the honorary officers. Already there had ceased to be an automatic acquiescence in the decisions of these honorary officers, and it took powers of persuasion to lead the Council in the direction where it was felt desirable it should go. At first this had been a tendency felt only at the synagogue level, and in discussions between local boards and the Executive Committee. But even at that level there were still sufficient personal links among all elements of the leadership for these difficulties to be comparatively minor. When, however, the new synagogues came rapidly into existence, and when they were controlled by new classes of individuals, there ceased to be such strong personal connections. Moreover, the new generation was less concerned with the United Synagogue as an institution, so that there was the possible danger of that 'shoolism' which had been present at the time of the original foundation.

These were not problems peculiar to the United Synagogue, and to some extent were, once again, probably inevitable in any organisation of its size and state of evolution. What gave them added importance was that they developed at a time when other institutions – such as the Chief Rabbinate – were also under close scrutiny. It is a matter of great importance that in these crucial and formative years the office of Chief Rabbi was held by a man of such courage and insight as Joseph Hertz. He was not always popular with the honorary officers of the United Synagogue, nor indeed could it be argued that he never made mistaken decisions or even understood the issues at stake. But in terms of his strong personality and above all in his conception of the office of Chief Rabbi he had an immense influence in preserving the cohesiveness of the Anglo-Jewish community, particularly that part of it in London.[1] His predecessors had been nominally Chief Rabbis of more than just the United Kingdom, but in fact their immediate influence had not extended much beyond London. They had been members of the Cousinhood, and very much part of the Establishment. In consequence, the arrival of an outsider, not even a British subject by birth, was a reflection of the way in which the immigrants had become more and more important. The contrasts between him and the older families were in some respects emphasised by his attitude towards Zionism. Despite the close connection between Lord Rothschild and the Balfour Declaration, most of the 'traditional' leaders of Anglo-Jewry were at best apathetic, but mostly opposed, to Zionist ideas. Hertz on the other hand was strongly Zionist, and lost little opportunity to preach his ideas. Some organisations in Anglo-Jewry followed him in welcoming Zionism, but the United Synagogue for one did not. There were many occasions in these years when the United Synagogue showed itself unwilling, as an organisation, to support Jewish settlement in Palestine, and there is no doubt that this, at a time when there was a growing recognition inside the wider Anglo-Jewish community of the importance of the Zionist cause, was yet another issue separating the honorary officers from the bulk of the United Synagogue membership. Above all, the fundamental difference between him and his predecessors lay in their differing concepts of their role within the Jewish community as a whole. The Adlers had not always approved of all that went on, but were broadly prepared to accept what they could not prevent. Hertz saw himself as a champion of certain principles and as a man responsible for the welfare of Jewish congregations as a whole and not merely those within the United Kingdom. He extended the concept of pastoral care to cover Jewish congregations in the British Empire, while there were some topics on which he fought battles on behalf of world Jewry. One example of many is the fight at Geneva on behalf of a true seven-day calendar. Through him, indeed, Anglo-Jewry gained a world status; there had been other figures who had a wide reputation as English Jews, such as Sir Moses Montefiore, but they had been recognised as figures in their own right, while he had a basis at once narrower yet also broader than theirs, as a representative of the new strength of Anglo-Jewry. All this was an aspect of the Chief Rabbinate with which the honorary officers could not deal, and the result was to make any differences between them the more difficult to heal. He could legitimately turn to other Jewish congregations for support, even when, paradoxically, they did not even recognise his official status, whereas the honorary officers could turn for support only to the customs and traditions of the United Synagogue itself.

These years saw yet another factor causing strain within the United Synagogue, a strain which could well-nigh have destroyed it as an institution. Two world wars, from 1914 to 1918 and from 1939 to 1945, placed burdens and responsibilities upon the United Synagogue which could never have been foreseen by its founders. Before the twentieth century, war did not necessarily and inevitably involve the civilian populations, save in a passive sense. Soldiers marched off, while civilians waved and, on occasion, remembered to send comforts to the troops. The myriad of border 'skirmishes' of Victorian England hardly affected the majority of London Jews, while even the fervent patriotism of the Boer War, combined as it was with the realisation that there were comparatively large Jewish communities in South Africa, still had little immediate effect upon a Jewish population that was not even largely of British nationality. The First and Second World Wars did have an immediate effect. Almost from the beginning the civilian populations were involved on a large scale, partly through conscription and partly of course because they increasingly became a major target for direct attack. This was less true of the First World War, of course, and in many ways this war had less of a strain on the institution as such. The deaths were not the less felt, and they hit the 'traditional' families more than others. Many of the immigrants were not naturalised or felt no need to volunteer their services, so that for some time the war meant nothing to them. From the point of view of the United Synagogue as an institution the comparatively little that was asked for was the supply of comforts to the forces, the making available of ministers as chaplains, and the granting of help to service families. The Second World War had much deeper effects, and these strained the United Synagogue very much indeed. The scale of relief in London, the need to provide religious services to members evacuated from the metropolitan area, the call on a much depleted staff to be available to carry a much greater burden, combined with financial problems and personal difficulties to make it possible to imagine the final collapse of the institution. None the less it was at this time that a fleeting vision was experienced of the United Synagogue extending its cover over the entire kingdom, and being reconstituted as a United Synagogue of Great Britain, providing for all the centres of Jewish population on a permanent basis the sort of service and assistance being provided on an *ad hoc* basis wherever, by chance, London Jewish evacuees happened to have found themselves. The vision was perhaps only a fleeting one, and the idea might never have been translated from theory into practice, but at all events there were personal feelings and jealousies which prevented it getting very far. On the other hand to the government of the day and to the civil service it was the United Synagogue which seemed in many ways to represent Anglo-Jewry, so that whether it was on detailed points of implementing food-rationing or on the proper bases for establishing the proper compensation for war-damaged synagogues it was to the United Synagogue, or to its leading officers, that the government turned for information about the 'Jewish point of view'. By the end of the war, then, the United Synagogue had passed through a generation of development and yet of consolidation. It had managed to absorb the earlier waves of immigrants, it had managed to establish itself as the leading force in Anglo-Jewry, and yet it was faced still, and indeed as never before, with essential questions as to where it was going and what should be its role within the broad field of Anglo-Jewry.

CHAPTER 10

THE EXPANSION
OF THE
UNITED SYNAGOGUE

Between 1912 and 1945 the most obvious change affecting the United Synagogue was its own physical growth. It was not only that thirty-four new synagogues came under the aegis of the United Synagogue in those years, nor that the range of activities under the umbrella of the United Synagogue developed widely, nor even that the number of members of the United Synagogue multiplied and that the central office staff of the United Synagogue expanded greatly – though all are true and need to be discussed. What was vital about this growth was the increase in the total area covered by the United Synagogue. The Jewish population of London was increasing rapidly, and moving equally rapidly away from those areas in which it had been established over the previous thirty years. This repetition of the earlier process involved very much larger numbers, and the new suburbs, into which the London Jews were flocking, were much more widely dispersed than the earlier quasi-suburbs had been. An extension into the suburbs carried with it all sorts of consequences for adherence to religious practice, demands for religious accommodation, and willingness – or lack of it – to pay for these religious functions. During the post-1945 period there was an even more marked expansion into north-west London and the far outer suburbs, but it was already posing questions for these earlier years, and the pattern established in these earlier years was that which the United Synagogue followed consistently in the years of the later development.

One of the issues at stake was the extent to which the United Synagogue was to continue to provide accommodation for these new communities. Elsewhere, as in the United States, there was a pattern of Jewish development out from an old residential centre into a suburb; but whereas American Jewish sociologists have traced a pattern of orthodoxy in the centre and a growing lack of it in the suburbs, that pattern could not fairly be traced here. The question is, of course, how far the United Synagogue was able so to adapt its image and organisation as to retain the loyalty of this increased dispersion from the central London heartland. The problems were in two forms for the United Synagogue. One of them concerned the future of the older congregations and their buildings, now increasingly under-used and subject to growing budgetary deficits. The other reflected the demand for the provision for synagogue accommodation from those who had earlier been members of either one of the founding synagogues or one of the new ones provided for such a new community. The first of these problems had already been before the United Synagogue in relation to the closing down of the Hambro' and its replacement by a new building. But that had been of comparatively little use as a precedent. When the new Hambro' was built, it was intended as a replacement for the old, and it was to be constructed as near as practicable to the older congregation. Now, however, a second of the founding synagogues was in difficulties, the New Synagogue, and the solution proposed was on much more radical lines. It was to be refounded on a site miles away from the old, and designed to serve the needs of an entirely different community, the members of which might originally have been drawn from the East End but had escaped from there into the new, more middle-class atmosphere of Stamford Hill. Technically the New Synagogue of Stamford Hill represents continuity with the 'old' New Synagogue; but it is a continuity in name only, and it represents a new foundation designed to serve the changing needs of the London Jewish scene. The replacement, however, had one enormous consequence. The sale of the ground represented an enormous capital accretion for the United Synagogue, and the creation of the St Helen's Court Fund made possible great schemes for expansion that previously would have been impracticable.

The scheme was developed by the Treasurers in 1920 and approved by the Council on 18 May. An offer had been made of £135,000 for the purchase of the site, and the Executive reported themselves as strongly in favour of the accepting of the offer. There were various schemes for the refurbishing of older synagogues or the erection of new ones, and these involved the United Synagogue in wide financial liabilities.

The Treasurers commented:

In the present state of the finances of the United Synagogue, the Council are confronted with a task of great difficulty in regard to the carrying out of these schemes, and to borrow money at the high rate of interest now demanded would mean financing these projects on very disadvantageous terms. The acceptance of the offer now before the Council will not only enable these important works to be carried out without recourse to a loan, but will place the United Synagogue in possession of a Fund available in the future for the most important of its functions, viz. to assist in the establishment of Synagogues in Metropolitan areas wherever they may be required by the growing Jewish Congregation.

This fund, the St Helen's Court Fund, played a vital part in the development of the United Synagogue between the wars. A brainchild of Sir Robert Waley Cohen, it amply fulfilled the hopes its founders envisaged, and it was not until the years after 1945 that the twin developments of inflation and the burden imposed by the development of one particular synagogue virtually reduced the St Helen's Court Fund to being merely the channel through which advances were made from other funds and balances to synagogue-building schemes.

Mention has already been made of one scheme for the expansion of the United Synagogue's influence, by the creation of the associate synagogues scheme. In fact this proved in the long term to be a failure. It certainly did encourage the development of various new congregations where none had been able to exist on a comparatively large scale before, and it helped at times of immense financial difficulty longer-established congregations which had run into well-nigh insuperable problems. But none of these communities was ever able to graduate to constituent status, and, as one report from the Executive also indicated, 'the Associate Synagogues have remained isolated units, without community of interest either with the United Synagogue or even, to any large extent, with one another'.[1] To all intents and purposes the associate scheme came to an end in 1928, although it was not until 1949 that it was formally brought to an end. The basic difficulty for the United Synagogue continued to be that this one organisation had to carry the responsibility for the maintenance of a wide range of communal responsibilities without ever having the financial assistance of a large section of the community either in the rest of the country or even, more narrowly, in London itself. The financial fortunes of the Chief Rabbinate fund provides, then and later, an outstanding example of this problem. The 1926 revision of the United Synagogue Act gave powers to the United Synagogue to carry its functions a little further in such a respect, and the annual reports of the honorary officers at this time hinted at the introduction of a scheme which might help to bridge the gap between the two major schemes and at the same time provide some assistance to the funds of the United Synagogue. The scheme that was evolved was the district synagogues scheme, whereby new congregations were not only to be given financial help but also were to be grouped together in a Council, parallel to that of the United Synagogue itself. The report from the Executive, discussed and adopted by the United Synagogue on 20 June 1927, made the situation quite clear.

> The Scheme . . . provides for District Synagogues to follow generally the methods of our Constituent Synagogues, save that no Synagogue is to be responsible for any deficit of another, except to the extent that the District Synagogues Fund may be able and willing to assist in such a case from the resources of a Contingency Fund. . . .
>
> . . . The Executive Council believe that the adoption of these proposals may prove to be of far-reaching importance to the London Jewish Community. For the first time the opportunity is being provided for the members of non-constituent Synagogues to join with the members of the Constituent Synagogues, and to take a part in bearing the responsibilities of Metropolitan Jewry.

So far as the individual member was concerned, one of the fundamental changes was that now all the members of these congregations were to be assessed members of the United Synagogue, and each congregation was to pay over to the Treasurers of the United Synagogue a weekly sum, out of which a reasonable amount was to go eventually to the general purposes of the United Synagogue.

The scheme proved to be a success; certainly it encouraged at the outset a further growth of congregations, and if the level of advances made by the new District Synagogue Council is any sort of reliable pointer to its welcome by the wider London Jewish population, then it should be remembered that the original limits of £20,000 from the St Helen's Court Fund had to be raised within a few years to £30,000, £50,000, £60,000, and eventually to over £100,000. Even more marked, corresponding also to the growth of population in the new suburbs, was the way in which several of the district synagogues changed status and were enrolled as constituent synagogues of the United Synagogue. On the other hand, there always existed the danger that these new synagogues and their Council would be regarded as not quite equal to the older ones, while there was the possibility that synagogues able to bear the financial burdens and responsibilities of full status were, selfishly, refusing to recognise their own full potentialities for growth. These problems were not at all evident at the foundation of this new body.

A further degree of sophistication was soon developed. In a very real sense none of these schemes mentioned created new congregations, as distinct from encouraging and permitting small existing congregations to come under the umbrella of the United Synagogue itself. There still had to be a great deal of spadework done outside the United Synagogue before any congregation could be admitted; this had always been true of the early congregations as well, even though some of the prominent members of the foundation committees had been leading members – and indeed usually honorary officers – of the United Synagogue itself. But with the growing spread into the more outlying suburbs London Jewry found itself increasingly faced with the situation that, instead of the community spirit resulting in the development of a synagogue and congregation, the official creation of a congregation had itself to create the community spirit. It was, in fact, almost certainly the early realisation of this by the honorary officers which made possible the continued religious affiliations of Jewish suburbia already mentioned in this chapter. It was still necessary to work round some small nucleus of Jewish sentiment in any particular district; but with the rapid development of building and the strong pressure from such areas as the East End and north London to move into the more salubrious areas of Balham, Harlesden, Wembley, Wimbledon, Dollis Hill, or Highams Park, it was not difficult to find such nuclei. Indeed, the new inhabitants of these districts who were already members of the United Synagogue through other synagogues were themselves seeking a method whereby they could continue to enjoy the advantages of United Synagogue membership and fulfil their own obligations as members. None of these groups could, however, expect to acquire even district status immediately, while the old associated status did not give them what they wanted. And so a new form of 'affiliated' status developed in the early 1930s. Links were established between these new congregations or groups and the nearest constituent synagogue, the minister of which would provide his services wherever practicable on such occasions as marriages, funerals, etc. The members would have the right to arrange marriages at such a constituent or to have their children received into the Hebrew classes there as full members. Connections would also be established at board of management level. The aim of the scheme, however, was to encourage the development of stable congregations, and so the essential feature was to give guidance to the possibly inexperienced board of the new group in such matters as the correct siting of its future building, and the avoidance of a multiplicity of small congregations never able to establish themselves satisfactorily. This of course had been a predominant theme of the United Synagogue since even before the discussion of the East End scheme. Another danger which it was sought to avoid was that by which the constituent synagogue itself might have its membership eroded by the transfer of individuals from one to the other, and so detailed provisions were made as to the acceptance of members by the small congregations. Each of the members of the group was expected, however, to make a payment to the United Synagogue, representing a contribution to the general work of the United Synagogue, a membership fee of the burial society, and a sum to be held by the United Synagogue in trust towards the establishment of a building fund. The memorandum continued:[2]

> The Honorary Officers of the United Synagogue hope it may be possible to allocate to the account of the Constituent Synagogue concerned a small portion of the above contribution. This is not intended as payment for Services rendered, but the Honorary Officers and Boards of Management of the Constituent Synagogues will realise that of much greater importance than the financial arrangements just mentioned are the principles underlying this Scheme. It affords, in a manner not previously attempted, means of linking with the Constituent Synagogues the smaller Congregations which modern conditions have tended to create; it introduces to their members the principles of ministerial guidance and leadership and of orderly religious organisation; it enables the local Committees to acquire at once a knowledge of the methods, ideals and traditions of Anglo-Jewry as they are preserved in the United Synagogue, and to secure some practical guidance both from the United Synagogue and the leaders of the nearest Constituent Synagogue; while so far as the Constituent Synagogue itself is concerned, the assistance which it affords to the smaller body will not only prove of benefit to the Community in the religious sense, but will enhance its own value to the Community as an active spiritual centre.

In fact, of the sixteen synagogues admitted under this scheme before the end of the Second World War, twelve progressed to a higher status quite quickly, four of them within three years, and four of them eventually achieved constituent status, so that the scheme was an outstanding success from the point of view of the United Synagogue as an organisation, as well as representing a considerable success in retaining for London Jewry the religious affiliations of groups who might otherwise have been lost completely. Some of the new synagogues came into the United Synagogue in rather peculiar ways. There was, for example, the case of the minister who refused to surrender the title deeds of the building even though his members had wished to affiliate; eventually the dissidents went ahead on their own and opened another building altogether. More important was the case of the Willesden Synagogue, which raised also the question of relations with the Federation of Synagogues. The Federation had begun tentatively to expand out into the suburbs, but all had not gone well. Earlier, on 15 December 1936, Sir Robert Waley Cohen told the Council:

> This is the second occasion in recent months on which a Synagogue connected with the Federation has amalgamated with another and the joint new body preferred to be affiliated to the United Synagogue. This naturally means that members of the former Federation Synagogue now have placed themselves under the aegis of the United Synagogue. The President of the Federation expressed the fear that this might represent a policy of competition between the two bodies. I have explained to him that there is nothing of that kind involved. The two bodies stand for different methods and principles. As one example of that, I may mention what is happening in the matter of Jewish religious education.
>
> Some two years ago, both Synagogal organisations, together with the other main bodies in the community, impressed with the urgency of the problems of Jewish Religious Education, undertook to provide considerable sums of money for the Central Committee for Jewish Education, the Talmud Torah Trust and other similar bodies by handing over for this purpose their share of the Shechita Board surplus and the proceeds of a tombstone tax imposed for the purpose. The United Synagogue is of course fulfilling this engagement and contributing very largely in this and other ways to the cause of religious education in the Metropolis.
>
> I am informed that the Federation have failed to maintain even their normal contribution of £1,000 per annum to the Talmud Torah Trust, that they have ceased to pay over to the Central Committee the proceeds of their share of the Shechita surplus, and that they have ceased to pay over the proceeds of the tombstone tax.
>
> It is only to be expected that large numbers of people would feel that they would wish to be attached to the body which is doing all that can be done to help Jewish religious education. Those who share our view

of the importance of Jewish religious education may very naturally transfer their allegiance to the United Synagogue, preferring to be associated with a body that in this matter, and perhaps in many others, may conform more closely to their conception of a more organised Anglo-Jewish Religious body.

I feel that the policy of the United Synagogue must be to accept membership from people who hold that view, notwithstanding our readiness, and even anxiety, to co-operate so far as possible with the Federation in all matters in which we can both be of service to the Community.

The situation in Willesden was acute. A newly opened synagogue there had found itself unable to pay the debts associated with its building, and, claiming that the Federation had refused any help, its board of management approached the United Synagogue for help. The United Synagogue honorary officers were unwilling to appear once again to be trying to 'take over' another Federation synagogue but were equally unwilling to contemplate a 'serious scandal' within the wider London Jewish community. The Federation did not come forward to accept any obligation and so the United Synagogue agreed to combine the Willesden district synagogue and 'the Willesden Green Federated Synagogue' into the new Willesden constituent synagogue, adding:[3]

> the Executive Committee cannot but regretfully add an expression of uneasiness as to the circumstances in which the 'Willesden Green Federated Synagogue', representing with its equipment an outlay of some £12,000, was planned and built upon such limited resources as to have caused the present grave situation to arise within a short time of its being opened. It is patent that, apart from any question of the Synagogue's ability to meet current expenditure, those responsible for its establishment had allowed serious obligations to be incurred with no provision for their being met.

The whole episode of the Willesden synagogue is of importance not in relation to the reactions of the Federation but in showing and emphasising the care taken by the United Synagogue in launching new synagogues and in making sure that newly founded congregations should be able to stand on their own feet financially.

Parallel to the growth of new synagogues was the problem of existing institutions, in financial terms and in terms of membership too. The position of the Hambro', for instance, at last became intolerable, and the final decision was taken, almost painlessly, to close it down and to bring its members into a special relationship with the Great Synagogue. But equally problems were now beginning to emerge for the communities that had been erected in north London. The discussion was precipitated by requests for help from two small congregations seeking a connection with the United Synagogue, on which a special North and North-East London Committee was set up to consider the provision of synagogue and classrooms accommodation in the district. It became clear that there was no lack of facilities for public worship in the area, the boroughs of Hackney, Islington, and Stoke Newington, even though all authorities agreed on a substantial increase of Jewish population there. But what also concerned the Committee was the future of the area. The members had to consider the question, 'Is the present concentration of Jews in the area in question likely to continue, or is it possibly . . . a merely transitory phase in the movement of the Jewish population through the metropolis?' The Committee came to the conclusion that 'it may be predicted with some confidence that the North and North-East of London will, notwithstanding a certain ebb and flow, remain a predominantly Jewish neighbourhood for the next twenty or thirty years'.[4] The report is dated, incidentally, June 1929, and displays a considerable amount of accurate foresight. This was shown too in a further comment.

> It is important, however, to note in connection with any quantitative estimate of the local Jewish population, that there are undoubted signs of a certain change in its composition. . . . Many of our brethren from the East End who have settled in some parts of the area since the war are of a somewhat poorer class, from the financial point of view, than those who settled there during the last century and the first decade of the present century.

In discussing the future needs of the area the Committee also reported on the way in which 'the younger men and women who are born and bred in London often prefer, if they join a synagogue at all, to join a United Synagogue type of synagogue', although pointing out the way in which many would join other types, partly because of the expense but also partly because of their 'genuine preference for the less formal and what they consider more orthodox atmosphere and ritual'. But to this Committee, as to so many others, the essential issue was that of finance. Four out of the five constituent synagogues in the area were 'deficit', a result not merely of the higher costs of maintenance and normal expenditure in these synagogues which were inevitably higher than those of the independents or even of the associates, but also because of the need for the United Synagogue to provide for a wide range of 'non-synagogue' activities. As a result the Committee urged very strongly that if there was to be any additional building for these synagogues it should be in such a way that it could be 'thrown into and form part of the synagogue'. The Committee concluded, however, by recognising that the area would continue to be predominantly Jewish for many years.

This being so, it obviously is desirable that these Synagogues should not only continue to function, but that they should, if possible, become even more vital and vigorous centres of religious and communal life than they are at present. It would not only be a blow to the United Synagogue as an Institution, but be in the nature of a communal calamity, if any of them should be compelled in the near future, for purely financial reasons, either to close down or to curtail its activities.

The finances of the United Synagogue were certainly continuing to give cause for concern. Attempts had been made by the honorary officers to exercise control over expenditure by insisting, for example, that not only were detailed estimates to be submitted annually in advance by all the spending committees but that monthly statements of the progress in expenditure were to be submitted. None the less, the Treasurers continued to complain of the difficulties they faced. It was, however, in the early 1930s that further action had to be taken. The first was as a result of the general financial crisis affecting the nation as a whole in the autumn of 1931. As usual, a committee was set up, 'with a view to investigating expenditure and making suggestions . . . as to economics in the Constituent Synagogues and other departments of the United Synagogue'.[5] The situation was certainly grave, for there had been a great falling away in offerings, while expenditure had certainly not decreased. The report went at length into the extent of the burden sustained by the United Synagogue on behalf of the 'general work of the London community', detailing the major headings of such expenditure over the previous five years. The report also detailed the extent of official contributions made by other bodies under the same headings, disclosing considerable deficits.

For convenience the report listed expenditure in tabular form as follows:

	Visitation	Discharged Prisoners' Aid Society	Welfare	Beth Hammedrash & Beth Din	Chief Rabbinate Fund
1927	882	1,133	3,683	3,975	3,877
1928	949	1,346	4,126	3,969	3,950
1929	1,076	1,287	4,152	3,966	3,909
1930	1,199	1,483	4,415	4,208	3,849
1931	1,269	1,556	5,058	4,353	4,001

'Towards this expenditure, the United Synagogue, including the Burial Society and Benjamin Levi Trusts, contributed the following amounts':

	Visitation	Discharged Prisoners' Aid Society	Welfare	Beth Hammedrash & Beth Din	Chief Rabbinate Fund
1927	600	500	3,135	2,693	2,915
1928	650	600	3,470	2,940	3,017
1929	650	650	3,420	2,925	2,875
1930	650	750	3,770	2,665	2,857
1931	696	650	3,878	2,780	3,127

'Unless an improvement takes place in the financial position, it would appear that it will be impossible for the United Synagogue to continue its contribution on the above scale.'

Other bodies contributed as follows:

	Visitation	Discharged Prisoners' Aid Society	Welfare	Beth Hammedrash & Beth Din	Chief Rabbinate Fund
1927	90	35	0	0	707
1928	120	35	0	0	688
1929	120	35	0	0	785
1930	120	35	0	0	742
1931	130	110	100	0	622

Attention was also drawn to those synagogues 'to which, as a matter of convenience, one must refer as "Deficit Synagogues"'; there were nine of them, and their pattern was disconcerting.

	Hambro'	Borough	East London	North London	Dalston
1927	654	522	449	493	281
1928	528	599	390	447	283
1929	543	353	410	455	353
1930	560	500	468	326	432
1931	617	491	596	277	541

	Hammersmith	South Hackney	Stoke Newington	Brixton
1927	284	407	10	466
1928	355	163	103	333
1929	453	333	127	312
1930	364	364	259	332
1931	621	588	299	408

Little was done immediately, but following various comments made at the budget meeting of 1933 by the Treasurers a special committee was set up to examine the overall situation, bearing in mind the additional statement that:

It is important to realise that a Constituent Synagogue which unfortunately has a deficit position may nevertheless be doing most valuable religious work in the district which it serves. Moreover all ... make regular contributions to the General Purposes of the Community through the United Synagogue, contributions that support many important communal purposes, and incidentally, prove of great advantage to many of our poor co-religionists not themselves members of the United Synagogue.

The basic recommendation was to increase the amount of canvassing for new members, particularly in the areas of these deficit synagogues. Indeed, each of the constituent synagogues was recommended to appoint a membership committee. Two years later the Council received reports, which pointed out that the greatest success for a membership committee had been achieved by the Hampstead Synagogue, although this was of course very far from being either a deficit synagogue or even one with unlet seats. This might also have been one indication of the transfer of population into the north-west of London, foreshadowing what became even more important in the years after the war.

What also emerges from the report by the Membership Committee in June 1936 is the extent to which the United Synagogue had actually suffered from a drop in membership. Figures for membership of constituent synagogues, as distinct from associate, district, or affiliated synagogues, show a decline from 7,860 men and 4,674 women members in June 1933 to 7,749 and 4,586 respectively a year later. By December 1935 the decline had been checked and showed an increase to 7,969 and 4,686 respectively, exclusive of the new Hendon Synagogue, but the Committee were still upset at the way in which some boards of management were unaware of the problem. To do the Membership Committee justice, there was a deep awareness that a worry over the level of membership was not only a financial worry.[6]

> The idea that a Synagogue is an organisation with the positive duty of trying in as many ways as possible to increase its religious influence and augment its membership came as an entirely new conception. Even now, this conception of the Synagogue as a live spiritual centre is too slowly replacing the old idea that the responsibilities of the Synagogue in this direction are adequately met by Addresses from the pulpit, an occasional interview with an individual newcomer (probably by the Beadle), and by the conversion of the Classrooms into an Overflow Synagogue for the recital of the Statutory Services on the High Holydays for those who are not interested at other times of the year.

Their hope was that an increase of the membership would result in 'the strengthening of the religious ties, the promotion of religious education, and the fostering of amity and concord'.

At about the same time as this report, the spring of 1936, the Treasurers produced a 'new financial scheme'. Quite high upon the list of recommendations came one to change the title 'deficit synagogue' into one of 'assisted synagogue'; the report commented:

> It is not at all desirable that Synagogues should be too readily labelled according to their annual financial results, for the religious work and influence of a Synagogue whose local income is unfortunately short of its needs may be no less valuable to the Community than that of another whose local income covers all its outgoings.

Another recommendation was to transfer a greater proportion of the administrative burden from the local secretaries to the central administration. In fact the net result of the scheme was to disguise the degree of deficit at the expense of the General Purposes Account of the United Synagogue. As the two Treasurers, Frank Samuel and Ewen Montagu, made quite clear:

> Inasmuch as the New Scheme does not add a single penny to the amount to be charged in any members' Synagogue Account, it follows that any improvement of the Final Surpluses necessarily entails a corresponding reduction in funds relating to the United Synagogue as a whole. In fact, the General Purposes Account of the United Synagogue will be the poorer to the extent of over £1,000 upon the adoption of the Scheme, and if the sole effect of the new Scheme were the bolstering up of the Final Surpluses of some of the Synagogues at the direct expense of those other branches of the work of the United Synagogue that are dependent on its General Purposes Account, no justification could be found for such a course.

The justification was that the greater confidence created amongst local boards of management and the increased membership would result in much higher revenue.

What sort of Judaism was the United Synagogue trying to maintain? It would be easy to turn, for example, to a minute of the Council of 13 November 1923, when the Bayswater Synagogue asked for a contribution towards the cost of maintaining the Mikvah there, and the Council were not inclined 'to depart from the principle hitherto guiding the United Synagogue, viz. that it is no part of its function to provide or manage Mikvahs for the London Community, or to enter into competition with private enterprise in this respect'. On the other hand, the Council did vote £25 not only on this occasion, but many other times afterwards, so that the item could be used to prove either the orthodoxy or the lack of it in the United Synagogue. But there were several issues that vitally affected the orthodoxy of London Jewry such as Shechita, or the maintenance of religious education, and on these the leaders of the United Synagogue adopted a stand which would have been endorsed by the majority of the religious leaders in London. On Shechita, for example, the Chief Rabbi and Sir Robert Waley Cohen worked closely together, Dr Hertz suggesting action which Sir Robert was quick to adopt and support. On education too, on which something has already been adduced, the leaders of the United Synagogue had positive recommendations to make. One of the consequences of the First

World War was the idea of a memorial to those who were killed, not in the form of stone but a fund to raise the standards of Jewish education and religious knowledge. The origins of the idea are surely to be found above all in correspondence between Robert Waley Cohen and various others directly or indirectly involved in problems of Jewish education. One of them, Joseph Prag, suggested that the United Synagogue should take over from the Union the general supervision of religious education of its own members. There should be an increase in the hours of tuition and the number of teachers, the funds for this to be met partly from an allocation from 'the Burial profits' and partly by an addition to synagogue bills. Waley Cohen felt that the problem ought really to be tackled on a broader front, and that it was not merely a question of providing more money. 'I do not think any synagogue classes are really restricted either in their numbers or in their standard by lack of funds, and I very much doubt whether we could get the children to attend for longer hours.' He continued: 'To my mind the Community must tackle the larger problem of religious education for the whole of the rising generation. . . . In the solution of that larger problem the United Synagogue ought to take an active and very helpful part.' Later in the summer of 1918 he put on record the notes of a discussion held with Frank Lyons and Adolph Eichholz 'on the subject of the re-organisation of the communal arrangements for religious education'.[7]

> They expressed their intention to try and create a Council of Jewish Religious Education which should embrace the whole of the work which is now being performed by the four or five other bodies who are now engaged upon religious education in the community. . . .
>
> I told them I felt sure the movement would certainly have the hearty support of the United Synagogue, and that we should be very glad to co-operate with it in every way . . . so that it could really put religious education in the community on a sound and permanent footing.

The question of financial aid direct from the United Synagogue as distinct from a voluntary addition to synagogue bills was a different matter, as was made quite clear.

The Jewish Memorial Council was launched after the end of the war, and, although its funds never reached the target that might have allowed it to attain all its objectives, the Council did proceed to establish the Central Committee for Jewish Education and to sponsor a Jewish Educational Conference which met in 1921. Individual synagogues helped to improve the finances of the Union by putting voluntary contributions on synagogue bills, and the decision of the 'parent' bodies of the Shechita Board to allocate its 'surpluses' to educational causes was a further help. On the other hand, the commitments of the Union continued to increase, and this was yet another example of the same feature of physical expansion of London Jewry already mentioned elsewhere. The 23rd Report of the Union described the situation from its own viewpoint, but in terms which paralleled the reports of the United Synagogue:

> The Union now consists of 40 sets of Classes, the same number as last year. Two sets of Classes withdrew their affiliation, though they have since made application to be re-admitted, and two new Units have been admitted, namely Hendon and Wembley. The normal growth of London demands a continuous policy of school extension on the part of the Union. The need for new Classes in the wider area that is being opened up was never so insistent as it is today, for, year by year, public housing schemes and private enterprise have turned green fields into regular townships. It takes time to form any religious organisation. The adults have no place of meeting where they can come together to worship and the children have no Religion Classes. Many of the newcomers, it must be regretfully recognised, are indifferent to these matters. A few public-spirited men, however, usually come forward and set about seeking facilities for worship and education. Generally, one of their first steps is to apply to the United Synagogue and Union, as they know that these Institutions are vitally concerned with their welfare and are ready to render them what assistance they can in establishing and strengthening religious organisation in their midst. At the present time applications for affiliation are under consideration by the Union from four different sets of Classes, in the North and North-West districts of London. The total number of children in these Classes is not very large, but it is growing, and a great deal could be accomplished if the Union could give all the financial help that is required. As it is, the Union's resources are already barely adequate for existing needs. They are fortunate in having secured a special grant this year of £100 from the Central Committee for Jewish Education for the purpose of assisting outlying Classes of this character.

Increasingly the United Synagogue found itself directly involved in such educational programmes. To an ever-mounting extent the Treasurers were requested for assistance in the building or enlargement of premises to be used as schoolroom or classroom accommodation and in 1937 it was even agreed that the Council of the United Synagogue should provide clerical assistance for the Union, on condition that reimbursement was given. Another step was the insistence by the United Synagogue that before a boy could read the *Haphtorah* on the occasion of his *Bar Mitzvah* he had to pass an examination set by the Union. While no one could claim that Jewish education in London before 1939 was completely satisfactory it was managing to continue at a reasonably high standard. The Judaism then which was sponsored by the United Synagogue was a middle-of-the-road Judaism which agreed well with the personalities of its lay leaders. As has been often pointed out, the predominating characteristic of the dominant personality of the United Synagogue, Sir Robert Waley Cohen, was that even if he were not strictly observant himself he would go to great lengths to make strict observance possible for others. In this, as in much else, the United Synagogue in the years between the wars reflected the personalities of its various leaders.

CHAPTER 11

THE OFFICERS
AND STAFF

In these years of growth and change the effective character of the United Synagogue continued to be created by those who served it, in paid and honorary capacities. The official head still continued to be a member of the Rothschild family; Lord Rothschild died in 1915, but to him in turn succeeded Leopold and Lionel de Rothschild, and although they were but little involved in the practical affairs of the United Synagogue their purses were open and their prestige remained high. At times of crisis they were brought forward and they launched appeals within the community, but it was understood that normally they remained above the hurly-burly of United Synagogue politics. In practice, however, the head of the United Synagogue was one of the most remarkable individuals to be concerned with its affairs, Sir Robert Waley Cohen.[1] If any individual could be said to have put his stamp on the modern United Synagogue it is he, and through his discovery of younger men to bring forward into the service of the organisation his influence persisted long after his own death. In many ways he was the last of the Grand Dukes of Anglo-Jewry, not merely in the way in which he belonged to the sacred Cousinhood – for there have been and still are members of that almost mythical group closely concerned with the United Synagogue – but in the way in which time and time again he persisted in his own way, dominating – almost domineering – over discussions and meetings, able to devote an inordinate amount of time to the affairs of the United Synagogue.

Robert Waley Cohen had family connections with the United Synagogue; his father had been active in its affairs, and had been largely responsible for the establishment of the associate synagogue scheme. But his own connections with Jewry, based partly on his membership of Polack's House at Clifton, and continued with the foundation of the Victoria Boys' Club, had not been particularly significant until he was invited to accept office as Treasurer, unusually, without having previously served in any more junior capacity. The correspondence which passed between him and his cousin, Albert Jessel, the senior Vice-President and Chairman of the Council, sums up their respective attitudes. In asking him to accept office Albert Jessel wrote:[2]

Of course I know you are very busy. We are all busy. You may ask if the work is so light, why trouble you? Well, my opinion is that the administration requires the presence of a practical businessman. . . . I sometimes feel that we are inclined to be a little meticulous and the tendency that way requires counter-acting. I think you will appreciate what I mean from your experience. . . . I will not enlarge on the family ties which bind you to the Institution, nor upon the very great pleasure it will give me personally to have you as a colleague. The important place the United Synagogue fills in the Community requires that it should be guided by the best available talent. . . . I omitted to mention that we know you are liable to be transported to distant places at short notice, but this will not create any practical difficulty.

Robert Waley Cohen replied:

My first impulse was to say 'no', because I feel that apart from the lack of personal qualifications . . . I really haven't enough time . . . but if the Hon. Officers feel – after I have told you of my special disabilities – that they cannot at the moment get anyone better, I shall feel it my duty to accept. I am, as you say, fairly busy, but apart from that, my time is not my own. . . . My work involves many meetings, the hours of which have to be fixed to suit the convenience of many people of whom I am the least important. The result of that is that I cannot ever be depended upon before 6.30 in the evening. That is a hard fact which cannot be got over in any way and I think you may feel it to be an insuperable obstacle. . . . [he concluded] I shall not feel in the least hurt if, when the Hon. Officers have heard of the inelasticity of my time, they feel that they can do better by another nomination. In any case it has been a great pleasure to me to receive your kind letter and if I am after all nominated and elected, I shall do my best to live up to the very high standard of the family tradition.

He was promoted to Vice-President in 1918, a promotion which not surprisingly under the circumstances caused some ill-feeling among his colleagues, one of whom, Leonard Franklin, resigned in consequence. He wrote, on 12 February 1918:

> My reason for resigning is one of principle. I hold that the office of Treasurer of the Burial Society with its many duties, dealing as it does with all kinds and conditions of men and women, not connected with the United Synagogue, also with other institutions having the same objects as ourselves, and public and Government officials, is a good training for those to whom should be intrusted the high offices, to conduct the affairs of the United Synagogue. I hold too, that those who have served as honorary officers for the longest time should have the offer of the higher offices and feel that unless this is done, it will be difficult to fill the troublesome and junior offices.
>
> This is no personal question. I have stood aside when the post of Treasurer was vacant and Mr Waley Cohen was elected and again when the late Major Evelyn de Rothschild was made Vice-President, but I feel that if I stood aside without protest now, I should be sacrificing a principle that would be detrimental to the Council and discourage the rank and file from giving service. Regretting that I have to sever my active connection with an institution that my family helped to found. . . .

The appointment was, however, a highly successful one, because it was 'Bob' who ran the United Synagogue for the next generation. He did not run it easily. There were, for example, perpetual arguments with the Chief Rabbi, while Sir Robert's well-known temper led him quite often into explosive scenes with many who came visiting him on official business. On the other hand, there is more than a suspicion that these outbursts were deliberately staged by him in order to create an impression, for he is known to have mentioned on at least one occasion to the Treasurers who had been with him 'a very good loss of temper that time'. What was outstanding about him was the time and energy he devoted to the United Synagogue. He may have had to defer coming down into the office until the evening, but once he arrived he threw himself into the work. A series of memoranda and dated comments still preserved in Philip Goldberg's papers[3] show how in the spring of 1942 he attended the offices of the United Synagogue at least three evenings a week, working till late drafting letters and memoranda, taking decisions affecting the work of the United Synagogue, and generally ensuring that the United Synagogue could continue under wartime conditions. There are series of papers entitled 'Matters for Sir Robert', and neatly attached to them sheets headed 'Decisions of Sir Robert'. All this was at a time when the Council was virtually in abeyance, so that the advice he could receive was restricted to his immediate circle; but perhaps that was not entirely to his distaste, for he was not altogether a lover of 'democracy', despite his remarks when he was being crossed by the Council: 'Well, the United Synagogue is, after all, a democratic institution.' He far preferred the idea of 'confidence from below', and disliked all decisions being liable to an upset from the Council. Once the honorary officers had been elected, he felt, they should either be backed or dismissed and he made no bones about making his attitude clear. On at least two occasions, in 1928 and 1939, there were meetings of the Council at which Sir Robert put into plain words these ideas of his. When in 1928 an alteration to the constitution was passed against the opposition of the honorary officers a special meeting was summoned, and in the summons they declared that 'unless arrangements can be made to maintain the Constitution we are not prepared to continue in office'; in his own speech Sir Robert put his principles fairly before the members of the Council. He defined the constitution of the United Synagogue; 'I think that it is right that our great religious organisation should not respond very easily to what may appear to be a new world but what may in reality be no more than a passing fashion.' The changes he opposed were designed to prevent any changes being introduced except by a two-thirds majority of the Council, thus making any further changes even more difficult; he felt that there were sufficient delaying mechanisms built in already.

> They do leave a real possibility open for our great historic body to keep 'alive', and to adapt itself as the generations proceed to the requirements of ordered evolution: . . . to maintain that carefully guarded and well-ordered road open and unobstructed is in our view vital to the United Synagogue if it is to continue to hold the great body of traditional Jews in this City. . . . If this proposal is put into effect it will destroy this institution as a living institution; it would drive large bodies of our fellow Jews – and these not the least intelligent or the least respected members – to join or to form other bodies which would very soon deprive the United Synagogue of its great place in the life of Anglo-Jewry.

He made his own position crystal clear.

Your Honorary Officers do not feel that they can carry on the work of
the United Synagogue except with the support of the great body of
the members expressed through the Council of the United Synagogue.
In the daily work of the United Synagogue with its many institutions
and thousands of members we are constantly called upon to take
decisions and executive action in accordance with our judgement of
the interest of this institution and of Anglo-Jewry. We can only do
that if we have behind us the goodwill and support of the main body of
this Council. . . . We welcome and appreciate constructive criticism
in this Council; here our problems are probed and thoroughly debated
and discussed, and we always hope for and often receive ideas and
guidance and help from your deliberations. But finally and in the end
in a matter of great principle on which we have convinced you as to
the vital needs of the institution we must be supported or we must be
relieved of the burden of carrying on.

The original draft read not 'convinced you' but 'given you our final
view'; that was apparently too strong meat even for Sir Robert when it
came to delivering his speech. He continued:

The United Synagogue has stood firm as a rock gathering to itself the
great body of London Jewry, maintaining those firm Anglo-Jewish
traditions which have made us the envy of Jewry in the East and in the
West – rejecting the extremists on each side who would either tear us
from our moorings on the one hand or kill our vitality on the other:
rising, too, above the destructive elements in our midst that would
overwhelm our activities in barren controversy. Rejecting these toxic
poisons we have maintained a healthy activity and in the last ten years
we have perhaps been able to render greater service to religion and to
Judaism in this land than at any other previous time in our history. I
pray that all this beneficent activity, broad-based upon our well-tried
Constitution, may be given a new lease of life tonight, and that future
generations may look back at this meeting not as the harbinger of a
devastating decay, but as the revindication of our principles – a
renewal of the determination of the United Synagogue to continue
with undiminished strength its beneficent and active life at the centre
of Anglo-Jewry.

He got his way.

A similar episode occurred in the summer of 1939, when the honorary
officers and the Chief Rabbi were enthusiastic about a scheme for special
services on Friday evenings in various constituent synagogues, the form

of worship being designed to attract many of the German refugees into closer association with the United Synagogue. In introducing the scheme Sir Robert made it quite clear that the idea had the full backing of the Chief Rabbi himself and that all were keen on it.

> There is one other matter which I feel it is only frank that I should tell you before this motion is adopted. The Honorary Officers and the Chief Rabbi have devoted a very large amount of time to studying this problem and arriving at their conclusion as to its solution. They have been elected by the Council as the Executive leaders of the United Synagogue for the time being and it is quite clear to all of us that if, in a serious matter of this kind, the Council is not prepared to accept their advice, it would not be right for them to continue to accept that responsibility. It is absolutely vital that those who are entrusted by the Council with the conduct of the multifarious executive work of the United Synagogue should hold the confidence of the Council and if, by your rejection of this serious, far-reaching and carefully considered recommendation you show that the Honorary Officers have lost your confidence, I say for myself, and I am requested to say on behalf of the other Honorary Officers that they will bow to your decision and cannot continue in office. . . . There may be those who, whilst they have *prima facie* doubts on this or that aspect of the proposals, still feel that they desire to show their confidence in the Chief Rabbi and in the Honorary Officers of the United Synagogue and in that event they will no doubt support the scheme and would wish, before expressing their views to the Council, to have a clear understanding of the position before our discussion proceeds.

The meeting was made the occasion for a trial of strength between the Council and the honorary officers, and the honorary officers were defeated. Immediately Sir Robert offered his resignation, and it was only the outbreak of the war which delayed its implementation.

In a lighter mood, one of his protégés, Ewen Montagu,[4] grandson of Samuel Montagu, recalled an occasion

> when a member of the Council moved a vote of 'No confidence' because of a ruling by Sir Robert from the Chair – one which he would not explain because it would have meant blaming a personality – Sir Robert put Frank Samuel in the Chair – the motion of No Confidence was carried by a big majority and there was a gasp from the meeting – which turned into a roar of laughter and applause as Sir Robert moved back into the Chair and said 'The next item on the Agenda is . . .'.

But if he was no democrat in the normal sense he was always eager to bring forward fresh blood into the service of the United Synagogue. As Ewen Montagu also recalled:

Sir Robert was always on the look-out for bright and able young men who might serve the Community – finding them, persuading or 'press-ganging' them as soon as they were ripe and then forcing their elders 'jealous of office' to accept them, give them their chance and promote them.

Philip Goldberg, then the secretary of the United Synagogue, left in his papers a note of such a memorandum:

Sir Robert said he was forwarding the names of two gentlemen who had spoken at the Hendon meeting who had made a good impression upon him as likely to be useful in connection with United Synagogue work. These names should be added to the Honorary Officers' list for future reference. The other United Synagogue Honorary Officers should be asked to act similarly whenever they attend Synagogue meetings, with a view to spotting talent for future use.

His colleagues remembered for long his skill as a draftsman – and indeed the draft letters and memoranda prepared for him contain ample evidence of the way in which he insisted on making changes before he was prepared to sign anything – and remembered too his foresight. This was demonstrated not only in the way in which he pushed the concept of centralisation of United Synagogue offices in Woburn House but also in the way in which he insisted on prolonging honorary officers' meetings if necessary until the early hours of the morning in order to make sure that the final decisions were such as he could have wished. On the other hand if his colleagues could convince him that he was wrong he was not impervious to criticism.

It was this attitude of wanting to have his own way which led to difficulties with the Chief Rabbis of his time. Chief Rabbi Joseph Hertz and Chief Rabbi Israel Brodie overlapped in time his tenure of office. Sir Israel Brodie never found him too difficult; Sir Israel was a much younger man of course and had made up his mind never to allow himself to be brought into a quarrel, so that relations there tended to be amicable. On the other hand Chief Rabbi Hertz's relations with Sir Robert were extremely difficult. This was in part a result of the particular structure of the United Synagogue. Its foundation had been that, while the honorary officers determined policy in 'secular' matters, they had to consult with the Chief Rabbi on 'spiritual' or 'ecclesiastical' matters. The interpretation of 'consult' was always liable to be difficult, if only because 'consult' did not necessarily mean 'agree with', and there was always the further problem of deciding what was 'secular' and what was not. It was all too easy for both men to expand their fields of interest until they each faced a direct confrontation with the other. If each, or indeed either, had been of an easygoing temperament, these problems could have been resolved without too much of a disagreement, but both were irascible to a high degree. Sir Robert's temper has already been described, while the biographical note on Joseph Hertz in the *Dictionary of National Biography* written by Cecil Roth commented on his 'combative conservatism' and added that he was 'somewhat bellicose' – it was once said of him that 'he never failed to seek a peaceful solution of a problem when all other possibilities had failed' – and so it became virtually inevitable that their disagreements should become almost violent. Sir Robert himself well understood this. In 1942, when the presidency of the United Synagogue was vacant, he was reluctant to accept the office. The honorary officers' minutes for 26 February note:

> Sir Robert has suggested that if possible it [the Presidency] should be offered to some other leading member of the Community on account of the difficulties created by the Chief Rabbi from time to time and the advantage of being able to introduce a person who was not actively engaged in the work of the United Synagogue. It appeared difficult, however, to find someone whose interests, outlook, and connection with our religious life rendered him suitable for the office of President.

The relations between them had deteriorated during the years of Dr Hertz's ministry. From almost its beginning issues had arisen over which the Chief Rabbi and the honorary officers had clashed, but gradually Sir Robert had come to personify all the various tendencies in Anglo-Jewry which Dr Hertz had most feared. It was not something which occurred overnight, and there were very many occasions, such as the maintenance of Shechita and Kashruth in general, when the two found themselves working very closely together. There were many occasions too when Sir Robert went out of his way to defend the entrenched position of the Chief Rabbi, upholding him against attacks from elsewhere, while Dr Hertz was prepared to pay many sincere compliments both to the United Synagogue as an institution and to Sir Robert as a person. In 1931, for example, at a Joint Anniversary Service on the occasion of the 75th Anniversary of Jews' College, the 70th of the Jewish Religious Education Board, and the 60th Anniversary of the United Synagogue, Dr Hertz said:[5]

In addition to building houses of worship in new centres of the Metropolitan Jewish population, and maintaining the various ecclesiastical and communal institutions of a world *Kehillah*, it has organised a wonderful network of 'Social Welfare' activities that extend far beyond the Metropolis; such as helping the helpless by visitation of hospitals, prisons, and reformatories; taking charge of the burials of the friendless poor, and coming to the rescue of the discharged prisoner; and, by means of its renowned Arbitration Court in connexion with the Beth Din, fulfilling in a striking manner the sublime duty of 'bringing peace between man and his fellow'. . . . And to these widely ramified services in the realm of worship and lovingkindness, it has in recent years added a new enthusiasm for *Torah*, liberally subventioning Jewish religious education, higher and elementary, both within and without its affiliated Synagogues.

He added an assessment of the United Synagogue with which afterwards he might not have continued to agree:

The United Synagogue has given its distinctive character to English Judaism. By its example and influence it has made Progressive Conservatism – i.e. religious advance without loss of traditional Jewish values and without estrangement from the collective consciousness of the House of Israel – the Anglo-Jewish position in theology.

The basic misunderstandings between the two resulted from their differing ideas as to how the decline in spiritual standards and in Judaism could be halted; Dr Hertz felt deeply that it was only by an insistence on religious observances that any standards could be upheld, while Sir Robert felt equally strongly that an undue emphasis on religious minutiae would drive many away from their faith. With the Second World War and the strains which that imposed on the United Synagogue their relations rapidly grew so much worse that the honorary officers of the United Synagogue had to try to convene conferences between the friends of Sir Robert and the friends of the Chief Rabbi which sometimes ended in compromise and sometimes where they had begun, in deadlock. Confidential records of such discussions, sometimes in the presence of the Chief Rabbi and sometimes only among the honorary officers themselves, which are still preserved either in the United Synagogue archives or among Philip Goldberg's private papers, show clearly the extent to which these differences had gone. To some extent also the detailed negotiations over the conditions under which Dr

Hertz's successor should be appointed indicate the earlier problems and difficulties.

These issues had an equally important impact upon the situation of the ministry in London between the world wars. Two issues came to the fore. One of these was the level at which salaries ought to be paid. There was in general terms an improvement in the general economic status of London Jewry, but at the same time there was a reluctance on the part of the community to make higher salaries available. In 1923 a committee, composed of representatives of surplus and deficit synagogues, was set up to examine the general salary levels of United Synagogue ministers and readers, and its report exuded a general air of self-satisfaction.[6]

In the opinion of the Committee it is not possible to say that a Minister's salary is or is not adequate. The service which the ideal Minister can render to a modern Anglo-Jewish congregation is so great that if it were to be measured by commercial standards it would be impossible to say that any salary that might be mentioned represents a greater value than the services to be rendered. But it is of the essence of the position of a Minister of Religion that he can only fulfil his task in life if his calling carries with it its own reward in the consciousness of the service he is rendering to his Congregation, to his Community, and indeed to mankind. No Minister can succeed in his task who enters upon it in any other spirit. We can, however, hope to relieve him from actual worldly anxieties, so that he may be free to devote himself to his labours with that detachment without which no Minister can render much valuable service to a modern congregation. The more we succeed in achieving that the more chance shall we have of finding men adequate to fulfil the office. Your Committee have observed with great satisfaction the immense progress which the United Synagogue has been able to make in that direction. Comparing the salaries of the Ministers and Readers of the United Synagogue twenty years ago with those established today, there has been an increase in the average individual salary of approximately 77 per cent. During the same period the salaries of senior members of the Civil Service have risen by less than 50 per cent., whilst there are few, if any, professional posts at the principal Universities in this country whose salaries have increased by 25 per cent. during the same period, and very few indeed who are protected by so generous a pension scheme as that of the United Synagogue. It may also be mentioned that the salaries paid by the United Synagogue to its Ministers and Readers are in advance of those paid by any other religious denomination in the country.

Taking these facts into consideration and using the phrase 'adequate' in this comparative sense, and not in the sense that we have in any way reached the limit of the salaries which we should like to offer if we had unlimited funds, the Committee, having examined the situation with regard to every Minister and Reader, have come to the unanimous conclusion that the salaries are adequate. . . .

The Committee desire to make special reference to the deputation which the Committee of Ministers sent to them. They had the pleasure of a conference, in which the Ministers set forth with great fairness some considerations relating to the salaries of Ministers and Readers, which received the close attention of your Committee. In the special circumstances of the present enquiry, we felt it right to lay before the representatives of the Ministry the fact which became apparent to the Committee at an early stage of our enquiry, viz., that no general increase of the salaries of our Ministers and Readers could take place without a corresponding increase in the annual amount of the Seatholders' Synagogue accounts. Your Committee were and are of opinion that Synagogue Accounts have already reached a very high figure, and that in the interest of our public worship it is most undesirable that they should be further increased. It should be recorded that in accordance with what might be expected of such men the representatives of your Ministers immediately concurred in this view, whilst fully realizing the effect which such a conclusion must have in debarring the possibility of raising the present scale of salaries.

Two specific recommendations were made for slight adjustments of salary, one concerning a minister who had entered the service of the United Synagogue in 1895 but who would not reach his maximum salary (of £630) until 1937. For him it was agreed that he should be allowed to reach it in 1930. It might perhaps be felt that the satisfaction of the report was a little marred by the need the Committee felt to draw attention to the Ministers' Salaries Augmentation Fund, the purpose of which was to make public the granting of additional money to those ministers whose salaries were otherwise inadequate; either the fund was intended to provide even more for the relief of deficit synagogues or else it was a recognition that something was wrong in the general salary levels.

The other issue which emerged was that of the status of the minister, in relation not only to his congregants but also to the other ministers serving the United Synagogue and above all the Chief Rabbi. The growth of new synagogues had led to a shortage of ministers particularly in the newer, small congregations which had often managed to find preachers but not ministers. There was also a danger that unless some sort of hierarchy were established the more experienced ministers would have increasingly become discontented at the lack of opportunities open to them, resenting their being put on a par with newly appointed ministers 'fresh out of college' and resenting equally the gap kept between them and the Chief Rabbi. The United Synagogue honorary officers attempted to meet these feelings by the creation of a system of district ministers, combining a number of synagogues under a Joint Board. The same Committee, having considered the range of duties laid upon a minister, reaffirmed the view that the minister should in general continue to act as the secretary of his synagogue, and it was not until the eve of the war, in 1937, that there developed any serious opposition to this view within the Council of the United Synagogue. The district ministry scheme was never fully developed. Too many of the existing ministers felt their status potentially threatened, and too many existing congregations resented either being apparently demoted in relation to other congregations in their district or losing the complete and undivided attentions of their own minister. Much depended on the personalities of the ministers involved, and not all of these were prepared to fit themselves into the scheme. Fundamentally, therefore, the essential problems of the ministry were not altered, and the years after the Second World War were to see the same problems forcing themselves over and over again on to the attention of the honorary officers.

If the tone of the United Synagogue was often reflected in its honorary officers and its ministers, much of its character was dictated by its full-time official staff. For most of these years the post of Secretary was held by Philip Goldberg; unlike both his immediate predecessor or successor he had not worked his way up the internal ladder of United Synagogue service but had been brought in from outside. While this meant that he had to learn the job from scratch, it had its advantages too, for it meant that he could bring a fresh mind to the task. In many ways, however, the combination of Waley Cohen and Goldberg was one in which Goldberg was very much the junior partner, for he was by no means a strong personality. As Sir Robert said after the interview to appoint the new Deputy Secretary (for such he was at first), 'X would make a first class Honorary Officer and not such a good Secretary, whereas Goldberg will make a first class Secretary and not such a good Honorary Officer.' After his death tributes were paid by the honorary officers and by those with whom he had worked. The President declared:[7]

He fervently believed in three great truths concerning the United Synagogue. That on the United Synagogue depended the stability and well-being of the Anglo-Jewish Community – that the United Synagogue was and must always be that great central 'umbrella' under which *all* who believe in our traditional orthodoxy can find spiritual comfort – that only the United Synagogue can, and consequently must, try to hold or bring back to the fold those who are drifting, or have drifted away.

Julius Jung, the Executive Director of the Federation of Synagogues, hit him off more precisely, in a letter written to Alfred Silverman on 14 August 1957:

> He . . . had made the organisation he served so well his main aim in life. His other interests were known to be limited. Not only at home, but even on train journeys, he was found to be coping with some problems of his office.

His private papers and his public attitudes confirm the impression above all that he tended to be a fussy man, liable to be swayed by the opinions of others and certainly deferring to the judgments of others. Perhaps the fairest comment on him would be based on the judgment that he spent so much time on minor issues, not so much neglecting the major ones as failing to differentiate between them and thus lacking a sense of proportion. The parallel could also be given of the long-drawn-out soul-searching through which he went before he volunteered for military service. On the one hand he held the conviction that he ought so to volunteer, but on the other hand there were members of his family dependent on him. He wrote round to all the people whom he thought he could consult, and, being a keen member of the scouting movement, even to Lord Baden-Powell, the Chief Scout. The latter refused to give him guidance and left the decision to him.

In many ways his actions after he became first Deputy Secretary of the United Synagogue, and then a year later succeeding Philip Ornstein as Secretary, bear out this same characteristic. He would have been an efficient chief clerk, and even his minor foibles evidence his personality. He had, for example, a passion for saving paper, and insisted on using the back of half-used sheets. Anyone looking through his memoranda would find it difficult to determine which is the important side of the paper; moreover he insisted on doing his own typing, and since he was never a very skilled typist the difficulty is the greater. His imprint is not writ large on the United Synagogue, and whatever effect he had was very much behind the scenes. Certainly many of the papers produced by the United Synagogue during these years were drafted largely by him. He noted, for example, on a copy of a newsletter produced in March 1941 by the United Synagogue, 'This was the only issue printed. The extreme Nationalist views of the editor Aaron Wright were becoming more and more threatening to an Organisation which was not meant to be an instrument of political Zionism, but a religious organisation.' It bore a message from the President, Lionel de Rothschild, and Goldberg wrote: 'The message was written by me, and Mr de Rothschild was delighted, and did not alter it at all.' Elsewhere he wrote: 'PG wrote this message for L de R who took it whole.' And certainly too the intense activity of Sir Robert would have been impossible without the assiduity of Philip Goldberg, for it was Goldberg's task to predigest all the materials coming into the office. Sir Robert's memoranda headed 'Decisions of Sir Robert' would never have existed without Goldberg's papers 'Matters for Sir Robert', and it was therefore just as well that there did exist in the United Synagogue offices a chief executive so devoted to its interests and yet unwilling to interpose his own personality between the institution and its 'managing director', a man capable of creating a strong pattern of orderly administration.

The amount of work falling on his shoulders was partially recognised by the appointment in 1926 of Henry Isaac as Joint Secretary, but the bulk remained certainly Goldberg's responsibility. As Secretary, Goldberg was never overpaid. As Deputy Secretary he had been appointed on a scale of £400–500 a year, and when he was confirmed as Secretary his salary was raised to a scale of £600 rising by £20 every two years to a maximum of £800. Admittedly it was increased by £100 in 1924 and by a further £100 in 1936, but this was hardly riches in terms of inter-war prices, and was the same salary that Asher Asher had received in 1880; indeed, in an organisation run by a group of extremely wealthy men, relative salaries were a mark of relative status. Other salaries in the United Synagogue were in proportion, and even though the amount of work falling on the staff increased greatly it took much battling before the honorary officers were prepared to increase the numbers of staff. It is small wonder that not all the officers were worthy of their trust and that some had to be allowed to resign prematurely without pension. Various minor changes and promotions were conceded by the honorary officers, but the biggest changes were inaugurated by a memorandum from the Joint Secretaries in 1934, at a time of great financial stress. They commented, 'we have done our utmost to avoid increasing expenditure until it has become imperative, but the need is undoubted.' They described the organisation of the head office.

The work is divided between the Joint Secretaries on fairly definite lines. Each has an experienced lady-typist, who is able to head off a number of telephone calls, and practically play the part of private secretary. She also acts as Committee Clerk to one or more Committees and has a junior typist to assist. The chief male clerk is Mr Wilsick, whose enthusiasm, tact and initiative, are deserving of high praise. Present salary, £330, and should be increased. Both Joint Secretaries have to rely on his relieving them, and a counterpart is urgently needed. Much of the increased work of the office in the last 3 or 4 years relates to District Synagogues Scheme and the small Congregations. Mr Wilsick knows well what is required in this connection and handles many of the questions arising, with the general guidance of the Joint Secretaries, but they and he are overloaded. We attempted to provide an Assistant a year ago, partly for this purpose and partly to deal with Defaulters' cases and other work. The appointee had some good qualifications, but lacked driving power and initiative, and we terminated the appointment. Provided that the Defaulters' work is handed over to the proposed new 'General Collector', we do not propose to replace the man who has gone, in addition to having the new Clerk.

There was a '3rd Clerk' and a '4th Clerk', a full-time shorthand typist, a temporary shorthand typist, two office boys, and a girl 'telephone-operator, with some additional duties'. The secretaries commented:

Our practice is not to employ people merely as typing-machines. They are expected to take an active and intelligent interest in the work of a particular department, and there is not, as in some offices, a group of typists employed solely as such, and sometimes busy and sometimes slack.

On the accounts side there were four persons.

When it is remembered that one of the Joint Secretaries is a fully qualified Accountant, and that the other has considerable experience in regard to the complicated finances of the United Synagogue, there is seen to be good ground for our view that the strengthening of the Clerical Side of the Office is much more urgently needed than changes in the Accounts Department.

Their further recommendations related largely to the surveyor's department:

The growth in United Synagogue properties leads to many incidental matters arising. The sale of a field, the letting of a house, the question of dilapidations of a leased workshop, an application for a licence to alter a shop – these are not matters of interest or importance to the general work and policy of the United Synagogue, but they call for a certain amount of technical knowledge and experience and they take up valuable time. We think that the Honorary Officers might consider whether the scope for the Surveyor's Department should not be enlarged to include the general handling of these matters, and, in some degree, the question of new sites for Synagogues.

They concluded:

If this memo seems to show a tendency to 'unload' some of the work of the Head Office it is to be borne in mind that the pressure here has become overwhelming and relief must be found. The move to our new Headquarters has proved a boon and enabled much long deferred re-organisation of the work to be carried out. But the constant increase of work creates many difficulties. The attached list shows the Congregational schemes already in negotiation or pending. Most of these schemes entail frequent interviews and require close watching, and some of them involve very difficult negotiations. In the old days the Synagogues generally found their own sites, and merely came to the United Synagogue for a loan. Nowadays, we do practically everything for them. In the cases of Hendon, Dollis Hill, West Willesden and Edgware we actually found them the sites or guided them in doing so. We carry on all the negotiations in fixing up with the Ground Landlords, developing the scheme, settling plans, obtaining tenders and putting up the buildings. Estimates have to be drafted and re-drafted; questions of officials and temporary officials require tactful handling, carefully phrased letters and other documents have to be prepared, memoranda for the Honorary Officers, Reports for Committees and Council.

There is, naturally, much work at the Head Office of a character that does not come too prominently before the Honorary Officers as a whole. The activities of the Welfare Committee and Visitation Committee have expanded very considerably. Such Schemes as the L.C.C. Visitation work, and the Fellowship Movement, occasion much thought and anxiety behind the scenes. The routine work of the Office continues to grow and includes many matters requiring careful guidance – Covenants, Bequests and Trusts matters, central buying of supplies, the general and local Synagogue finances, election matters, questions of the appointment, salaries and pensions of about 80 officials. The number of Committees and Sub-Committees grows whilst practically none of the old ones drop out. It is also a fact that in relation to the Constituent Synagogues, the position of the Head Office has altered considerably in the last 14 years. It is expected to do in many ways what it was at one time expected to refrain from doing.

We conclude these notes with an expression of gratitude to the Honorary Officers for their confidence in us, and their never-failing support, and – not least – for the free hand they have given us in regard to Head Office staffing, a factor of great importance to us in securing efficiency; and we, in turn, desire to record our appreciation of the loyalty and devotion of the members of the staff.

The Council agreed to the recommendations of the Executive Committee, framed in a report which mentioned the steady increase of work in such diverse fields as checking membership lists and transfers from one synagogue to another, the need to create a special property department, and the necessity for extending the amount of accommodation on the third floor of Woburn House. The Council's agreement was expressed, however, largely in terms of finance.

> The Council leave it in the hands of the Honorary Officers of the United Synagogue to take, at a cost not exceeding £1,100 per annum, all such steps as they may deem necessary or desirable in relation to the matter of additional staff and accommodation as outlined in the foregoing Report of the Executive Committee.

Three years later the property department was given a reorganisation to bring it into line with the Joint Secretaries' suggestions.

The picture which emerges from a study of the full-time salaried staff of the United Synagogue in these years between the wars is that of a group of overworked individuals who never received the rewards which their work warranted. That the United Synagogue actually managed to continue at all to recruit staff was tied very closely to the general overall situation of clerical employment, and the potentialities for professional advancement elsewhere. Undoubtedly, however, the poor salaries and even more the few potentialities for the development of a 'civil service' in Anglo-Jewry had their effects in depressing the status of the officials as against the part played by either the honorary officers or even the 'rank and file' of the Council. It was as well that there were men as capable as Waley Cohen to run the United Synagogue, for conditions certainly militated against any important part being played by the officials.

CHAPTER 12

THE UNITED
SYNAGOGUE AT WAR

The two world wars had very different effects upon the United Synagogue. The First World War certainly presented no particular problems of organisation; members of the Council and the office staff volunteered or were called up for military service, and the minutes of the Council record with gloomy regularity votes of condolence to members whose sons had been killed at the front or, occasionally, to the families of members of the Council who had been killed. The services of chaplains were called for, and a special committee was established to meet the needs of Jewish servicemen. Other committees too felt the problems of the families of servicemen left to try to make ends meet on the pitifully small allowances which were all that could be made. But just as in the world around them there was a wide gulf between the world of the United Kingdom and the narrow world of the trenches, so that London could be gay at a time of long lists of casualties in Flanders, so also the Anglo-Jewish world could continue in London almost regardless of the impact of the war on Anglo-Jewish youth. Perhaps too it could be suggested that the war had a little less impact upon the Jewish than upon the non-Jewish world. Of the vastly increased Jewish population many of those of military age were, after all, not of British nationality and could have felt very little impulsion to volunteer and fight for that Russian government from which so many of them had fled, while even after the conscription laws came into effect many were not directly affected until the summer of 1918. That is not to say that a large number did not volunteer, and that the Anglo-Jewish community did not pay its share of the 'blood-tax', but that the impact of the war itself did not go very deep, and it might well be conjectured that it was this which led to a comparative failure of the scheme for a Jewish memorial pushed so vigorously and earnestly after the end of hostilities.

The Second World War had an immeasurably different effect, for its effects were to be felt from the very beginning. This was much more a 'total' war, one in which the civilian population was involved as much as, if indeed in some ways even more involved than, the military, and so right at the outset the United Synagogue was faced with the need for radical changes both in personnel and in organisation. It was not merely that the United Synagogue was involved in the war but through such circumstances as the bombing on London the United Synagogue and its organisation had to undertake tasks that were novel, and for which the whole of the United Synagogue structure had to be reshaped and readapted. Not least among the problems which faced the United Synagogue at the outbreak of the war was the fact that all the honorary officers were serving out their resignations. The events of the summer of 1939 over the question of special services for refugees had culminated in the insistence by Sir Robert Waley Cohen that he and his colleagues had no alternative to resigning. This was on 17 July 1939, and so little had been done by the United Synagogue in consideration of war precautions that at that same meeting the agenda recorded:

> The question of Air Raid Precautions is well-known to be one that has unusual complications and difficulties. There are, however, certain aspects of the subject that require consideration, and for this purpose the Executive Committee recommend the Council to resolve:—
>
> That the Council appoint a Special Committee to consider and advise what steps are necessary or desirable in relation to the United Synagogue in the matter of Air Road Precautions.

The next recorded meeting of the Council, however, was that held on 7 September 1939, at which the President and nineteen other members of the Council were present and at which emergency arrangements had to be made. It was agreed that it was undesirable to hold meetings of the full Council, and so the normal machinery of the United Synagogue was suspended. In its place the honorary officers were given all powers of all committees, and all standing orders were suspended with the sole exception of the standing order permitting the requisitioning of a meeting of the full Council by not less than twenty of its members. The meeting also expressed its pleasure that the honorary officers had agreed to withdraw their resignations 'and hopes that in the future they will continue to serve – just as the Council will continue to serve – to the best of their ability'. It was not until the summer of 1942 that the full panoply of Council meetings was resumed, and even then they were held only every three months, so that for the bulk of the war the greatest burden of administration fell fairly and squarely on the shoulders of those honorary officers who were not called away for war service outside London, and on those members of the permanent administrative staff who were left behind at Woburn House. The burden on them all was enormous, and it is little wonder that after the war was over Philip Goldberg retired prematurely from his office as Secretary. Not all of the work came immediately, but it came soon enough. What came immediately was evacuation; masses of children, and indeed many of their parents as well, were removed from the London of regular organisation of religous life into provincial centres for which there had been very little preparation of any sort, to say nothing of any specifically Jewish preparation. A great deal has been written of the general confusion brought about by the mass of this evacuation and the social impact it created in the 'host' areas. The impact on London Jewry was even greater. The needs for kosher food, for Jewish religious education, for any sort of Jewish observances, would have taxed any organisation, however efficient it may have been. But it had to be handled by an organisation which itself had had to be evacuated, from the files and office routines of Woburn House to the outer fastnesses of the Edgware Synagogue Hall. Almost overnight London Jewish communities disappeared, ministers and secretaries (still too often the same people) were unable to keep track of their members, not knowing where their members had gone, not able to collect dues from them, unable to organise any sort of religious services for their members. The officers of the United Synagogue were faced therefore with problems that seemed almost insuperable. The history of almost every individual synagogue would tell the same story at this stage, of the impossibility of maintaining the statutory services, of ministers either being called on to act as chaplains to the forces or finding themselves obliged to meet new commitments in a wide variety of ways. But for the officials at the centre the problems were multiplied many times over. The summer of 1939, for example, had as usual found the United Synagogue engaged in its normal programme of physical expansion, to meet the growing needs of London Jewry. Not all of these building schemes could be abandoned overnight, so that orders had to be given for the completion of some building schemes even though others were stopped. But whether they were stopped or not, all had still to be paid for, and the crying need was to try to find money. The United Synagogue had rarely had much of a float on either capital or current account, and that was hardly the best possible time at which to sell shares. On the other hand few members were prepared to pay their half-yearly synagogue bills then falling due, so that from both sides there was immediate pressure. There were indeed additional expenses forced by the move to Mowbray Road in Edgware; extra fares were incurred and the United Synagogue agreed to meet these, hoping however that some of the employees would be able to travel on cheap 'workers' tickets' or somehow or other minimise the cost. Even so, the Treasurers were certainly at their wits' end on finance. General economies – such as closing down any paid choirs and dispensing with much part-time auxiliary assistance – were made. Even so, by the end of 1939 income was down by over £9,000 compared with the end of 1938, and the honorary officers had to contemplate a reduction in all ministerial and officials' salaries which, it was decided, should come into effect by April 1940. Although in practice a straightforward cut could not be enforced, and there had in time to be comparatively substantial increases, the fact that it was even contemplated is an indication of the problem. After the war in Europe was ended one of the Treasurers disclosed the extent of the problem. The additional deficits for 1939, 1940, and 1941 came to over £12,000 and this was despite the greatest possible economies. The gap was met by heavy and repeated borrowings from the capital funds of the United Synagogue, but overall the United Synagogue was fortunate in that there had been such effective 'follow-up' on arrears that by 1945 the leeway had been made up.

The evacuation had been the result of a widespread belief that the outbreak of war would be the signal for a catastrophic series of air raids on the metropolis; when these did not occur at once many of the population, and of course Jews included, began to drift back into London. Where this return resulted in a renewal of synagogal life the old strands of the United Synagogue could be resumed. But in many cases the evacuees began to demand that they should be able to continue Jewish observances and their former style of life in the new areas in which they now lived. In some of these there were already Jewish communities, and the United Synagogue had to make arrangements so as to ensure that the United Synagogue secured some of the membership dues that were being diverted into the coffers of, say, Brighton or Worthing. But in many others no communities of any significance existed, and if the United Synagogue did not take steps to offer them some help then these members would have been lost, either through assimilation or through following ministers not acceptable to the Chief Rabbi or the United Synagogue. The response of the honorary officers was the recognition of a number of 'membership groups', in such obvious places as Eastbourne, Brighton, or Worthing as well as in such others as Bath, Beaconsfield, High Wycombe, Blackpool, Llandudno, Macclesfield, or Welwyn Garden City. As the war went on these communities became more and more regularised and their relations with the United Synagogue were formalised. Buildings were secured for them, affiliation fees became standardised, and attempts were made to find for them a regular system of ministerial attention or visitation. It was almost a fourth or fifth scheme of United Synagogue membership, parallel to the constituent, district, and associate schemes. The initiative had come partly from the groups themselves and partly from the United Synagogue, but certainly these communities showed a great eagerness to maintain their links with the United Synagogue and with traditional Judaism. As the war went on the size of individual congregations waxed and waned. The communities on the south coast became rather less popular after the German occupation of the French Channel coast, while at other times less salubrious areas declined as the war seemed to be receding from the immediate neighbourhood. None the less, there were in all some twenty-two of these groups, and some of them remained in being after the war came to an end, applying eventually for status as affiliates of the United Synagogue.

The growth of these groups immediately brought into prominence a further problem for the honorary officers. Their development promised eventually, for example, to bring some relief to the finances, while even the fact that former members wished to resume their connections with the United Synagogue meant obviously that some attempt could be made to clear off some of the arrears of membership contributions. But their proliferation meant an immediate demand for ministerial help, and that was one thing of which the United Synagogue possessed very little. Many ministers were called on almost immediately for service as chaplains, and although there were some very highly esteemed ministers, teachers, and rabbis, who had escaped from Nazi Germany, many of them were ineligible or unsuitable for service in the United Synagogue if only because they were not British subjects and could not speak English, let alone being unable to understand the habits of thought of the average member of the United Synagogue. At the height of the Blitz, for example, many ministers were unable to give help and guidance to their congregants in the shelters since they themselves, from their accents and origins, were highly suspect to the police and ARP wardens. Some of the ministers of the United Synagogue performed prodigies; Harris Swift was to be found as virtually Mr United Synagogue (peripatetic), and wherever there were any difficulties of personal relationships or of ministerial shortages he was almost inevitably sent out by the honorary officers in order to find some solution. This problem was further deepened by the increasing need for the United Synagogue to find a large number of chaplains for the forces. In the First World War four ministers, including Michael Adler, served full time as uniformed chaplains in the field, while many others served part time in an honorary capacity to army encampments near their own congregations. In the Second World War, however, the need was far greater and many more were invited to accept full-time chaplaincies. The request could not be denied, of course, but since almost all the ministers available for service came from the ranks of the United Synagogue, this organisation once again had to accept a burden that really belonged to the Anglo-Jewish community as a whole. The gaps left by these departures could not be properly filled. There were only a few graduates coming from Jews' College, and to this number could be added a number of refugees looking for some means of livelihood. But not all of this second group were regarded as suitable for posts in the United Synagogue and in any case no permanent vacancies could be recognised for filling; all appointments had to be regarded as temporary, since the employees called up (or volunteering) had by law to be reinstated after the end of the war. Under all these circumstances it is indeed surprising that there was any degree of normality in the arrangements of the United Synagogue. Not all ministers, it must be confessed, fulfilled their obligations as they should have done; some refused to return to London, while others engaged in a series of disagreements with either their local boards of management or even the Chief Rabbi. But by far the great majority of ministers rose nobly to their responsibilities; many stayed on long after their official retiring dates, while the threatened, and in some cases implemented, salary cuts which were only slowly restored by cost-of-living bonuses, meant that the ministers, the backbone of the local administration and indeed the very life of the United Synagogue, were not given the return which might have been normally expected for them.

Whatever normality of arrangements there might have been restored by the summer of 1940 was very quickly disturbed by the events which followed, the physical disruption of London Jewry caused by the Blitz. The 'phoney war' of 1939–40 had been followed by an intensive aerial bombardment of London, at first of those areas close to the docks but then more indiscriminately, and naturally the civilian population suffered greatly, many being killed, others injured, while many more were rendered homeless. The problems of the dead and their burial were obvious; even though the numbers involved were less than had been originally dreaded, they were substantial enough, and there were difficulties encountered, e.g., of reconciling problems of Jewish law with the immediate physical difficulties of providing mortuaries and funerals. One such problem was the occasional need for mass funerals. Naturally the United Synagogue was involved through its Welfare Committee with all of these problems; for although the responsibilities lay with national and local government all welfare organisations were brought into play. The Jews' Temporary Shelter and the Board of Guardians were equally invited to participate not only in purely Jewish reception centres but in many that were technically non-denominational. The problems once stated were obvious; there was a need for provision for and the maintenance of Kashruth and the need to replace all the wants of a kosher household, and once the need had been demonstrated to uninformed, even if potentially sympathetic, officials the need was recognised. But they had to be stated by a recognised authority such as the United Synagogue. In many cases too the United Synagogue was the necessary liaison with these non-English-speaking victims, although at the same time many of the United Synagogue's officials suffered from their own lack of an English accent. As already mentioned there was a great deal of suspicion of these foreigners moving about the East End at the height of the Blitz, and this hampered their activities. Another aspect of the work of the United Synagogue was the way in which the officers had to participate in the activities of the air-raid shelters. A curious troglodyte existence developed in these years in London; the underground system was gradually used for night refuges, and gradually a quasi-civilisation developed round them. Other religious organisations extended their ministrations to shelter-dwellers, but arguments developed over whether ministers of the United Synagogue could be associated with other faiths or even indeed other 'varieties' of Jews in parallel work.

These activities, however much of the officers' time they may have taken, were not as spectacularly disruptive of the routine work of the United Synagogue as was the fundamental disruption of services in the synagogues of the United Synagogue. From the very beginning – the autumn of 1939 – problems were created by the impossibility of 'blacking-out' the buildings in time for the High Holyday services and particularly for Kol Nidre night. Unthinkable it might have been to advise against the holding of services, undesirable it undoubtedly was to advise the concentration of large numbers of people in buildings especially vulnerable to bombing at times when bombings were particularly expected. Not only during the Blitz of the autumn of 1940 but throughout the winter of 1940–1 this remained a constant fear of all concerned. Certainly this represented yet another element in the breakdown of communally organised religious life which many feared they were seeing in these years. A fear of possible disruption of services was accompanied in too many cases by actual destruction of buildings. No synagogue was hit while in use for service, and so no heavy loss of life was sustained directly, but the list of properties destroyed or severely damaged was a long one. Not least of the damage done was that to the synagogues themselves. Two of the founding synagogues were completely destroyed – the Great and the Central – as were others more recently consecrated, while many others were damaged to a greater or lesser extent. Bayswater, Borough, Hampstead, Hackney, Brondesbury – all suffered major damage as did smaller buildings equally representing lively communities and a great deal of sacrifice in their original building schemes. Cemetery properties – mortuaries, prayer halls, and even tombstones – as well as other more mundane properties suffered damage. From the purely administrative point of view – and disregarding all the sentimental or psychological issues involved in the importance or the unimportance of more material property, or those involved in the loss of all the religious appurtenances of the various buildings – each incident involving damage had to be recorded, the damage assessed and described, and claims lodged for the eventual compensation to be paid over at some date in the future. In some cases it was necessary to provide some form of interim repair, in order to prevent further deterioration and to secure payment for this from the government. All this was essential for the future of the United Synagogue, and future generations could not have accepted an argument that it was less important than other aspects of the work of the United Synagogue. Any ignoring of this aspect would have imposed even greater future burdens on the United Synagogue. It was not only the United Synagogue of course, or even London, that suffered such damage, and it took some time before an effective organisation was set up. Conflicts between various organisations, not least between the United Synagogue and the Board of Deputies, as to whose organisation should present joint claims to a government which cared little for differences between Federation or United Synagogue, or even between Board of Deputies and Beth Din, but was concerned only with getting one body for negotiation with the appropriate government department, make almost unbelievable reading in the minutes of the bodies concerned, and it was not until 1943 that a Synagogues' War Damage Committee could be set up on behalf of all of Anglo-Jewry. A report submitted by this committee's chairman to the

United Synagogue (on 29 May 1945) listed some 350 incidents involving damage. Some were of course to the same properties which suffered several times over, but, as the report also pointed out, some buildings were affected indirectly by damage to foundations and so on which might not be apparent at the time. The effect of the document is to give the picture of a tremendous effort of work on a property department already depleted by a withdrawal of personnel, either because they had been called up for military service and could not be given deferment by the Ministry of Labour or because they were needed for re-employment within the United Synagogue in order to replace others who had been taken away. On occasion permission was given to recruit staff who were exempt from the armed forces (or had been discharged for medical reasons), but not all such appointments were happy, and sometimes the result was to create even more difficulties. At the same time there were admittedly some curious activities proceeding. On several occasions, for example, gifts of stained-glass windows are recorded, and some were actually installed while the war was on.

In addition to the problems caused to the organisation of the United Synagogue by the evacuation and by the physical destruction which resulted from the attacks on London, there was a further set of problems imposed on the United Synagogue not because they particularly affected the United Synagogue but because the United Synagogue represented the largest single body representing large numbers of Jews. There were questions of rationing, for example; it was as a result of its close connection with the Beth Din that the United Synagogue was brought into the problems associated with the use of flour and the provision of matzoth for Passover and the rationing scheme for biscuits, and it was through its connection with the Board of Shechita that the United Synagogue was involved with meat rationing. Eventually the answer was found in the appointment of Sir Robert Waley Cohen as Kosher Food Adviser to the Ministry. But the United Synagogue was also brought into controversy over the unwarranted attacks on Jews as black-marketeers. Unfavourable, though understandable, publicity in certain cases of breaking rationing regulations led to demands from within the United Synagogue that action should be taken, and although the United Synagogue as such could do little, nothing was put in the way of individual congregations introducing by-laws which forbade offenders from holding office in local boards of management or from receiving any honours in the congregation.

As shown, the problems were widespread, and the burden on staff at all levels was extremely great. It was during this time that, as already shown, Sir Robert was in the office of the United Synagogue most evenings working systematically through the materials prepared from him by the Secretary and attempting to keep the United Synagogue running smoothly. None the less all did not run smoothly for him. These were, after all, the years in which the arguments between Sir Robert and the Chief Rabbi were coming to a crescendo. The relations between them had never been easy, and although there had been several times before the war when the cracks had been smoothed over, and even though there had been occasions when the two men had worked closely together, presenting what had seemed like a united front to the outside world, their personalities prevented this from becoming permanent. Looking at the conditions of the war years, and bearing in mind the strains of the years before the war, when it must have seemed that many of the trends and tendencies of Anglo-Jewry were taking English Jews largely away from traditional religious practices, it must certainly have seemed doubtful whether even the pre-war standards could ever be resumed in Britain. Difficulties in maintaining services in synagogues, difficulties in maintaining any standards of Kashruth among evacuated children, difficulties in maintaining any standards of Jewish religious education, must inevitably have created the need among religious leaders to have seen some sort of 'Recall to the Synagogue'. It was unfortunate that this should have been the occasion for a further series of angry exchanges between the Chief Rabbi and Sir Robert, in the course of which each lost something far more important than dignity. Their disagreements went back in some respects to the years after the First World War, but they came out most strongly after the outbreak of the Second World War.

During the two or three years after this outbreak, when the disorganisations consequent upon the various evacuations were at their height, there were very many who had fears for the continuance of Judaism in Britain. There were many, like the Chief Rabbi, who had seen a decline even before the war and who found many instances of an acceleration thereafter. Attempts had been made to give evacuated children full provision for Passover, but apparently all that the honorary officers of the United Synagogue had been prepared to offer was help in the provision of matzoth; it was alleged that some of the honorary officers had denigrated Passover observance and had even made extremely contemptuous remarks about the survival after the war of any kosher practices. Although attempts had been made to create a scheme of Hebrew classes and religious education both for evacuated children and for those left behind in London, there were many complaints that these had been far from adequate and that not enough money was being devoted to these purposes; the arguments on the other hand were that the United Synagogue was giving all that it could and that there was not enough for all the calls on the United Synagogue's resources. But even more important than any of this was the allegation that the honorary officers of the United Synagogue were doing all they could to sabotage any attempts made by the Chief Rabbi to induce a religious revival and that instead they were trying to sweep away all distinctions among Orthodox, Reform and Liberal Jews. It was alleged that Sir Robert had gone out of his way to summon conferences on Jewish education for which Norman Bentwich and Lily Montagu, acting on behalf of these other two organisations, had been co-chairmen, and that it was intended to throw all Jewish education into the hands of these people, excluding all orthodox Jews. For their part the honorary officers attempted to defend themselves, pointing out that it had been the honorary officers themselves who had become alarmed at a growing alienation of many people from Judaism and who had set up the committee which had eventually suggested a campaign for a return to Judaism. Their objections were, however, to a campaign which seemed to concentrate on the observance of ritual to an exclusion of deep moral and ethical points which might better attract those who had become apathetic or even antagonistic.

The details of the arguments were in themselves not incapable of compromise; but by early 1941 the protagonists had become personally abusive. Hertz was described as being, at best, still not recovered from the effects of shock following an air raid, while for his part the Chief commented on Sir Robert as being 'a self-appointed autocrat' and being opposed to orthodox Judaism. The ill-feeling extended to long discussions between the honorary officers and delegations nominated by the Chief Rabbi to represent him and to speak on his behalf, and in the course of these arguments both sides niggled over small issues which at other times would have been unimportant. Both sides calmed down, the more so since after the death of Lionel de Rothschild – he was succeeded as President by Sir Robert Waley Cohen – neither side was able to appeal to an impartial Chairman, and it became possible for each side to co-operate with the other and not least to meet each other without immediate recriminations. But any old friendships had by now gone, and Sir Robert had come to believe that the Chief Rabbi had allowed himself to be influenced by persons who were not under the aegis of the United Synagogue but more concerned with religious organisations far removed from the sort of tradition which had made the United

Synagogue. For his part Chief Rabbi Hertz felt isolated, and lamented on one occasion to Dayan Lazarus that his only solace in life was his son-in-law, Rabbi Dr Schonfeld: 'he had no one to fall back on at all, and he had therefore made Dr Schonfeld his right hand man in everything.'

Differences between Sir Robert and the Chief Rabbi were paralleled by difficulties further down the organisation. Particularisation would be invidious, but there were certainly personality problems between various representatives of the United Synagogue at either Woburn House level or local level on the one hand, and ministers on the other. It was almost at times as if the war brought out not merely the best but the worst in people as well, and differences of opinion which might well have been settled at local level, or indeed even have been passed over as being inconsequential, erupted over and over again, culminating in law suits, challenges to the authority of the Beth Din, motions of 'no confidence' in the honorary officers of the United Synagogue, and in general an overall malaise.

It would seem therefore that the rows, difficulties, and bad relations between Sir Robert and the Chief Rabbi are of greater than merely personal interest, as reflecting and creating a general atmosphere in the United Synagogue, and therefore they warrant discussion from the point of view of the United Synagogue as an institution. It would be too facile indeed either to ignore them or to go from one extreme of blaming them solely on the personalities of the protagonists, to the other of showing that they merely illustrate the results of ever-shadowy demarcation of communal responsibilities – though they do that too. It might well be said that these quarrels show what happens when one side is responsible for 'spiritual' and the other for 'temporal' matters without a careful definition of the two terms. It might also be too easy to point out that whereas the Adlers had been willing to accept domination by the Rothschilds, Joseph Hertz was determined to be no Adler to a man who was himself not a nineteenth-century Rothschild. All these points are true, and yet they are inadequate as full explanations of the reasons for the difficulties which existed and which were in consequence created for the London Jewish communities. In a sense two different philosophies of Judaism were at stake. Hertz, who must indeed have been troubled for some time over many of the directions in which it appeared Anglo-Jewry might well be travelling, was brought into very close contact with influences seeking to counteract those tendencies and found himself at odds with Sir Robert who in many ways epitomised one possible end-product of those tendencies. But for whatever reasons the two found themselves at odds, the result was the same. The United Synagogue found itself in effect without that strong secular and religious leadership which it had a right to expect. In the crisis of the mid-1940s the rows, and the memories of rows, made it difficult for either the spiritual or the secular leaders to exercise control over the organisation. And at a time when new generations were coming to the fore in the service of the United Synagogue, strong leadership was more essential than ever before. This was possibly one of the unforeseen results. The war years and the general upheaval – social, financial, personal – changed the United Synagogue in many ways, not least of all in the direction in which outside society was changing too. New sorts of people were coming to the fore, new sorts of leader, whose claims were not based on hereditary position or social prestige. Just as in politics so in the Jewish community, these new elements took over responsibility. But whereas in the past the older elements in Jewish society might have been able to persuade the new leaders to follow in the well-trodden steps of their communal predecessors, in these post-war years neither President nor Chief Rabbi could expect the same automatic response.

PART FOUR

THE
FOURTH QUARTER
1945–1970

The post-war world of London Jewry found itself faced with an enormous number of problems, for which its pre-war experience had not at all equipped it. These problems lay partly in the field of physical construction and reconstruction and partly in the spiritual areas, in the re-examination of the purposes of the United Synagogue and the reasons for its very existence. It was during the 1950s and 1960s, however, the last two decades of its first century, that all these problems seemed all at once to descend upon the organisation altogether, and seemed to present the United Synagogue with one enormous crisis. There was a crisis of finance and building policy, a crisis of conscience, and above all, perhaps transcending and yet including all the rest, a crisis of leadership. It is not too much to say that it was in the fourth quarter of its first century that the United Synagogue found itself faced with decisions that would dominate the next fifty years, if not indeed the whole of its possible second century.

CHAPTER 13

RECONSTRUCTION
AND EXPANSION

Dominating much of the immediate post-war period were the purely physical problems of rebuilding and of coping with changing patterns of London development. The war itself had left, as already indicated, two major sets of problems. On the one hand many synagogues had been either destroyed or severely damaged, and decisions had to be taken quickly either about their rebuilding on the original site or about their compensation being used for the erection of new buildings elsewhere. On the other hand, and of course closely connected with that second possibility, the mobility of the Jewish population had been very greatly accelerated.

Old communities had begun to decay, or even a decay originally forecast and previsioned had been accelerated, while during the wartime standstill on building newer areas had developed out of all recognition. This was in addition to those temporary centres of the diaspora which had come into being through the membership groups; some of these withered away as soon as the emergency which had given them birth, but others remained almost obstinately active, calling for official integration into the general structure of the United Synagogue. Schemes tentatively put forward during the war for the creation of a United Synagogue which would cover the entire country had proved abortive, but in the years after the end of the war the United Synagogue entertained schemes for the admission of congregations in such outlying areas as Worcester, Peterborough, or Windsor, or for the making available of United Synagogue facilities to other communities such as Colchester or Chatham. That there was any possibility of including these areas as far-flung outposts of the United Synagogue empire was one result of the scheme for affiliated synagogues, introduced before the outbreak of the 1939 war.

When this scheme had been originally introduced it had covered small groups in growing areas where, it was confidently anticipated, larger congregations would eventually emerge. As already indicated, of the fifteen admitted before 1945 under this category, twelve were 'promoted' within thirty years. With the ending of the war there was, however, a rush of formal applications for this status, this time from communities which did not necessarily anticipate an accretion of members. For its part the United Synagogue was not unwilling to accept new members, but once again had to bear in mind the necessity of securing some assistance towards the burden of communal financial responsibility laid upon the United Synagogue alone. It was as a consequence that the honorary officers presented a report to the United Synagogue Council suggesting ways of rationalising the various categories of status and at the same time improving the financial position of the United Synagogue as a whole. Of the various categories of non-constituent synagogues, that of associate synagogue was now felt to be completely anomalous. As already shown, it had been established to assist 'residents of the poorer London districts to establish places of worship and to afford them membership of the Burial Society'. Their per capita contributions to the United Synagogue were very low and in effect they made virtually no contribution to the general running of the United Synagogue. None had been admitted to the scheme since 1927, and several of those admitted before then had already applied to be given district status. Now the whole category was abolished and those in it – eight congregations – were offered the chance to change either to district or affiliated synagogue status. Of the eight, two seceded, one closed, and the others transferred. The scheme had been successful so far as it went, but it had never quite managed to fulfil all that had been hoped for it, and above all had never been a magnet to draw off from the old East End those immigrants who would otherwise have been members of the Chevras.

The honorary officers also turned their attention to regularising the whole position of the affiliated synagogues which had as yet had no direct impact upon the United Synagogue as a whole; this had not been considered necessary since theirs was envisaged as only a temporary status. Now, however, it was suggested that any congregation could become an affiliated congregation 'even if the membership is quite small' under certain conditions such as that it was obviously going to be of a permanent nature, or it included most of the local Jewish residents.

Regular contributions were to be made by these congregations to the general funds of the United Synagogue and individuals would thereafter be recognised as 'assessed' members. At the same time the Affiliated Synagogues Council was set up, to give an opportunity for making representations and having some degree of influence. There was, however, a further part of the report. The honorary officers pressed very strongly that synagogues in one category should somehow be encouraged (or persuaded) to change from one status to another:[1]

It is obvious that the interests of the Community can be adequately served only if each of the smaller Congregations of the United Synagogue makes every endeavour to reach the stage of development when it can undertake full partnership as a Constituent Synagogue, and pending such development, it should accept the greatest degree of responsibility which its size and other factors demand. For a District Synagogue, having reached the necessary stage of development, to be unwilling to apply for admission as a Constituent Synagogue, or similarly for an Affiliated Congregation to be unwilling to seek enrolment as a District Synagogue, is unquestionably harmful not only to the interests of the United Synagogue, but to those of the Community as a whole.

The whole question of change of status was to continue to concern the honorary officers, particularly with regard to ways of inducing congregations to transfer from district to constituent status when they had reached an adequate size, usually about 600 or 700. One refused to transfer its status even when it had a membership of over 2,500.

Not all these changes were accepted by the United Synagogue immediately, but the results of the new scheme are to be seen in the growth in the number of affiliated congregations and in the way in which not a few have progressed further. The basic attitude, however, with regard to these congregations continued to be what it had been earlier: 'the initiative in establishing a new congregation must come from the local residents, who would then be encouraged to find premises in which to hold Services and when their numbers were sufficient they would apply for affiliation to the United Synagogue and in due course appoint a minister'. On occasion this had to be modified and not always with the results envisaged. In 1965, when the Ilford congregation appeared to be getting beyond manageable size, it was agreed to appoint ministers for possible satellite congregations.[2]

The Executive Committee feel sure that the Council will recognise that what is now proposed is a major departure from the practice which has been followed in the United Synagogue for nearly 100 years. That practice, it is felt, is by no means diminished in value because of the present proposals – it has proved itself time and time again and in fact is currently proving itself in other areas. In the Ilford area, however, there is a new situation and that is, that in two thickly-populated Jewish areas there are already sufficiently large numbers of existing members of the United Synagogue to form separate viable congregations. The Executive Committee desire to place on record the view that, contrary to popular belief, the United Synagogue is always ready to meet any new situation and a situation such as that created at Ilford is one which should be accepted as a challenge.

One of the consequences was to give the honorary officers of the Ilford congregation an excellent further reason for seeking a deferment of that congregation's upgrading.

The growth of the affiliated synagogues was, however, only one small part of the major problem of the provision of synagogues, and the major issues of these years concerned the boom in communities and the need to maintain a balance between the replacement of old, damaged synagogues and the building of new synagogues to meet the needs of expanding congregations. That there had been a growth in the affiliated synagogues has already been mentioned; in 1945 one had been admitted, in 1946 four, 1947 four, 1948 eleven, and in 1949 five (of which three were transfers from the old associate synagogue status). The changes in the district and constituent synagogues were more significant. In 1947 and 1948 there were three new district synagogues of which two had earlier been affiliated and one a former associate. In 1949 five were admitted as district, one of which was a completely new congregation, and the others had been either affiliated or associate; thereafter the pattern remained of transfer from affiliated to district. As for the constituent synagogues, in the ten years after the end of the war four new congregations were admitted, all of them in the north-west suburbs; each of them had been originally district synagogues and three had come up all the way from having been affiliated. The expansion in these areas was even more marked, for some of the newer congregations had had to split. Just as Ilford had divided itself, so, for example, Harrow and Kenton had split into two congregations and Edgware had divested itself of the Stanmore and Canons Park area.

All this involved heavy building programmes at a time when not merely money was scarce but, even more important, all building was strictly controlled by government action. Before the war all that was needed was to persuade the United Synagogue honorary officers that a case had been made out satisfactorily for a new synagogue and that the financial basis for the new congregation was sound; once that had been done the honorary officers would give their blessing and all would be well. But in the post-war period government permission had to be given and that was far from easy. As the honorary officers pointed out in a debate as late as January 1952, the building allocation for the whole of the United Synagogue for one year was £35,000 and that included repairs and maintenance. The comment by the Chairman that the amount was 'woefully insufficient' was an understatement. In a report indicating in detail the extent of building schemes then under consideration, he declared:

> The Honorary Officers of the United Synagogue are much concerned at the pressure exerted for works of different kinds to be undertaken at the various Synagogues, each Synagogue regarding its own project as meriting the highest priority and regardless of the needs of other Congregations, some of which completely lack any facilities for Services or classes.

The list then presented showed a total of £846,000-worth of building projects for which, when a government ban on building was lifted, £28,500 would be available.

In the debate members of the Council complained of seeing 'satellite towns being built, but there was no provision for synagogues'; another indicated that the problem was one of priorities, trying either to provide something for everybody or concentrating where the need was at its greatest.

> Three congregations stood out in the list, viz. Edgware, Hampstead Garden Suburb, and Wembley. It was intended to spend money on outlying Congregations where the membership was 120 or perhaps 200, but there were Congregations where there was a membership of 900, but accommodation for only 300, and therefore some 500/600 families were being ignored. The point he felt so strongly about was that the nearer one was to London the greater the distractions to young people. His feeling was that money should not be spent on enlarging synagogues but on Synagogues lacking in Religion Classes and youth movements. Money was being spent to encourage life in outlying districts but the large number of youth in the Metropolis was being ignored.

The existence of the backlog and the building up of pressure for new synagogues led to one inevitable result; when licensing of new building was removed overnight, the honorary officers already had applications for over a million pounds' worth of new building and were being pressed to enter immediately into large financial commitments without being able to see where this money could be obtained. The financial pressures which resulted, and to which further reference will have to be made, meant that for some time to come the emphasis of the United Synagogue was much more on meeting its continual financial difficulties than on anything else, and certainly not with any new schemes, however significant, if they involved large expenditures.

This need to provide new synagogues was closely linked with the need to repair war-damaged, or rebuild war-destroyed, synagogues and with the need to keep an eye on the older congregations, seeing how far they remained viable. From the technical point of view, the making good of war damage was quite straightforward; the bulk of the work that needed to be done was to be met eventually by compensation payments through the government's war damage scheme. However, it was possible to transfer these payments from one site to another, and to replace a synagogue destroyed in one area by an entirely new one elsewhere, and so the issue as to whether a synagogue should or should not be rebuilt on its original site assumed entirely different proportions in the conditions of financial stringency. So this problem, too, became caught up in the fundamental one of the shifting centres of the London Jewish population. It was not a new issue since it had been at the basis of the United Synagogue's very existence from the beginning; but in relation to specific areas the problem had been brought to the attention of the United Synagogue as early as 1928, when a special committee had been appointed 'to consider the question of Synagogue and Classroom accommodation in North and North-East London'. That committee's report, which has already been quoted, drew attention to the problems of the four deficit synagogues in that area and, notwithstanding its belief 'that the North and North-East of London will . . . remain a predominantly Jewish neighbourhood for the next twenty or thirty years' remained doubtful about the longer-term future, adding merely that it would be wrong if any of the synagogues was forced to close through purely financial reasons. But with population changes during and after the war so altering the character of the area the problem became not one of finances but of whether the congregation was still viable in any real sense at all. It was a problem which had been faced before the war with the old New Synagogue and on several occasions with the Hambro'.

The Hambro' had eventually been amalgamated with the Great but allowed to keep its own identity, even to the extent of electing honorary officers and board of management. After the war the problem recurred in two main areas, partly in south London but mainly in the old heartland of London Jewry. The Borough Synagogue had been in difficulties for some time, confining its activities to its hall and giving up its main synagogue building; but in 1961 it was finally agreed to amalgamate it with the Brixton congregation. Elsewhere two other smaller congregations, Hoxton and Shoreditch, and Poplar, closed their doors in 1949 and 1951 to expressions of regret from the United Synagogue Council. The continued changes in north London were however much more serious, threatening as they did the existence of some of the oldest and most prestigious congregations. They were heavily in debt, but could not balance their financial drain on the United Synagogue by a vibrant, spiritual life. Their membership dropped off in numbers, their elections failed on occasion to secure a full board of management, and they failed even to maintain the statutory services.

Just as one of the earliest branch synagogues to be set up was the North London so it in turn became the first in this group to suffer a change of status; it was a leasehold property and was in any case under suspended threat, but it was also now becoming difficult to maintain it, and there was no real objection raised to its being amalgamated with the not-too-distant Dalston congregation in 1958. The problem went deeper than just this one synagogue, however sincere the regrets were at its closure, and the committee's report went carefully into the nature of the issues.[3]

> The area was no longer popular with Jewish people and . . . although for some time to come some Jews would continue to reside there, with the effluxion of time their numbers must continue to diminish to the point at which positive action would be bound to be taken by the Council. . . .
>
> Another fact . . . was . . . that the normal social pattern of the Anglo-Jewish Community was no longer operating in the area. That is to say, orthodox Jews moved into the area, joined the Synagogue, brought up their families, who in turn married, joined the Synagogue and, more often than not, stayed in the area or, occasionally, moved away sometimes to be followed by their respective parents and other relatives. The Committee found that in the area under review, the replacement of these members was no longer forthcoming; either the newcomers were non-Jewish or, and this was a disturbing feature, they were 'just not interested' in joining a Synagogue. . . The

Committee further elicited the information that many of the members of these Synagogues were leaving the area to move to the outer suburbs and, of course, the almost 'mushroom' growth of Synagogues in areas such as Ilford confirmed this fact.

The committee recommended that the Dalston Synagogue be amalgamated with Stoke Newington, and although the implementation of this was delayed to give the local honorary officers a last chance, the final decision was taken in 1967. The committee had also expressed surprise that nothing had been said earlier by anybody and recommended the setting up of a standing committee on the movement of Jewish population. This committee began its work by going carefully into the position of various synagogues, and pointed out that already some of the newer, north-west congregations were beginning to lose members, and that their declining surpluses were being succeeded by mounting deficits. As against that, the committee also illustrated in detail the emergence of a large number of peripheral communities, and the need to have resources at hand for their needs. Indeed, during the discussion of this report there was a strong element demanding that the United Synagogue should not necessarily wait until a request had been made for help but should take the initiative itself in activating a new congregation. This would have represented a great change and one that on the whole the United Synagogue was not prepared to make. The problem of the future of these congregations – Willesden, Brondesbury, and Cricklewood – went very deep indeed and to the heart of the financial structure of the United Synagogue. These big synagogues had in the past been sources of strength to the United Synagogue as a whole. If they began to crumble there would be no way of seeing the United Synagogue keeping its position in London Jewry. There was, too, one further feature of all the schemes for new buildings in the suburbs; every one of them was becoming very expensive. One of the ways in which the United Synagogue had been able to keep its programme of building in step with increased demand had been by borrowing heavily from outside sources. The capital funds of the United Synagogue largely became empty during this period, and such sources as the St Helen's Court Fund which had played so important a part in the building work of the United Synagogue had to be replaced by funds made available through normal commercial sources. Since these had to be paid for at normal, or near normal, commercial rates the strains on the newer constituent synagogues became correspondingly greater, for their members had now not only to repay capital as in the past but also pay off interest on both long-term and short-term advances. The result was that it would no longer be possible to rely on the newer constituent synagogues to find final surpluses to balance the deficits in the assisted synagogues. Although in the centenary year, for instance, fourteen of the constituent synagogues were in surplus, only five of them were in a position to be able to make a substantial contribution to the deficits of others, and as early as 1958 the warning had been given that even the addition of further constituent synagogues would do nothing to alleviate general burdens, that because of mounting capital costs even wealthy congregations would be unable, or unwilling, to accept the burden of helping less fortunate synagogues, that all that could be hoped for was that they would shoulder the burden of general communal responsibilities. Even that was not necessarily to be true, as was to be shown with the tangled picture of religious education.

This was the background against which the story of two particular congregations had to be pictured in the 1960s, the closing decade of the first century. These were the Bayswater and Marble Arch Synagogues. The Bayswater Synagogue had been one of the oldest in the union; indeed it had been one of the five original congregations and had contributed much of value to the history of London Jewry and the United Synagogue in particular. Many of its members had been prominent in communal affairs, while its ministers had included many of the leading luminaries of religious life. But during the 1960s it had been threatened from two directions. Its congregation had been beginning to decline as a result, there too, of changes in the neighbourhood, and although it had remained, technically, a surplus synagogue this had on occasion been almost as a result of accident, and opposition had been expressed to the filling of ministerial vacancies. In the post-war climate of rationalistion, this congregation was obviously to be high on the list for regrading and reconsideration. It was at this stage that local government plans threatened its physical existence, its site being required for road development. Obviously, compensation would be payable; if the synagogue were to be rebuilt elsewhere in the area the local authority would pay for complete reinstatement, but if no rebuilding were contemplated a lesser sum would be paid to the United Synagogue funds. The tripartite negotiations between the United Synagogue, the honorary officers of the Bayswater Synagogue, and the Greater London Council, were protracted, but basically the Bayswater honorary officers were not prepared to see their congregation disappear, while the United Synagogue honorary officers were not sure that a rebuilt synagogue would be desirable for either spiritual or financial reasons. Allegations and counter-allegations of bad faith, of bad judgment, and of malpractice were exchanged, and eventually the honorary officers of the United Synagogue were taken to court by a warden of the Bayswater Synagogue in an action which ended with an undertaking by the United Synagogue to rebuild the Bayswater Synagogue on a site provided by the Greater London Council. It was clear, however, that this whole episode would lead to bad blood for some time to come not only among the parties directly involved but also with others whose participation had been decisive but unexpected. From the point of view of the United Synagogue honorary officers, the possible closing of the Bayswater Synagogue would undoubtedly have helped to rationalise the provision of synagogue accommodation in the West End of London and also the whole unstable financial structure which had emerged, partly as a result of the development already mentioned but also as a result of the Great Cumberland Place Development Scheme which had increasingly become a millstone round the neck of the United Synagogue as a whole.

The whole history of the Great Cumberland Place Development Scheme is in many ways an excellent example of how an idea, good in itself, begins to develop and escalate so as to acquire a momentum of its own. At each stage the logical next step appeared clear, and yet if comparisons were to be made between the original concept and the final stage it is almost certain that those who thought of the scheme in the first place would have been aghast at the way in which it eventually developed. The history of the idea of a synagogue at Marble Arch went back to 1946–7 when it was reported to the honorary officers that there was a growing centre of population there without any synagogue provision. Services were held in Crawford Place for the High Festivals in 1947, but it proved impossible to repeat this in the following years, there being no halls available. A further report was made in 1951 urging that there was a potential demand for a synagogue there, the more so since other nearby synagogues were unable to cope with the demands made upon them. At the same time the property department had been trying to find a site in a very expensive neighbourhood, which was also scheduled by the local town-planning authority as a purely residential area. When eventually a site was found the negotiations were complicated by an initial need for secrecy, but a later need for formal approval by the Council, accompanied also by the desire for the vendor to secure an office building on a part of the site for the purposes of the rest of his estate. The understanding was that the United Synagogue would build the block and then lease it to the vendor at an agreed rent. Within the United Synagogue, however, two complications had arisen. Representatives of neighbouring synagogues feared that their own membership would be eroded by the new synagogue, while the sudden lifting by the government of building restrictions, combined with pressure from a large number of other congregations for their own building schemes to be approved, meant that the United Synagogue would have difficulty in finding the large sums of money involved in getting the large building programme under way. Accordingly the honorary officers agreed to the setting up of a select committee to make an urgent report on the whole issue, while in the meantime the vendor was persuaded, reluctantly, to agree to a further delay. Eventually one of the honorary officers of the United Synagogue bought the lease of the central part out of his own pocket on the understanding that he would be repaid when funds became available. The committee went into some detail on the need for a new synagogue in this area, including also taking the comments of the neighbouring synagogues, particularly stressing the opinion of the Bayswater honorary officers that their own synagogue was wrongly sited and that if the new congregation were called the 'New Bayswater Synagogue' they would be willing to co-operate fully. But they also discussed the financial implications of the scheme. The site would cost £35,500 plus legal costs; on two-thirds of it would be built a synagogue, etc., at an estimated cost of £170,000 and on one-third an office block costing an estimated £115,000. It was against this cost that the committee envisaged the transfer of the war damage payments for the Great Synagogue and the proceeds of the sale of the whole of the Cree Church Place site. It was only by the use of a very expensive site that the full value of the Great Synagogue compensation could be used. Needless to say, the honorary officers of the Great Synagogue were deeply opposed to the scheme despite the hopes of the committee that the traditions of the Great would be transferred to the new site and that this new synagogue would be used for communal services and for 'State Occasions'. The committee reported:[4]

> The Great Synagogue, which was the focal point of our community, has been destroyed and, as we have said, can never be revived on its old site in its old glory. We earnestly hope that this new Synagogue can in its turn and in its central situation, become that focal point. If the Great Synagogue will rise to what we feel to be its great opportunity . . . bring its great prestige and tradition to this new Synagogue as, perhaps, 'The New Great Synagogue', it can once again become the heart, inspiration and focal point of our Kehilla.

The need for speed in the final signature with the owners of the site in effect meant that prolonged discussion was hardly possible, and the United Synagogue Council agreed with the basic recommendations of the committee; it was a year later that the new congregation formally applied for registration as an affiliated synagogue, one of the Treasurers becoming Chairman, and the Secretary of the United Synagogue, Alfred Silverman, becoming also acting secretary of the new congregation.

As time went on the scheme became altered in some of its important details. The cost of the site went up by £1,000, the cost of the buildings crept up gradually, and parts of the synagogue accommodation (such as the hall) were changed from being intended for the local congregation into accommodation which could serve as 'the focal point of major metropolitan Jewish social functions'. Indeed one of the arguments used consistently concerned the amount which the new congregation could possibly contribute to the finances of the United Synagogue.

With continued escalation in costs serious doubt arose as to the viability of the whole scheme and accusations were levelled as to whether the honorary officers of the Marble Arch Synagogue had met all their commitments. Statements to this effect by the then Treasurer led to bitter recriminations and to the setting up of yet another special committee of enquiry specifically into the Marble Arch Synagogue scheme. The picture which emerged was quite clearly one in which the local committee had had little or no say in the details of the building as it was being constructed and where a large number of extras had been imposed by the United Synagogue central administration, extras amounting to a virtual doubling of the synagogue cost. One of the recommendations of the special committee was that there should be no repetition of the appointment of the Secretary of the United Synagogue as secretary of a local synagogue. What also was clear, however, was the lack of any real idea at the centre of what was involved; the minutes of the committee of enquiry record, for instance, one leading individual confessing: 'in 1955 we really and truly had not a clue to what the costs were really going to be . . . We had not really a clue to the thing at all.' This was in 1962, and in 1970 the synagogue's finances were still creating difficulties. Even a cursory look at the United Synagogue accounts shows that the indebtedness of the Marble Arch Synagogue was increasing rather than decreasing; despite substantial annual repayments the original long-term advance had increased substantially.

The whole story of the Marble Arch Synagogue, linked also with the vast building programme of the post-war period, emphasises the financial problems already illustrated in this chapter. Indeed, for the United Synagogue entering into its second century, this was already clearly one of the major problems. The organisation had originally been set up to deal with problems of finances and building, and a century after its foundation these remained substantial problems. Though the finances were in difficulties the need for building remained an expanding one. The growth of new congregations inevitably meant a continuance of requests for financial help, and if the United Synagogue was to continue as the leading communal organisation it could not refuse such requests.

What this crisis also showed, however, was that there was a far deeper malaise in the United Synagogue. It was almost as if there was a failure of collective leadership at the top, and the parallel political crises in the United Synagogue would seem to point the same way.

CHAPTER 14

NEW GENERATIONS

The years after 1945 were years of financial stringency and building difficulty and also years in which the United Synagogue had to face other serious problems. They were essentially problems of leadership, both lay and religious, and it was in this period that the United Synagogue had to face a complete revolution in the personnel of its leaders. There was an unusually large turnover of Presidents – four in twenty-five years – and there were also two Chief Rabbis who took office during this time; at a different level there were three Secretaries of the United Synagogue. It was not, however, merely that there was a much larger number of leaders who caused the revolution; the sort of people who were now available for election as honorary officers were different from their predecessors, and because they were different they had entirely different concepts of the United Synagogue as an institution from those held by their predecessors. These were the years that saw the end of the Grand Dukes in United Synagogue affairs and the attitudes that went with them. Two reasons had caused the change. It was no longer possible for the great families to devote their whole time to United Synagogue affairs; they too had their incomes to make, and as the *Jewish Chronicle* pointed out, 'to combine honorary office in the United Synagogue with full-time business or professional activity would be onerous at the best of times; the present structure of the institution makes it doubly so'.[1] In any case there were fewer members of these families, with all their long traditions of service over several generations, willing or even interested enough to serve the London Jewish community in this way and at the same time the effects were being felt, at last, of the immigrations of the end of the nineteenth century. It had, broadly speaking, taken two generations for the immigrants to make their way. At first they were interested only in their immediate surroundings and in making their livings. As time went on, and they escaped from the East End or north London to the salubrious and more 'respectable' north-western suburbs they had sought, and secured, a larger share in the running of their own individual synagogues. They had still been prepared to leave the running of the United Synagogue as a whole to the honorary officers, but there developed an incursion at first into the Council and then into the Executive Committee, of individuals increasingly reluctant to accept without question rulings by honorary officers. Increasingly, the honorary officers found it difficult to persuade the Council or even the Executive to follow their advice. Indications of this are not hard to find; one such is the way in which the honorary officers had increasingly to make various votes issues of confidence in order to get their way. This, which had been rare before 1939, became much more common after 1945, and illustrates a lack of control by the honorary officers. There was also a growing groundswell of opposition in the Council to 'undemocratic' leadership by the honorary officers, and increasing attempts made to 'curb' the President's powers. Members of Council objected to 'rubber-stamping' honorary officers' recom-mendations, even in such matters as backing recommendations for election as honorary officers. Various Presidents tried to urge that it was necessary for the smooth working of the United Synagogue, as an institution, for the honorary officers to work well as a team, for the senior honorary officers to have experience of the working of the more junior positions, that the President, like a Prime Minister, ought to be able to choose his team and select the persons whom he thought to be most suitable for the particular posts. This worked for most of the time while Sir Robert Waley Cohen was President, although even he found difficulty in finding exactly the men he wanted. One observer from within the administration commented of one post-war nomination:[2]

> he was rich but difficult and cantankerous . . . but he was the only one possible. This is the pattern which has since prevailed, with the election – on occasion – of an Honorary Officer who had all these defects and wasn't even well-to-do.

They never wanted to nominate an 'employee', feeling that an employee could never devote sufficient time to his United Synagogue duties and never generate enough prestige.

Under Sir Robert's immediate successor, Frank Samuel, there was little direct conflict between the Council and the honorary officers, but with the appointment to office in 1954 of Ewen Montagu, grandson of the first Lord Swaythling, Samuel Montagu, the fundamental differences in attitudes which had been developing between honorary officers and Council began to show themselves openly. The clearest example of this came with the events of the summer of 1961, when Ewen Montagu was anxious to secure the re-election of Alfred Woolf and Asher Wingate, the outgoing Treasurers. Wingate's re-election was thought by the President to be particularly important at a time when there were great financial difficulties and there were in progress delicate negotiations with various banks. At the ordinary election meeting Wingate was defeated, but in order to create a vacancy for him a reshuffle of officers took place. One of the Vice-Presidents, Sir Bernard Waley-Cohen, resigned, Alfred Woolf was nominated as Vice-President, and Wingate was nominated as Treasurer. There was intense canvassing – itself something new – and Ewen Montagu sent out a letter to all members of the Council:

> Our expenditure in each year, including capital investment in building schemes, is over a million pounds a year. Our margin of income over expenditure in any one year is but a very few thousand pounds. You will appreciate that, operating on so comparatively small a margin, which any comparable business concern would consider derisory, the utmost care and capability is required – even one ill-considered, or ill-administered building scheme could do almost irreparable damage.
>
> As President of the United Synagogue, I am regarded by our members, by our Ministers and others employed by us, and by the public as primarily responsible for seeing that our affairs are stable and properly conducted. I cannot and will not accept that responsibility unless I can feel confident that I can rely on those who serve under my leadership as being capable, and able and willing to spend enough time and energy, to ensure that sound administration. . . .
>
> Democratic control is essential for the United Synagogue. But as Sir Robert Waley Cohen rightly said at a time when our affairs were infinitely less complex – true democratic control has to be exercised not by the choice of administrators according to the chance of popular ballot, but by the fact that the Honorary Officers have to submit their policies for scrutiny and acceptance by the Council before they can be implemented.

In one of his counter-canvassing letters the other candidate, George Gee, who had stood and been heavily defeated at the previous election, took up a position of high principle:

In my previous letter to you I referred to my opposition to rubber stamp methods and my preference for more co-operation between committees at all levels in trying to secure what is best for our places of worship. . . .

We are now faced with a situation in which the same methods for forcing views on the United Synagogue and its constituents are being applied to the election of its honorary officers. The moral pressure to which you have been subjected, coupled with threats of resignation if you do not submit to authority are against all the democratic principals on which our great institution has been founded.

I offer my services, and I am not without a good record of endeavour and experience in the communal interest, on the same principals as before. I am confident that should the Hon. Ewen Montagu persist in his threats to resign unless my opponent is elected, a member of one of our leading families would be ready to take over the reins of Presidency.

I am deeply regretful that our President has been so ill-advised to follow the course he has chosen and has reduced what is normally a dignified procedure to a personal issue.

In the event Wingate was again defeated – by one vote – and Ewen Montagu carried out his declared intention. In his letter announcing his resignation he made various pointed comments about the extent of the work necessary on the finances and his colleagues.

When I considered my colleagues after the recent election no one remained who could spare the time and had the particular abilities to carry out the financial planning and many, many hours of negotiation needed by this side of our vast and complex organisation. The Community owes an immense debt to the great abilities and devoted work of my colleagues – and I personally owe them a debt which I can never repay – but there was none who could cope (apart from their other commitments) with the work that Mr Wingate has done, excellently as they have carried out their own important allotted share in our work. . . . I cannot face the United Synagogue and the Community as responsible for an administration as to the soundness of which I cannot pledge myself. If I were to do so I would not be a person worthy of your confidence and I could not live with my conscience.

The issue on which he had resigned was only one example of growing differences of opinion; the sight of honorary officers differing in public and speaking and voting against each other at Council meetings had saddened him as demonstrating the loss of that harmony which had prevailed earlier under Sir Robert, while the emergence of people who actively desired office as an end in itself, as against the tradition of communal service and being virtually dragged into office by Sir Robert, meant that he was far from happy about his colleagues. In one of his letters written at this time commenting on his motives, he added: 'a pity that I can't be more specific – but even if successful, a libel action is costly to defend'.

His withdrawal was short-lived; many members of Council expressed intense dismay at his action and after considerable pressure a specially requisitioned meeting of the Council was held at which he was asked virtually unanimously to withdraw his resignation. Technically that was not possible, but he was re-elected by acclamation in the autumn of 1961. Within a year, however, he again resigned, making it clear that he had originally intended to return for only a limited period and that after having been an honorary officer for twenty-seven years, and President for eight, he now needed a complete rest. In any case the fundamental reasons which had induced him to return had by then been cleared out of the way. The Council agreed to the election in his place of Sir Isaac Wolfson. The immigrant families had arrived. On the face of it these differences might well appear to have been connected with different attitudes towards religious practices or from personal difficulties among the honorary officers. It is, however, quite clear that there were deep-rooted differences. This particular issue throws a great deal of light on the way in which the whole pattern of social structure – and even of religious structure – was changing in the United Synagogue. This was to be seen also with reference to the Chief Rabbinate and above all in what became known as the 'Louis Jacobs affair', an episode of which the implications went much deeper than the individuals concerned, indeed perhaps to the very root of the United Synagogue itself.

The story of the Chief Rabbinate in these years opens with the last year of Joseph Hertz. The difficulties which arose between him and Sir Robert Waley Cohen have already been told, and it is sufficient to repeat that even in this last year there were open breaches, as for example over a summons by the Beth Din of the honorary officers of the Finchley Synagogue; over a telegram by the honorary officers of the United Synagogue countermanding instructions given by the Chief over mention to be made about Jewish refugees' entry into Palestine, this constituting 'political' interference; or a pronouncement by the Chief Rabbi and Beth Din against intermarriage. This decree, which sought to prevent those who had married 'out' from holding office in a synagogue, was felt to be equivalent to *Cherem* (excommunication), and such action was forbidden to the Chief Rabbi under the terms of his appointment with the United Synagogue. Although some attempt at reconciliation was once again attempted, Dr Hertz died before anything could be done. When the machinery of election of a new Chief Rabbi was set in motion various ideas were put forward in an attempt to prevent such clashes occurring in future.

As was usual on such a vacancy, various informal meetings were held among interested parties before the main conference was formally summoned. For these meetings Philip Goldberg, 'who had been appointed Secretary despite his having retired from the United Synagogue secretaryship, prepared various memoranda which laid stress on the sorts of situation which had occurred in the past and which ought to be prevented in the future. Such memoranda include allusion to these difficulties:[3]

It would be foolish to gloss over the fact that during more particularly the last years of the Chief Rabbinate, irrespective of the cause or causes, there were at times misunderstandings and difficulties of a serious character, and hard to dissolve when the incumbent of that high office no longer had the robust health, mobility, the clarity of vision, deep insight, patience and understanding which are all necessary to smoothing away the difficulties, intensified by long periods of global warfare, and by conditions still far different from those of normal years. Desperately difficult indeed must be the position of any highly-placed Religious authority weighed down with responsibilities so widespread and persistent as those which faced our late Chief, but desperately serious too becomes the position of the elected leaders of the Community if the approach to him and the normal procedure of 'taking sweet counsel together' are blocked by circumstances outside their control, whether it be the Rabbi's ill-health or any other causes. There is not, and cannot be, a Pope in Israel, nor can 'sanctions', at any rate of an earthly character, be employed against the ordinary Jew or Jewess or Jewish organisation. The extent to which the Chief Rabbinate in this country and the Empire will be assured of loyal support and respect, depends entirely on the hold which the individual, whom the Community shall choose, is able to establish by his high ideals, his exemplary character and life, his ability to promote co-operation and concord in the Communities, and the maturity and wisdom of his judgement in dealing with the affairs of

British Jewry on lines that are at once in conformity with the basic principles of our Traditional Judaism and the well established order and procedure of Jewish congregational life in the 'free' countries of the Diaspora.

More specifically, memoranda drew attention to such previous difficulties as 'uncontrolled movements and residence, particularly during the war, during a great part of which the Chief Rabbinate removed itself to a Provincial town' or 'retention of office beyond the age of 70 and in serious ill-health'. Other points were 'Lack of Co-operative spirit', 'Tendency to papal infallibility', 'Arbitrary and sudden rulings', and 'desire to be unhampered even in expenditure payable by the United Synagogue or Community (e.g. printing)'. Another issue on which the United Synagogue felt strongly was relations with the Federation, particularly since history was repeating itself. Just as with the preliminaries to the election of Dr Hertz, the Federation had at first declared its willingness to make substantial contributions to the maintenance of the Chief Rabbinate and then had paid virtually nothing; now the Federation declared its interest. Philip Goldberg commented:

Historians – and the public today – may . . . marvel at the somewhat strange sequence of 'moves' by the Federation when Dr Hertz lay on what proved to be his death bed:–

(1) On 26th July 1945 – that is to say, 32 years after the installation of Dr Hertz, and less than six months before he passed away – the Executive of the Federation of Synagogues 'approved the principle that the cost of and the responsibility for the Chief Rabbinate and the Beth Din should be shared by the whole Community'. It was, perhaps a little late in the day!

(2) But less than three months later, the Federation of Synagogues (which for some 20 years had dispensed with any election to its vacant office of 'Chief Minister'), decided to appoint a Rabbi to be designated 'Principal Rabbi of the Federation'. . . . The Federation President . . . stated that they were doing nothing to weaken the position of the Chief Rabbi. . . .

(3) They also proceeded to recommend the appointment of *an outstanding Rabbinical authority whose duties will include acting as the authority on matters of Din.*

Goldberg added, 'if the new Chief Rabbi is not one of its own newborn spiritual overlords, the Federation "won't play" – and won't pay, either, towards the future Chief Rabbinate'.

In the meantime there was no formal gap, for Dayan Lazarus was appointed to act for the Chief Rabbinate. The appointing committee also gave particular attention to the practicability of appointing a council which might exercise control over the future Chief Rabbi's actions, to the need for a formal retiring age and for specific provision in case of physical incapacity if this were to be certified medically. Fundamental differences arose, however, as between the United Synagogue and the Federation, over the extent to which the Chief Rabbi should be bound by any decisions of the Beth Din. The Federation maintained that he was merely one of the Beth Din, while the United Synagogue held that it had always been the Chief Rabbi himself who had been the unfettered ecclesiastical authority for the United Synagogue. A form of words was devised, allowing any group of synagogues whose constitution allowed it to refuse to be bound by a Chief Rabbi's decision unless it had the backing of the Beth Din, but the Federation was unable to agree to this, and it was on this issue, rather than any arguments over the number of votes to be allocated to any organisation or group of synagogues that the Federation withdrew. Further issues were also discussed. Should the new appointment be for five years at a time? Should there be a considerable pause before an appointment being made be announced so that there could be some watch on how potential candidates were behaving? There was a strong opposition to the five-year term; it would not have a real effect on 'moderating' the attitudes of a Chief Rabbi in practice, and in any case it would prove difficult to find someone willing to take on the office under such circumstances. The opposition to a six-month 'pause' was much less strong, for although no such pause was officially announced, in practice the gap between the death of Dr Hertz and the announcement of the choice of his successor was over two years.

There were several candidates in the field; one eminent Israeli Rabbi declined the offer that was made to him, leaving some six more or less in the running. Some were ruled out as not being British, and therefore in the climate of opinion at the time unsuitable, or else having become unsuitable because of alleged incidents during the war. Rabbi Kopul Rosen was another who was considered, but it was felt that he was still too young, that in some fifteen years' time he would be much more suitable. Sir Robert Waley Cohen was very much in favour of the appointment of Rabbi Israel Brodie, a man who had earlier been pushed strongly for a vacancy on the Beth Din, and who had obviously been considered for some time as a potential Chief. At all events, at an informal meeting in September 1946, Sir Robert was reported as urging Rabbi Brodie's claims on his colleagues.

He was a determined person, with personality, and his association with the younger people, more especially the 25s to 40s in the Services, had created an excellent impression and had won their confidence. The Chaplains working under him were all impressed by his leadership. He was a firm holder of orthodox opinion and his scholastic attainments were quite high. . . .

He [Sir Robert] had come to the conclusion that it would be the right thing for a call to be made to Rabbi Brodie. He supposed that they should all think over this matter, and expressed the hope they would all be able to support the suggestion.

Sir Robert did not get his way on this immediately, since those present at the meeting insisted on considering all the possible candidates. On the other hand the committee agreed that there ought not to be a contested election. As the draft report of a sub-committee stated:

Everybody knows in 1912 the occasion lost some of its high significance when it degenerated into a contested election, by more than one name being put forward, and surely the Committee would prefer that there should be only one candidate to avoid all the ill-feeling and bitterness that a contested election would inevitably arouse among various sections of the Community.

If it is the feeling of the Committee that one name should be put forward to the Conference, then let us confine ourselves to that issue agreeing that the question of voting rights in the circumstances is a matter of no significance at all. Then we would be left with steps to be taken to select and appoint a Chief Rabbi, and this we suggest should be to report to the Conference that we feel that a call should be given to one man.

It was in the spring of 1948 that opinion came down on the side of Dr Brodie. He was not all that happy, however, about what seemed to be restrictions on his powers, particularly by the terms of reference of the proposed advisory committee which seemed to introduce 'shackling and restraint of "the unfettered and ultimate decision of the Chief Rabbi".' He objected not to consulting with others but with having to do so. Sir Robert's reply was friendly, conciliatory, but quite firm, insisting that there could be no alteration in the conditions of appointment and that it was essential to have Dr Brodie's reply. Given verbal assurances and written confirmation that his authority was unfettered, Dr Brodie agreed to accept an invitation to become Chief Rabbi.

During Dr Brodie's Chief Rabbinate there were no obvious and public clashes between the Chief Rabbi and the honorary officers of the United Synagogue as there had been during his predecessor's time. But, as he himself once commented, 'it takes two to make a quarrel', and he was determined not to see such events as had occurred earlier. Sir Robert was perhaps less involved directly than earlier, while both Dr Brodie and Ewen Montagu had too much respect for each other to indulge in near-public slanging matches. On the other hand there were complaints made that Dr Brodie was too much inclined to turn for guidance to his Beth Din, leaning on them perhaps to a greater extent than would have been expected. There were, for example, great arguments over the transfer of the office of the Beth Din from the East End to Woburn House, and the move was only accepted after long discussion and ingenious compromises in the course of which it was made clear that the only alternative was the closing down of Woburn House as the official centre of much of London Jewry. It must also be said that once the move had been made, and the Chief Rabbi had found that the results had not been the harming or the weakening of the authority of the Beth Din, or the loss of its autonomy to the United Synagogue, he was prepared to admit that Ewen Montagu had been in the right.[4] Perhaps the only complaint that could be made was that Dr Brodie was too prepared to avoid a clash and unpleasantnesses, that rather than make a decision which would cause harsh repercussions he would try to avoid such a decision, and that this could too often give the appearance of vacillating. Only in one case did this lead to serious trouble within the Anglo-Jewish community, and that was over the 'Jacobs affair'. This, which attracted a great deal of publicity at the time, surely struck deep at many of the problems of post-war Anglo-Jewry which contemporary observers felt as basic.

It was inevitable that the United Synagogue should have been affected by the sorts of question which supporters and opponents of Rabbi Louis Jacobs felt were involved in the public and private controversies, if only because many of the leading figures in these controversies were also leading figures within the United Synagogue itself. None the less, the United Synagogue as such was only involved in a narrow and restricted sense, and even though through that involvement many fundamental issues about the United Synagogue were aired it became clear that the problems which arose from the United Synagogue's involvement could be effectively separated from the issues which the 'affair' raised in its own right. These wider issues are irrelevant to a history of the United Synagogue and were dealt with extensively by the contemporary press, Jewish and non-Jewish alike.

Dr Jacobs was originally appointed minister at the New West End Synagogue in 1954, but resigned in 1959 to take up an academic post at Jews' College with a view to becoming eventually its Principal. Even before he took that post he had come into public view as the author of a work on Jewish theology – *We Have Reason to Believe* – which did not always conform to doctrine as traditionally accepted. Other theological writings followed, and there were many who felt as a consequence that he was unsuitable for a major post at the college. In 1962 it was made known that despite a quite general expectation to the contrary he would not be appointed Principal of the college. He resigned his post, and in 1964 on a vacancy occurring in the ministry at the New West End his name was put forward for election. It was at this point that the United Synagogue as an institution became involved. The legal position was quite clear. No minister could legally be appointed a minister of a synagogue within the United Synagogue unless a certificate of moral and religious fitness had been issued on his behalf by the Chief Rabbi: without that he could not even don 'canonicals', sit in the minister's place, or preach a sermon. The principle had been upheld in the past and there was no suggestion of argument against that point. What carried weight at another stage was whether Dr Jacobs's original certificate enabling him to take up his first appointment at the New West End Synagogue was still valid. Either it had never been withdrawn, it was claimed, or else no valid grounds had been put forward for withdrawing it. The conclusive argument seemed to be, however, that certificates applied to particular individuals for particular synagogues; that they ceased to be valid if a minister changed from one synagogue to another, having then to be reissued; and that when a synagogue changed its status, as for example from district to constituent, the certificate lapsed even though in practice there was no gap of time between the one and the other. Under these circumstances the issues became much more narrow and much clearer – from the legal point of view. Could a synagogue insist on having a minister of its choice against the wishes of the Chief Rabbi and therefore against all the rules, by-laws, and constitutions of the United Synagogue, or was the United Synagogue to continue to affirm that the Chief Rabbi was the sole ecclesiastical head of the United Synagogue, and that once he had made a decision that was to be the decision of the United Synagogue as well? The question was, of course, fundamental to the entire concept of the United Synagogue for it went right back to the decisions of the founding fathers and their discussions before the Act as well as the Deed of Foundation and Trust. Indeed, once the issue had been stated in those terms, and once the majority of the members of the board of management of the New West End Synagogue had insisted that come what may they wanted Dr Louis Jacobs as their minister, the decision was clearly foreseeable, and all the arguments that were used at the Special Meeting of the Council called for 23 April 1964 were virtually irrelevant.

Much more than that was at stake, however, and it was a realisation of some of those issues that made that meeting of the Council so memorable. The press was formally excluded, and the debate developed into a far-ranging, 'no holds barred' discussion. The President had circulated a lengthy statement giving in full the correspondence which had passed and the stages by which the crisis point had been reached. The official motion called for the board of management of the synagogue to be replaced by officers nominated by the United Synagogue Executive Committee, but most of the debate took place on a motion introduced by Edmund de Rothschild that the issue be referred back, 'in order that a further opportunity be given for the pooling of the collective wisdom of the United Synagogue'. None the less in doing so he declared that he was not undermining or even, he hoped, seeming to undermine the authority of the Chief Rabbi. Many of those supporting his amendment made it quite clear what they thought either of the action of the New West End Synagogue's board of management – 'Every one of us . . . are agreed that the New West End Synagogue, in taking the step which they did, . . . were unconstitutional and acted definitely with malice aforethought' – or of the need to prevent anarchy within the organisation. Many echoed the call of one member who had served for many years, 'ask your own conscience as to whether you agree that there is no place somehow or other for a man like Louis Jacobs under the umbrella of the United Synagogue', and there were many who could declare as one did, 'I sit in the New West End in a seat in which a member of my family has sat since the Synagogue was opened'. But the issue on which the Council had to decide was not whether Dr Jacobs should be able to secure a pulpit within the United Synagogue. One member put the issues facing the Council fairly and squarely.

This meeting . . . is both a historic and a sad meeting. Historic because it is, in my opinion, the first time in the history of the United Synagogue that we are being asked to force the resignation of Honorary Officers and the Board of Management of one of the most important and oldest Constituent Synagogues. It is also sad because there is a danger that this great institution, of which we are all so proud

and to which some of us have devoted a quarter of a century of loyal
and devoted service, is being divided and cut through the middle. At
the same time . . . there is no doubt whatsoever in my mind that all of
us must vote in favour of this Resolution because it cannot be allowed
that anarchy prevails in the United Synagogue. We dare not create a
situation, a precedent, when any Synagogue can appoint its minister
without the over-rule of the Chief Rabbi and of the Ministerial
Appointments Committee.

The motion to refer back was lost, and the resolution to remove the
synagogue's board of management was carried.

The arguments did not end with the debate, for it was continued at
length in the columns of the *Jewish Chronicle*. As printed, the letters
betray a great deal of acerbity, and show only too clearly how deep went
the rancours. Personal abuse and subsequent apologies became almost the
small change of communal affairs for some time thereafter, and it took
some time before all the public disagreements were publicly assuaged.
So far as the United Synagogue was concerned, there was a further issue
caught up in the discussions. It was not merely that the New West End
Synagogue was one of the oldest in the United Synagogue, nor indeed
that many of those who spoke at either the general meeting of that
synagogue or the Council of the United Synagogue bore names that had
played prominent parts in the history of London Jewry in general or of
the United Synagogue in particular. It was the combination of this with
the changing balance of forces within the United Synagogue, the
'takeover' of the United Synagogue by the new generations and the new
families, already mentioned, which gave particular emphasis to the
arguments. Without there being any conscious decision by the former
Grand Dukes of Anglo-Jewry, it was almost as if many of the
representatives of the older, pre-immigration families had turned to this
issue, preferring to support the New West End congregation in a sort
of unilateral declaration of independence from an institution they had
created but which had since developed in ways they found unpleasant.
The point must not be pushed too far, for many who supported the
actions of the followers of Dr Jacobs retained their membership of the
United Synagogue and indeed hold office within it. Yet it must be
admitted that the founding fathers would certainly have felt at home in
the synagogue of which Dr Jacobs became the minister, the New
London Synagogue, if only because that congregation found itself the
owner of the former St John's Wood Synagogue, vacated when the
members of St John's Wood opened their new enlarged structure in

1965. The irony is of course the greater, since the original New West End Synagogue and the original St John's Wood Synagogue had been founded at the same time as alternatives to enlarging the old Bayswater congregation.

At the time the controversy bid fair to be the harbinger of a split within the United Synagogue, or of the disappearance of the Chief Rabbinate as an institution. Neither happened, although certainly it did nothing to strengthen either institution. On the other hand it did point to one essential weakness in the position of any would-be dissident congregation. The union was indissoluble. Even if all the members of the New West End congregation had wished to take themselves out of the United Synagogue it would have been difficult – perhaps even impossible – for them to retain control of their buildings. Thus the New West End continued in being under the direction of the officers appointed for it by the United Synagogue until such time as it was felt that a local board of management could safely be elected, while it was the dissident group of members who went in search of a new physical presence, who had to found a new congregation, and who had to start from scratch.

By the time of the appointment of Dr Brodie's successor there had been changes in the leadership of the United Synagogue: Sir Isaac Wolfson was now President, and undoubtedly his strong personality became more prominent in the choice of the Chief Rabbi. Indeed the statement was often heard at the time of election that Sir Isaac had promised 'to find a Chief Rabbi'. Sir Isaac put a great deal of effort into interviewing candidates, discussing qualifications with those well qualified to know, and trying to eliminate those who were patently unsuited. It was equally true that he tried very hard to ensure that public debate be kept to an absolute minimum, and that there should be no vote as between various candidates. Only in this way could the prestige of the Chief Rabbinate be kept at its highest; in other words, Sir Isaac was trying virtually to repeat the unanimous call, as made at the previous election, rather than permit the semi-public voting, as had occurred at the election of Dr Hertz. It must be admitted, however, that the impression could well be given that the President was trying to 'choose' a new Chief Rabbi, and there were some who complained about this. There were no formal candidates for consideration; only one had been formally nominated – and he had nominated himself – while the others had been suggested informally by various prominent members of the community.

During the discussions, it became clear that the candidate who was most favoured was Jacob Herzog, who had received *semicha* in Israel although he had never actually exercised rabbinical offices there. He was invited by the conference, accepted the office, and then was compelled by ill-health to withdraw his acceptance shortly after his agreement had been announced and plans had been made for his installation. Bereft of the acceptable candidate, the conference had to be recalled and a new candidate decided upon. Once again the whole procedure was repeated, and this time one of those considered earlier was brought forward as a unanimous choice, Dr Immanuel Jakobovits.

CHAPTER 15

NEW PROBLEMS – THE UNITED SYNAGOGUE IN AN 'AGE OF AFFLUENCE'

The years after 1945 were not uniformly years of affluence, nor were all the individual members of synagogues within the union uniformly affluent. But certainly so far as many members were concerned they had greatly improved their material living conditions as compared with those of some fifty years earlier, and enough has been shown already in earlier chapters of the emergence of new sorts of leaders and of the dispersion of London Jewry into the newer suburbs to show the extent to which that affluence had percolated into many elements of the membership of the United Synagogue. At the same time there was another aspect of this age which equally strongly and increasingly affected the United Synagogue as a collective body and the individuals which composed it. Within the larger setting of British society generally the post-war years brought with them a growing inflation, and many observers of the wider scene commented increasingly on the emergence of that phenomenon characterised by many as 'public squalor within private affluence'. This was as true of the United Synagogue as of any other semi-public body, and in terms of the United Synagogue had certain key results. Above all, there was the failure to realise soon enough that the old-fashioned ways of paying for the commitments of the United Synagogue were grossly inadequate. This has already been illustrated through the building policy of the United Synagogue. At first the problem was masked by the great difficulties in securing licences for repairs or new construction; but when the flood gates were opened after the removal of controls, it became clear that the normal capital resources were inadequate and that money had to be borrowed at near-commercial rates of interest. This meant that individual synagogues, and synagogue members, had to find crushing burdens of capital repayment before they could even begin to make provision for any other needs of the United Synagogue. This was not a process caused, or even begun, by the Marble Arch scheme, but undoubtedly the mounting cost of that scheme – in itself a result in part of external inflation – drew attention to a problem which the scheme itself contributed to in no small part. In other fields this was equally true: commitments were entered into without a close analysis of the eventual consequences of those commitments in purely financial terms; expectations were created for the future and when they were broken the resultant uproars were even greater than if they had never been made. The result undoubtedly was that there came increasing demands on the purses of the individual members of synagogues merely to maintain those standards of synagogue service to which they had become accustomed, demands which were resented not unnaturally by those whose own incomes had not kept pace with inflation but which were not welcomed even by those who had entered into this new affluence.

In addition, however, standards themselves were not standing still. With a changing world had come also changing demands, new concepts for which the United Synagogue had to find answers, so that all in all the United Synagogue found itself faced with a new sort of society, new sorts of needs, and above all a necessity to find new sorts of solutions and new channels of endeavour and inspiration if the United Synagogue were to continue to represent the aspirations of London Jewry. This then was the basic problem of these post-war years, and of course fundamental to it was the question of money. Over and over again the cry came that there was not enough money available to meet the needs of the organisation as a whole. As a consequence of that came further complaints, either that particular schemes were draining the United Synagogue of its life blood, or that individual synagogues were suffering unduly in order to uphold the deficits of other congregations that could no longer cover their own financial needs. Inevitably, then, all the basic activities of the United Synagogue had to be discussed, and will have to be discussed here, in terms of financial provision. None the less, in this discussion finance must play initially a secondary role to the more pressing question of the extent to which the United Synagogue recognised the way in which the old world had changed.

In the first post-war budget speech, that delivered on 4 June 1945, the Treasurer surveyed not only the finances of the United Synagogue but also its general work, commenting in the words of Simon the Just that 'the life of communities rests on three pillars – education, religious worship, and philanthropy'. These three pillars remain as signposts for the twenty-five years following that budget speech, and the phrase remains as true throughout the century as it ever did. Perhaps the field in which the United Synagogue changed most was that of education, a process of change which certainly had begun in the later years of the nineteenth century but which saw most dramatic and drastic changes in the years after 1945. The end of the war found the United Synagogue compelled to take drastic steps and completely reconsider its approach to educational matters. Two crucial decisions were then taken by the United Synagogue which dominated the next quarter of a century. The first was that education in the Hebrew classes associated with the synagogues should be paid for communally out of contributions from the major synagogal bodies. No longer, it was claimed, was Hebrew education to be regarded as a charity, dependent on the odd crumb or pittance. Instead it was to be a primary charge on community resources, and the United Synagogue agreed to levy a religious education rate equal to one-third of the membership contributions, while other bodies agreed to make equivalent grants from their own resources. The second crucial decision was to continue the system whereby there was to be a unified education system, covering the work of the Union and of the Jewish Religious Education Board and also of the Talmud Torah Trust, the Central Committee for Jewish Education, and the Association of Non-Provided Schools. Once again the United Synagogue had shown itself prepared to cater for its own particular needs and at the same time to bear in mind the needs of the larger community within, and even at times outside, the Great London area. The idea was an inspiring one, and in an address delivered by Nathan Morris to a special meeting of the Council of the United Synagogue in 1946 – probably the first occasion that a non-member had been allowed to address the Council – great play was made of the way in which Jewish education was to be 'liberated from the crippling anxieties of charity – finance'.

Unfortunately within three years there were once again financial difficulties facing the new London Board, while at the same time, once again, the United Synagogue found that other bodies did not always act with the same spirit that had imbued the United Synagogue itself. At the same time too the United Synagogue itself was beginning to find itself in those financial difficulties which were to beset it all through these twenty-five years. By 1951 the Council was faced with the need to meet a rapidly growing deficit, and turned towards the $33\frac{1}{3}$ per cent religious education rate, proposing to reduce this to 25 per cent instead. Although, as a result of rescheduling of seats, the amount of money paid over to the

London Board continued to increase there was never enough, and the taking from it of various sums, even for such laudable purposes as grants to the Kosher School-Meals Service, tended to worsen the situation. The United Synagogue itself was also increasingly under strain, and the consequence was the setting up of the 1955 Committee on Jewish Religious Education. This report, calling for changes in the constitution of the London Board, was accompanied by complaints that other bodies were not contributing their fair share of communal taxation, but also maintained that the United Synagogue had the duty still of continuing to uphold religious education for the community in general rather than merely for members' children in particular.

Within four years the general situation had worsened even more for the United Synagogue, and once again the United Synagogue had to turn to some pruning of the amounts paid out by the United Synagogue to other bodies, particularly the education rate. The occasion was the vast financial burden caused by new building schemes, and the rationale was that increases in membership contributions caused by repayment and servicing of such capital sums should not pay the rate. The argument was logical, but its adoption in practice involved a cutting back of the effective religious education rate to some seventeen per cent, and by 1968 the Board was once again facing pressure both from its own financial problems and from those members who sought to disband the London Board and replace it with an education department of the United Synagogue itself.

Quite clearly, then, finance dominated the question of education provision. The same can be said of the other activities of the United Synagogue as well. Welfare, for example, a field which covered a myriad of communal activities, displays the same picture. Before the Second World War the Welfare Committee had been made responsible for the work of the Jewish Institute and various other functions of the Beth Hamedrash Committee of the United Synagogue. Direct representation on it had been given to the various East End synagogues and to all others undertaking special welfare work in the East End, and it was hoped that 'more helpers who can and will put their hearts in the work will come forward and assist those who are already striving to better the lives of our brethren in East London'. Eventually the work of the Welfare Committee included the provision of lectures, concerts, library facilities, as well as an Advisory Centre and a Poor Man's Lawyer Service, these latter two comparable to the later Citizens' Advice Bureau which became so prominent after 1945. All this was of course in addition to a wide programme of youth work, particularly through the Buxton

Street Settlement. The destruction of much of the old East End by the 1939–45 war, and particularly the physical destruction caused by the Blitz, removed the original geographical centre for much of the Welfare Committee's work, but so far as the United Synagogue was concerned this was followed by a broadening of the committee's activities, and a physical extension from the East End to the wider London Jewish community.

The activities of the Welfare Committee in the post-war period changed emphasis with the new economic status of the community. The deprived classes of the community came increasingly to be seen less in terms of the old East End and more in terms of those elements unable to find a place in the organisation of the United Synagogue. Thus many of the activities were associated with children and with youth. The years immediately after the war saw a series of short reports embodying a fresh look at some of the activities of the United Synagogue, especially in the fields of welfare and social concern. That by the Welfare Committee, embodying various recommendations for its own reconstitution, sought to introduce schemes for 'Youth Fellowship', 'Youth Adult Membership', and 'Youth Ministers'. There was emphasis in that report on the way in which over the previous twenty-five years 'the Welfare Committee, ever alive to the social welfare needs of the younger members of the Community, and the growing emphasis placed on the Service of Youth, have constantly striven to help Jewish Youth Organisations preserve their Jewish heritage'. The reports of the Welfare Committee, faithfully presented annually to the Council – usually towards the end of a meeting which more often than not had become sparsely attended – certainly demonstrate the attempts being made in these spheres, even though not all of them, begun with such high hopes and enthusiasm, have ever managed to make further progress. Indeed, these reports show that the most successful activities of the committee have been precisely in those areas where the early founders of the United Synagogue had themselves shown most enthusiasm. Just as Lionel Louis Cohen had each year carefully devoted a great deal of time and effort to maintaining services at the High Festivals for the poor and those unable to find places in the synagogues, so the reports show impressively the way in which the new deprived were being given a proper place in the religious aspects of communal life. And yet even here the committee felt bound to set up periodic enquiries to discover why attendances were falling and why there seemed less interest than in the past.

Lacking in headline appeal, but equally part of the general attention given by the United Synagogue to social welfare, were such other activities as marriage guidance, friendship clubs, and, above all, the activities of the Visitation Committee, a body older than the United Synagogue itself, but not one which carries such prestige in itself. The ministers of the original constituent synagogues had always 'visited' prisons and hospitals, so that it was natural, on the first union, for these duties to be carried on by them. Only gradually was the membership of the 'Prisons, Etc. Visitation Committee' extended until it embraced not only the United Synagogue itself but the whole London Jewish community, receiving financial support from the overwhelming mass of London synagogues. The visiting of hospitals and prisons, the after-care of Jewish prisoners after release, the superintendence of the spiritual care of Jewish children in council homes, residential, and approved schools are in themselves important and arduous activities, and they receive their due share of credit in the annual reports, but they scarcely can be said to attract over-much attention.

These then were the day-to-day mundane matters in which the United Synagogue was as much concerned as the much more attention-drawing problems of finance and of education difficulties. They failed to attract attention and in many ways they failed to recruit sufficient members of the community to provide for their adequate continuance; and yet these were the issues which had, in earlier generations, most attracted the attention of the leaders of Anglo-Jewry, so that the problems of the individual synagogues, the difficulties of one congregation as against another, had been continually attacked in the *Jewish Chronicle* as 'shoolism', the undue attention paid to minor issues which did not vitally affect the community as a whole or the basis of a full religious life. In the years of the immediate post-war era, before the age of affluence had opened, the honorary officers were imbued with the desire to recreate. It is no accident that the late 1940s saw a series of reconstructions of various social and welfare committees. A short brochure on *The Religious and Social Welfare Work of the United Synagogue* was issued, in an attempt to make members of the United Synagogue more aware of what was being done in their name.

The average Shool member has only a vague conception of the fundamental purposes which the United Synagogue serves in the Anglo-Jewish Community. He knows that the United Synagogue builds Shools, that Divine Service and Religion Classes are held, that it has a Burial Department and its own cemeteries and that if a Shool bill is not paid there is usually a reminder from the Financial

Representative. But what does the average Shool member and his family know of the large share which the United Synagogue takes in the social and philanthropic work of the Community?

Charitable and social welfare work has from time immemorial found its inspiration and expression in the Synagogue. So far as the United Synagogue is concerned much of this work was already being actively carried on by the Great Synagogue and two other City Synagogues (Hambro' and New), well before the foundation of the United Synagogue in 1870. In addition, the City Synagogues were instrumental in 1858 in forming the Jewish Board of Guardians, whose first President was Mr Ephraim Alex, an Overseer of the Great Synagogue.

There is no evidence, however, that the brochure had either a wide distribution or much effect.

In some ways the United Synagogue was faced with challenges which did not involve financial burdens, and in these there was undoubtedly evidence that as an institution it did not merely stand still or mark time. In 1970, for instance, there was set up an Israel Committee, reversing in a sense the conscious ignoring of Zionism which had been so marked a feature of some years between the wars, and even of the years immediately after 1945. But it must also be pointed out that, if the United Synagogue as an organisation had refused to be tied officially with the Zionist movement, many of its leaders, not least of them Sir Robert Waley Cohen, had contributed in practical ways towards the upbuilding of the State of Israel, and that appeals for causes associated with the Zionist cause had never been far away from the synagogue. A response to what was to be termed in the 1970s 'Women's Liberation' also found expression in these years. The question of votes for women who were members of the United Synagogue in their own right had been grumbling in the background for many years, finding a modified expression even before the First World War. After 1920 it became much more prominent, and a Special Committee was set up to discuss this question, among others. It recommended that men and women should have equal voting rights, save that women should not be eligible for election as wardens or financial representatives. It should perhaps be pointed out that women had for long been eligible for election by the Council itself to various committees where they had done invaluable work. The committee's recommendation, approved by the Council, was in 1926 put before a Conjoint Meeting of the Council and of delegates elected by the constituent synagogues, but was turned down. Among the arguments used during the debate was the declaration by various rabbis outside the United Kingdom that the measure was wrong, and although the Chairman ruled that these opinions were out of order, they must certainly have had an effect.

Before a second attempt was made to alter the constitution the opinion of the then Chief Rabbi had been sought. He gave a ruling which managed to straddle both sides of the fence on the issue:[1]

1. There is no objection whatsoever in Jewish Law to the granting of such voting powers to women as were included in the Resolution submitted to the Conjoint Meeting on October 31st last.

2. At the same time, I feel it necessary to say that this is a religious question, as is every measure affecting religious administration of the Synagogue or its allied institutions. My opinion should have been officially ascertained by the Honorary Officers on behalf of the Council.

3. In the minds of many people, this proposal is bound up with other measures, and some of these are religiously questionable. The Deed of Foundation and Trust which remains, other amendments notwithstanding, binding upon the United Synagogue, provides that the opinion of the Chief Rabbi upon each and every one of these measures if and when they arise, be officially ascertained.

4. At the Conjoint Meeting on October 31st last, there was brought forward an alleged declaration of several rabbis of other countries who have no official standing in the United Synagogue – a procedure that was rapidly ruled out by the Chairman as unconstitutional. Otherwise, a declaration by an outside source or sources might easily be brought forward on some future occasion in support of quite other policies.

At the same time Dr Hertz had been far from happy on the matter, and fearing that the sponsors of the motion wished it to be taken much further he let it be known to at least one prominent member of the Council 'that it was "the thin end of the Wedge" and that he [this member] should fight it tooth and nail'; at the Conjoint Meeting in 1928 which again discussed the possibility of amending the constitution in this sense the motion was fought 'tooth and nail' and was defeated.

After the war, however, the issue was brought up once again, and various constituent synagogues asked the Council to consider the matter once more. Before the debate was held the Chief Rabbi, Dr Brodie, was asked his opinion, and his reply reaffirmed that provided women members were not to be voted for, that is, that they were not to be eligible for election to Boards of Management or as honorary officers or to the Council, they could vote at meetings of members of synagogues if they were members in their own right. The proposal was strongly supported but equally strongly opposed, one speaker expressing 'pained surprise' at the Chief Rabbi's attitude; 'the Council was not bound to accept the Chief Rabbi's opinion. Time and again in the history of the Council, a Chief Rabbi had recommended a certain step which the Council in its wisdom and judgement had refused to follow.' Another suggested that 'it was only a few "busybody" women who wanted the vote. If women were interested in synagogal work, there was surely plenty of opportunity for them in the Ladies' Guilds'. A committee was set up to investigate and report back; within six months the committee had unanimously agreed that women should get the vote under safeguards to which both sides represented on the committee had agreed. The procedure for change was long drawn out, and it was not until February 1954, three years after the change had been first mooted at the Council, that the necessary Conjoint Meeting could be held. Even at that there was still opposition; one member maintained that the enfranchisement of women was 'the beginning of an age which would drift away from Judaism, and the cry was back to traditional Judaism, not to grant the vote to women'. None the less the change was agreed to overwhelmingly.

The pattern of the last twenty-five years has shown that the prime need of the United Synagogue has been that of finding adequate finance. Almost inevitably the realisation of growing inflation came too late, so that the Treasurers were never able to keep up with ever-mounting costs. Whenever synagogues were able to reschedule membership contributions they did so largely in terms of existing debts and deficits rather than in terms of projected future costs. Moreover, on top of that came an entirely different pattern of growth, caused by this same inflation, and the need among younger couples to move out into the suburbs less as a result of growing family wealth than as a result of an inability to maintain life in the more expensive inner suburbs. The position was stated quite clearly by the President at a Council meeting on 9 March 1959.

The fundamental concept of the United Synagogue which has made it the pride of this community, and the envy of all others, is that it was recognised by our founders that there would always be Synagogues which, whilst giving a vital service to the lives of their members, could not maintain themselves, and that the Synagogues more fortunately placed should subvent these less fortunate congregations. That magnificent conception of our forebears is, as I have said, the whole basis on which the United Synagogue exists.

Until the War, the pattern of the United Synagogue had developed steadily. As our members prospered, they tended to move to new areas and new Synagogues were founded which consisted very largely of some of the wealthier members of the community and became what we call, for convenience, 'Surplus' Synagogues. These Synagogues, one after another, took up the main burden, though we are proud to say that they did not regard it as a burden, of maintaining the poorer Congregations, and so we saw the pattern develop – St John's Wood, New West End, Hampstead, Golders Green, and Hampstead Garden Suburb – to name but a few – successively took on the major share of the burden. These were the conditions existing when our calculations for the Religious Education Rate were made in 1946.

After the War, the situation developed in a manner that we had not envisaged. First of all, many of the new Synagogues which had to be built were, for the first time, for large Congregations with many members and alive with enthusiasm, but not on the whole consisting of wealthy persons who had necessarily moved their homes with increasing prosperity. Secondly, the cost of building rose astronomically, and out of all proportion to past experience. Thirdly, until they were relaxed, the restrictions on building held up the construction of the new Synagogues; this resulted for the first time in our own funds being insufficient to finance the necessary building, and recourse had to be made to outside sources with the consequential payment of high interest rates.

Let us now see how these factors have affected the position of the United Synagogue. Instead of the newly-established Synagogues successively providing the main support for the poorer and declining Synagogues, the reverse was the picture. Let me, as an example, tell you the story of Edgware. I think it will be agreed that Edgware is not really a wealthy community, although it is undoubtedly a large community and a live community set in an attractive suburb and extremely representative of the United Synagogue as a whole. They produced a seat schedule for the new Synagogue which the local Board of Management considered was as high as their community could bear, and every effort is genuinely being made to implement it. In 1957, before the new seat schedule, the Synagogue showed the greatest deficit that had ever been known in the United Synagogue and, if I may give away a Budget secret, the 1958 Account, in spite of the new seat schedule, will not be very substantially better. This story can be repeated again in large measure in the case of Wembley.

Apart from these striking cases, when our Surplus synagogues have to be re-built to provide for an expanding membership, and we consider how their budget will appear, we are faced with the fact that the re-building will involve capital charges so great as to turn them from Synagogues with big surpluses to Synagogues with considerably smaller surpluses even with considerably higher seat schedules.

From such examples as these, it will be seen that the annual funds available from the newer and wealthier Synagogues are in danger of no longer providing for the needs of the poorer parts of the community.

Why is this? The reason is, is it not, as I have informed you on many occasions, and as the Treasurers informed you at the last Budget Meeting, when they illustrated their point with a graph, the growth in membership contributions has not kept up with the growth in expense and, as you know, even if our less interested members may not know, the sole income of the United Synagogue is the contributions of its members?

The Honorary Officers have naturally been regarding this situation with considerable anxiety for some time, and they have studied the steps which have been taken over the years to meet this trend.

Perhaps the most important problem of all those raised by the 'age of affluence' was one which had been present from the very beginning – the status, remuneration, and the recruitment of ministers. Various reports from the honorary officers in the 1950s and 1960s served merely to repeat what was clearly stated in the 1880s. The 1953 report indicated that out of the 114 students who had entered Jews' College between 1925 and 1952, over half had not entered the ministry, and that the reasons for the failure of potential entrants to the ministry had not altered over the previous seventy years. A decline in religious enthusiasm had been one factor.[2]

The number of parents who are anxious that their sons shall adopt a career in which the Sabbath and Festivals can be strictly observed has lessened, with a corresponding effect upon the number of students who enter Jews' College. In former generations this was a strong motive which induced some fathers to think of the Ministry as a career for a son, but it has been losing weight. There does not appear to be, either among parents or their sons, the sense of a call to service for

Judaism. Even where a youth does feel a desire for Holy Service, he is frequently discouraged by his elders.

But an equal weight was put upon two other factors. One was the financial disadvantages of the ministry:

> As the average member of the Community grew in affluence, his ambitions for his sons took a higher flight. Certain professions offered better remuneration and an allegedly superior social standing than the vocation of Rabbi, Minister or Teacher; consequently preference has been increasingly given to the lay professions.

The second was a clear recognition that the ministry held no prestige within the community at large.

> It has been made clear that dissatisfaction exists among the Clergy. In particular they suffer from a sense of futility and frustration. They feel that they are denied the full opportunity of spiritual leadership in their Congregations. . . .
>
> Ministers come to wonder for what purpose they applied themselves to intensive study over a lengthy period, since they have little occasion to make use of their acquired learning. Most of their energies are spent in work for which this arduous scholastic preparation is quite unnecessary. Moreover, they are usually not even consulted about matters connected with the Synagogue, and decisions are taken, or their own views overridden, by laymen who are unhampered with Jewish knowledge. . . .
>
> There has grown within the Community a tendency to disparage the Office of the Ministry which reacts upon the attitude of the average congregant towards the Minister. For example, in conversation he may be spoken of in disrespectful language within the hearing of the young.

That these problems were not confined to the Anglo-Jewish ministry but could be found expressed just as forcibly by various non-Jewish communities in relation to their own clerical shortages was of little consideration. Socially and culturally the United Synagogue might well have been assimilated into the host society, but its problems remained very real indeed.

CONCLUSION AND
RETROSPECT

However much the historian of the first hundred years of the United Synagogue tries to maintain an impartiality, he must inevitably be more than a mere chronicler. Even the way in which the raw materials of the history have been handled implies a series of value judgments, but in addition it would be unusual if he had not drawn specific conclusions from his studies. Some of these conclusions become apparent from the form in which the history is compiled. During the years covered by this study the United Synagogue has had to face a number of problems, some of which were relevant to one generation alone while others have found short-term solutions only to reappear in the later generation. Inevitably, indeed, some of these problems could never have had more than a short-term, interim solution, but the question which must remain to be faced is the extent to which the United Synagogue has been able to find answers to its various difficulties, and whether it will be able to continue to meet the challenges of its contemporary environment. Obviously the answers to these facets of that question are tied up with issues of personalities and of internal 'political' arrangements, and to that extent the historian as such cannot even begin to give any answers; but to the extent that the past history of the institution can give any pointer to the way in which it is likely to develop he is perhaps entitled to draw his conclusions.

In its beginnings the United Synagogue came together to provide a financial framework and overall structure for a number of growing communities, and to make it possible from the common resources of London Jewry for the continuance of the communal responsibilities which each synagogue had recognised but found difficult to maintain on its own. As time went on the nature of those responsibilities may well have changed, sometimes out of all recognition, but the principle of joint responsibility had always to be accepted, and taking the century as a whole the institution can be found shouldering that burden. The corollary of that acceptance in principle has been, however, that in each generation each part of the institution, having willed the end, had to be prepared to will the means; in practice that usually, though not invariably, implied a growing financial provision, either by increased communal taxation or by drawing on other resources open to the community. It would be unfair to criticise the United Synagogue, as was done for example by Israel Zangwill, for being unduly concerned with balance sheets and finances without recognising the impossibility of its taking any of its other activities far without a sound financial basis. Similarly, one of the aims of those who first planned the new organisation was to induce the members of each individual community to look beyond the narrow boundaries summed up in the word 'shoolism' to the interests of the community as a whole, seeking not the immediate benefits of one small part but the longer-term interests of the whole. The question, to what extent has the United Synagogue fulfilled the hopes of its founders, becomes one which is very difficult to answer, for it ignores one further factor in the situation. The community which the United Synagogue was created to serve has in itself altered so markedly as to be almost impossible to recognise. Certainly the founding fathers would have found it almost impossible to envisage in its geographical spread, its sheer size of numbers, and its complexities of organisation. How far they would have considered that the organisation they set up could have been at all appropriate to the altered circumstances is impossible to answer.

At all events there are certain features of the original scheme which had a crucial importance. There was, for example, a continued emphasis on financial stability. The continuous worries over the Hambro' Synagogue are evidence of that, combined as it was with a recognition of the spiritual vitality; not until it was in danger of spiritual death was it in serious danger. Similarly, when the East London Synagogue was being planned it was made clear that although it was unlikely to be able to make an important contribution to the general financial work of the United Synagogue it was an important element in the religious life of the community. At the same time, the early additional synagogues had always to be financially sound, and no new synagogue was admitted into the united community unless it showed that it was not only financially sound at the date of its admission but likely to continue so for the likely future. In consequence there was always a strict financial control over these branches of a single organisation; in practice the number of congregations was limited; problems of capital investment for new buildings did not arise; but there was also a lack of flexibility when there developed a need for new congregations with social and financial backgrounds different from those of the founding fathers. It was to be a remarkable feature that for the first three-quarters of a century the United Synagogue was able to meet these sorts of challenge, adapting its formal structure but retaining the essential purpose of enabling poorer congregations to continue with help from the richer. When, however, the original clarity of purpose seemed to become lost, so that what had originally been castigated as 'shoolism' re-emerged at the expense of central objectives; when the earlier refusal to accept new synagogues without a clear exposition of the needs for the potentialities of such congregations was replaced by a willingness to bring them into precipitate existence; when individual congregations were able to take advantage of interim status and diminish burdens of contribution to central purposes – these emerging features would seem to indicate that the organisation was in danger of losing its way and failing to respond to the developing needs of the wider community.

Two other features have also in the past marked the developing United Synagogue. The founding fathers, Grand Dukes all, had a certain effortless superiority which arose from their social and economic position within the Jewish and non-Jewish communities. As the patterns of the non-Jewish world altered these individuals lost their place in the Jewish world too, at the same time as Zangwill's 'Children of the Ghetto', the second generation of immigrants, were coming to the front. They had absorbed some of the *mores* of the community into which they had come but not all, and the end of the first hundred years of the history of the United Synagogue has not yet seen a full clarification of the extent to which these newer rulers of London Jewry have determined what they want out of its institutions. Closely connected with that problem has been the parallel issue of the part to be played in the United Synagogue by its full-time lay and religious officials. The United Synagogue, from the time of Asher Asher, has always been closely connected with the personality of its Secretary and its other administrative staff, in the same way as its spiritual tone has been set by the quality of the ministers who serve the individual congregations, but as with the civil service of the wider host community few pains have been systematically taken to recruit and train for communal service the best available talent. Such men have entered communal service, but by accident rather than by deliberate recruitment, and as the organisation becomes larger and its responsibilities wider the question will sooner or later have to be faced as to whether the old machine can be continued unchanged. In one respect the situation is little changed over the years. Recruitment to the ministry is a constant problem, and the reasons advanced for this failure in the early years of the United Synagogue are largely identical with those adduced in the last decade of the century. Repeated committees of enquiry have spelled out diagnoses of the situation, but their clear recommendations have had little direct effect.

And yet, despite all weaknesses and potential difficulties, the United Synagogue continues, and its successes in London have led other, provincial communities to seek to emulate it and establish their own united congregations. It has managed to weld the many disparate elements in London Jewish life into a coherent whole and in doing so has absorbed an enormous mass of migrants not only into the patterns of Anglo-Jewry but also into the full stream of life of the host communities which accepted these migrants. This has been the great contribution of the United Synagogue, the 'acculturisation' of all these migrants. The challenges have altered, but they are still there, while the opportunities are also still there for those who are able and willing to make use of them. What is essential above all is that those who have the destinies of the United Synagogue and of London Jewry in their hands should have a clear understanding of the factors which brought it into life and which enabled it to continue for over a hundred years. By the nature of his vocation the historian will obviously hope and expect that such a clear understanding will enable these leaders to bring their institution into line with the needs of its second century. It has been that hope which has been the constant spur to the historian.

NOTE ON SOURCES

Over forty years ago Cecil Roth was invited to prepare a report on the archives of the United Synagogue. His catalogue still remains the fundamental introduction to the papers of the pre-1870 individual synagogues and to the papers of the various bodies of delegates bringing the union into existence. For the period after 1870 the archives of the United Synagogue consist in part of the minute books of the Council or of the various committees and sub-committees reporting to the main body. There are also various series of 'Green' and 'Orange' folders created on an *ad hoc* basis by the United Synagogue secretariat, containing extracts from Council minutes, rearranged under subject headings. These collections of minutes, folders, balance sheets, and printed reports have obviously not been arranged for the benefit of historians, but in practice it is possible to use the Council minute books as the basic points of reference, so that wherever a quotation appears in the text without a specific attribution it can usually be traced to the relevant Council minute. Even the printed reports from sub-committees have been pasted into the minute book, so that whatever rearrangement might be made in future it will still be possible to trace the original.

It is impossible to cite all the secondary works that have been consulted for the centenary history of an institution which, like this, covers an enormous community. The standard works of Anglo-Jewish history – Cecil Roth, *History of the Jews of England* (3rd edn, Oxford University Press, 1964); Vivian Lipman, *Social History of the Jews in England, 1851–1951* (Watts, 1954); James Picciotto, *Sketches of Anglo-Jewish History* (2nd edn edited by Israel Finestein, Soncino Press, 1956) – could be added to over and over again into a bibliography comparable to those of Cecil Roth, *Magna Bibliotheca Anglo-Judaica* (Jewish Historical Society of England, 1937), or Ruth Lehmann, *Anglo-Jewish Bibliography, 1937–1970* (Jewish Historical Society of England, 1973). Where necessary, books have been given individual citation, but lack of mention does not imply lack of use.

NOTES

CHAPTER 1 THE FOUNDATION

1 There were other synagogues at this time, but most of them were of less importance. See Cecil Roth, 'The Lesser London Synagogues of the Eighteenth Century', *Miscellanies of the Jewish Historical Society of England*, III, pp. 1 ff.

2 A full analysis of this process can be found in V. D. Lipman, 'The Rise of Jewish Suburbia', *Transactions of the Jewish Historical Society*, XXI, pp. 78 ff., and in his *Social History of the Jews in England, 1851–1951*, Watts, 1954.

3 Minute Book of the Great Synagogue Vestry, quoted by Cecil Roth, *History of the Great Synagogue*, Goldston, 1950, p. 278.

4 Ibid., p. 280.

5 Minute Book of the New Synagogue Vestry.

6 Ibid.

7 See V. D. Lipman, *A Century of Social Service, 1859–1959: The History of the Jewish Board of Guardians*, Routledge & Kegan Paul, 1959.

8 Minute Book of the Great Synagogue Vestry.

9 Ibid.

10 Ibid.

11 Ibid.

12 'Case for Master Jacob Waley', Hambro' Synagogue Vestry.

13 Minute Book of the Great Synagogue Vestry.

14 Ibid.

15 Ibid.

16 Minute Book of the New Synagogue Vestry.

17 Minute Book of the Great Synagogue Vestry.

18 These are included in the Great Synagogue delegates' version of the minutes.

19 Delegates' minutes.
20 Ibid.
21 Ibid.
22 *Final Report of the Delegates*.

CHAPTER 2 THE NEW ORGANISATION

1 Although the term 'Vestry' was the official title of the Council until 1880, it would be pedantic and confusing not to use 'Council' in these earlier years.
2 It was at the rate of one per fifty qualified members. The Great had six (for 324 let seats), the Hambro' three (for 161), the New five (for 283), the Central Branch five (for 260), and Bayswater seven (for 359).
3 *Report*, 1876.
4 14 June 1876.
5 3 May 1881.
6 Executive Committee Minutes, 13 July 1876.
7 Ibid.
8 *Report*, 1874.
9 6 April 1889.
10 8 May 1878.
11 J. H. Stallard, *London Pauperism amongst Jews and Christians* (Saunders, Otley, 1867).

CHAPTER 3 THE FINANCIAL STRUCTURE

1 The quotations in this chapter are taken, unless otherwise indicated, from the Treasurers' Annual Report of the relevant year.
2 Approved 11 November 1886.
3 Hambro', New, Borough, East London, North London.
4 Great, Bayswater, Central, St John's Wood, West End, Dalston.

CHAPTER 4 THE FOUNDING FATHERS

1 *Jewish Chronicle*, 1 July 1887.
2 Ibid.
3 V. D. Lipman, *A Century of Social Service*, Routledge & Kegan Paul, 1959, p. 72.
4 *Jewish Chronicle*, 1 July 1887.
5 *Jewish Chronicle*, 1 January 1889.
6 Ibid.
7 *Some Notes and Articles by the Late Asher Asher, M.D., 1837–1889, with reprints of his newspaper obituaries, etc. . . . .*, London, 1916.
8 *Jewish Chronicle*, 18 February 1881.

CHAPTER 5 THE GROWTH OF LONDON JEWRY

1 See V. D. Lipman, 'The Rise of Jewish Suburbia', *Transactions of the Jewish Historical Society*, XXI, pp. 78 ff., and L. P. Gartner, *The Jewish Immigrant in England, 1870–1914*, Allen & Unwin, 1960.

2 For a detailed discussion of their impact upon the non-Jewish world, see B. Gainer, *The Alien Invasion*, Heinemann, 1972.

3 See A. A. Goren, *New York Jews and the Quest for Community: the Kehillah Experiment, 1908–1922*, Columbia University Press, 1970.

CHAPTER 6 DEVELOPMENT AND GROWTH

1 See *Jewish Chronicle*, 2 September 1870.

2 The adjective 'Minor' disappeared within two years.

3 7 January 1890.

4 *Jewish Chronicle*, 8 May 1891.

5 'Scheme for Associate Synagogues', Minute Book, 5 December 1899.

CHAPTER 7 THE ROUTINE OF THE UNITED SYNAGOGUE

1 Albert Jessel to Sir Robert Waley Cohen, quoted R. Henriques, *Sir Robert Waley Cohen, 1877–1952*, Secker & Warburg, 1966, p. 179.

2 Memorandum of Conference, 27 June 1910. .

3 Collected edition, Globe Publishing Co., 1925, vol. I, p. 332.

4 See V. D. Lipman, *A Century of Social Service*, Routledge & Kegan Paul, 1959.

5 Jewish Religious Education Board, *First Annual Report*, 1895.

6 *First Report of the Union of Hebrew and Religion Classes*, 1907.

7 See M. Goulston, 'The Status of the Anglo-Jewish Rabbinate, 1840–1914', *Jewish Journal of Sociology*, X, 1968, pp. 55–82, and his unpublished thesis, University of London Library. See also S. Sharot, 'Religious Change in Native Orthodoxy, 1870–1914', *Jewish Journal of Sociology*, XV, 1973. pp. 57–78 and 167–87, and his 'Native Jewry and the Religious Anglicisation of Immigrants in London', ibid., XVI, 1974, pp. 39–56.

CHAPTER 8 RELATIONS WITH SOME OTHER BODIES

1 On the office of Chief Rabbi, see Cecil Roth, 'The Chief Rabbinate of England', in *Essays in Honour of the Very Rev. Dr J. H. Hertz*, Edward Goldston, 1942.

2 *Report of the Executive Committee on matters connected with the appointment of the Rev. Dr Hermann Adler as the Delegate of the Chief Rabbi . . .* , December 1879.

3 *Jewish Chronicle*, 25 July 1890.

4 Memorandum of Conference of June 1910.

5 Cecil Roth, *The Federation of Synagogues, 1912–1937*, Federation of Synagogues, 1937, p. 9.
6 Privately communicated.

CHAPTER 9   LONDON JEWRY 1912–1945

1 For a fuller, if perhaps controversial, assessment of Rabbi Hertz, see my Commemorative Lecture delivered on 25 September 1972 and published by the United Synagogue.

CHAPTER 10   THE EXPANSION OF THE UNITED SYNAGOGUE

1 *Report on the District Synagogue Scheme*, 20 June 1927.
2 *Report by the Executive Committee on the Affiliation of Small Congregations*, 14 December 1932.
3 24 October 1938.
4 *Report of the North and North-East London Committee*, 4 June 1929.
5 *Report of the Special Committee*, 7 April 1932.
6 24 February 1936.
7 Prag to Waley Cohen, 15 April 1918; Waley Cohen to Prag, 17 April 1918; Waley Cohen to Philip Ornstein, 20 July 1918.

CHAPTER 11   THE OFFICERS AND STAFF

1 His biography by Robert Henriques does him justice in all fields save one, his Jewish connections and activities.
2 R. Henriques, *Sir Robert Waley Cohen, 1877–1952*, Secker & Warburg, 1966, p. 179.
3 Anglo-Jewish Archives, Mocatta Library, University College, London.
4 Privately communicated.
5 *Joint Celebration of the 75th Anniversary of Jews' College, the 70th Anniversary of the Jewish Religious Board, and the 60th Anniversary of the United Synagogue*, 1931, p. 11.
6 *Report on Ministerial Salaries*, 24 November 1924.
7 Goldberg papers.

CHAPTER 13   RECONSTRUCTION AND EXPANSION

1 *Non-Constituent Synagogues – Relationships with United Synagogue: Report . . . of the Honorary Officers*, 29 November 1948.
2 25 January 1965.
3 *Report of the Special Committee of the Council of the United Synagogue set up to*

examine the position of certain synagogues in North and North-Eastern London, 19
July 1965.

4 *Interim Report of the Special Committee to enquire into the building policy of the
United Synagogue*, 28 May 1965.

CHAPTER 14   NEW GENERATIONS

1 28 September 1962.
2 Private communication.
3 Goldberg papers. Anglo-Jewish Archives, University College, London.
4 Private communication.

CHAPTER 15   NEW PROBLEMS – THE UNITED SYNAGOGUE IN AN 'AGE OF AFFLUENCE'

1 Dr Hertz to Lionel de Rothschild, 10 January 1927.
2 *Report on Recruitment . . . for the Anglo-Jewish Ministry*, 8 June 1953.

HONORARY OFFICERS OF THE UNITED SYNAGOGUE
1870–1970

PRESIDENTS

Sir Anthony de Rothschild, Bart.,
1870–1876
Sampson Lucas, 1876–1879
Nathan Mayer, Lord Rothschild,
1879–1915
Leopold de Rothschild, 1915–1917
Lionel de Rothschild, 1918–1942

Sir Robert Waley Cohen, 1942–1952
Frank Samuel, 1953–1954
Ewen E. S. Montagu, 1954–1961
F. A. Rossdale (Acting), 1961
Ewen E. S. Montagu, 1961–1962
Sir Isaac Wolfson, Bart., 1962–1973

VICE-PRESIDENTS

Lionel L. Cohen, 1870–1887

Henry Lucas, 1887–1910
Felix A. Davis, 1911–1916
Albert M. Woolf, 1917–1925
Samuel Moses, 1925–1934
Sir Isadore Salmon, 1934–1936
Frank Samuel, 1936–1953
H. Gledhill, 1953–1959
Frank A. Rossdale, 1959–1965
S. S. Levin, elected 1965

Sampson Lucas, 1870–1875
Nathan, Lord Rothschild, 1876–1879
Baron Henry de Worms, 1880–1882
Sir Barrow H. Ellis, 1883–1887
Benjamin L. Cohen, 1887–1899
Albert H. Jessel, 1899–1917
Evelyn de Rothschild, 1917
Sir Robert Waley Cohen, 1918–1942
Ewen E. S. Montagu, 1942–1954

Sir Bernard Waley-Cohen, 1954–1961
Alfred Woolf, 1961–1973

TREASURERS

Solomon Schloss, 1870–1872
Baron Henry de Worms, 1872
Charles Samuel, 1873–1875

Assur Moses, 1870–1873

Hyman A. Abrahams, 1874–1876

David Davis, 1875–1896

Assur Keyser, 1876–1879
Frederick W. Halford, 1879–1883
Henry Lucas, 1883–1887
Henry E. Beddington, 1887–1893
Hyman A. Abrahams, 1893–1900

Felix A. Davis, 1896–1911
Evelyn de Rothschild, 1911–1917
S. H. Emanuel, 1917–1925
Sir Isadore Salmon, 1925–1934
Ewen E. S. Montagu, 1934–1942
Henry Gledhill, 1942–1953
Maurice Hyams, 1953–1957
Asher Wingate, 1957–1961
F. M. Landau, 1961–1971

Woolf Myers, 1900–1906
Carl Stettauer, 1906–1913
Robert Waley Cohen, 1913–1918
F. D. Benjamin, 1919–1929
Frank Samuel, 1929–1936
Percy M. Rossdale, 1936–1937
Dr M. Epstein, 1937–1946
Frank A. Rossdale, 1946–1959
Alfred Woolf, 1959–1961
George M. Gee, 1961–1973

OVERSEERS OF THE POOR (TREASURERS OF THE BEQUESTS AND TRUSTS FUNDS)

Henry Solomons, 1870–1874
Joseph M. Isaacs, 1874–1876
Maurice Hart, 1877–1895
Albert Woolf, 1895–1916
Samuel Moses, 1916–1925
Frank Samuel, 1925–1929
Otto M. Schiff, 1929–1934
Dr M. Epstein, 1934–1937
Stephen B. Cohen, 1937–1943
Edmund de Rothschild, 1946–1950
Alfred Woolf, 1950–1959
S. Boxer, 1959–1969
Victor Lucas, 1969–1973

Charles Samuel, 1870–1873
Noah Davis, 1873–1899

R. Sonnenthal, 1899–1901
Lewis Levy, 1901–1913
N. S. Lucas, 1913–1947
I. D. Goldberg, 1947–1955
S. S. Levin, 1955–1965

Raymond Goldwater, elected 1965

TREASURERS OF THE BURIAL SOCIETY

Samuel Levy, 1872–1879
Morris Van Thal, 1879–1881
Simon Simons, 1881–1899
Leonard B. Franklin, 1899–1919

Arthur L. Lazarus, 1919–1927
Lawrence Levy, 1927–1936
Henry Gledhill, 1936–1942
Maurice Hyams, 1952–1953
A. Wingate, 1953–1957
R. Kandler, elected 1957

Jacob Levy, 1872–1875
Joseph Magnus, 1875–1898
Isaac A. Joseph, 1898–1902
W. T. Leviansky, 1902–1916
Sir Herbert B. Cohen, Bart., 1916–1919
Joseph Prag, 1919–1929
A. J. Jacobs, 1929–1937
Frank A. Rossdale, 1937–1946
Sidney Spanjer, 1946–1955
Mark Kleiner, 1956–1974

CHAIRMEN OF THE BUILDING COMMITTEE

Edward A. Beddington, 1871–1876
Barnett Myers, 1876–1879
Samuel Montagu, 1879–1883
Henry E. Beddington, 1883–1887
Charles Samuel, 1887–1893
Woolf Myers, 1893–1900
Frank I. Lyons, 1900–1901
R. Sonnenthal, 1901–1916
Isidore Salmon, 1916–1924

James Rossdale, 1924–1933
Joseph Freedman, 1933–1935
S. J. Goldberg, 1935–1945
P. M. Rossdale, 1945–1951
I. W. Goldberg, 1951–1955
A. Wingate, 1955–1961
George M. Gee, 1961–1967
Victor Lucas, 1967–1973

CHAIRMEN OF THE VISITATION COMMITTEE

N. S. Joseph, 1872–1880
Louis Davidson, 1880–1915
S. H. Emanuel, 1916–1919

Dr Clarke S. Myers, 1919–1932
Dr Dennis Geffen, 1932–1959
Frank E. Ellis, 1960–1969
Dr M. N. Oster, 1969–1971

CHAIRMEN OF THE WELFARE COMMITTEE

Albert M. Woolf, 1913
Dr N. S. Lucas, 1913–1918
Ernst H. Schiff, 1918–1919
Dr Israel Feldman, 1919–1923
Ernest Lesser, 1923–1932
John Lewis, 1932–1941

T. H. Fligelstone, 1941–1943
(Acting Chairman, 1941–1947, John
    Lewis)
Sidney Spanjer, 1947–1954
Arthur Snowman, 1954–1959
Raymond Goldwater, elected 1959

SECRETARIES

Dr Asher Asher, 1870–1889
Philip Ornstein, 1887–1920
Philip Goldberg, 1920–1947

Henry Isaac, 1926–1940 (Joint)
Alfred Silverman, 1947–1968
Nathan Rubin, appointed 1968

STATISTICS OF MALE
SEAT-HOLDERS OF THE
UNITED SYNAGOGUE
1870–1970

This table has been compiled by Mr J. Julius, Assistant Secretary of the United Synagogue. Not even his patient assiduity has been able to fill all the gaps here revealed. Each Synagogue has been listed in the order in which it was admitted to the United Synagogue, irrespective of its status, then or later. The list however, when used in conjunction with the various maps, makes it possible to chart the varying fortunes of each of the synagogues and the ways in which London Jewish communities moved about. It was judged sufficient to choose a ten-year period of time for the sampling process, except for the initial entry which, save in the ten instances of a synagogue admitted in one of these 'sample years', represents the number of male seat-holders at the date of admission. This figure is printed in brackets to indicate that it does not follow the pattern observed elsewhere.

Synagogue	Date of Admission	1870	1880	1890	1900	1910
Great	1870	324	400	449	459	410
Hambro	1870	161	162	102	199	212
New	1870	283	358	294	318	204
Bayswater	1870	359	318	377	365	306
Central	1870	260	380	334	355	380
Borough	1873	(162)	170	152	167	177
St John's Wood	1876	(53)	79	298	373	317
East London	1877	(221)	227	272	345	340
North London	1878	(247)	252	163	235	235
New West End	1879	(179)	202	260	322	317
Dalston	1885	—	(268)	269	365	368
Hammersmith & West Kensington	1890	—	—	57	175	295
Hampstead	1892	—	—	(141)	384	486
Hackney	1897	—	—	(155)	252	352
Poplar	1902	—	—	—		
East Ham & Manor Park	1902	—	—	—		
S.E. London	1902	—	—	—		
Stoke Newington	1903	—	—	—	(221)	434
Brondesbury	1905	—	—	—	(170)	316
West Ham	1907	—	—	—		
Brixton	1913	—	—	—	—	
Richmond	1916	—	—	—	—	
Chelsea	1917	—	—	—	—	(52)
Hornsey & Wood Green	1920	—	—	—	—	—
Walthamstow & Leyton	1920	—	—	—	—	—
Ealing & Acton	1921	—	—	—	—	—
Golders Green	1922	—	—	—	—	—
Sandys Row	1922	—	—	—	—	—
Upton Park	1923	—	—	—	—	—
Mile End & Bow	1927	—	—	—	—	—
Hoxton & Shoreditch	1927	—	—	—	—	—
S.W. London	1927	—	—	—	—	—
Becontree	1927	—	—	—	—	—

1920	1930	1940	1950	1960	1970	Remarks
522	445	577	608	310	294	
211	207	—	—	—	—	Amalgamated with Great 1936
654	702	607	1022	1119	729	
366	338	293	406	419	191	
353	374	351	467	685	657	
246	313	274	200	134	—	Amalgamated with Brixton 1961
368	397	544	904	938	991	
397	383	359	411	467	376	
313	317	291	301	—	—	Amalgamated with Dalston 1958
365	393	381	535	562	406	
340	355	306	402	463	—	Amalgamated with Stoke Newington 1967
362	375	347	456	402	265	
511	613	713	767	833	773	
404	314	565	767	770	582	
140			80	—	—	Closed 1951
			315	287	184	
			186	196	181	
450	458	351	568	511	343	
522	540	515	518	401	250	
		457	561	523	296	
252	356	473	508	614	526	
		111	235	222	180	
			75	145	125	
			106	129	87	
150			—	—	—	Seceded from U.S. 1949
(68)		129	284	342	311	
	533	639	959	1011	829	
			—	—	—	Seceded from U.S. 1949
		159	177	237	169	
		382	353	292	208	
			—	—	—	Closed 1949
		144	233	230	173	
			—	—	—	Amalgamated with Barking 1949

Synagogue	Date of Admission	1930	1940
Cricklewood	1931	(50)	663
Willesden	1931	(51)	281
Wembley	1931	(57)	244
Highams Park & Chingford	1932	(124)	120
Dollis Hill	1932		
Edgware	1933		247
Harrow	1933		80
Finsbury Park	1934		167
Palmers Green & Southgate	1934	(63)	146
Hendon	1935		561
Finchley	1935		279
Highgate	1935	(59)	81
Kingsbury	1936	(38)	67
South Tottenham	1936		176
Ilford	1936	(70)	192
Hampstead Garden Suburb	1937	(199)	
South Hampstead	1938		77
Catford & Bromley	1938	(86)	100
Edmonton & Tottenham	1938	(100)	99
North Finchley & Woodside Park	1943		
Hounslow	1945		(62)
Staines	1946		(87)
Stanmore & Canon's Park	1946		(57)
Streatham	1946		(52)
Sutton	1946		(66)
Ruislip	1947		(45)
St Albans	1947		(112)
Wanstead & Woodford	1947		(25)
Barking (& Becontree)	1948		(152)
Cockfosters & North Southgate	1948		(146)
Dunstable	1948		
Elm Park	1948		(48)
High Wycombe	1948		(68)
Kingston & Surbiton	1948		(80)
Peterborough	1948		(25)
Pinner	1948		(51)
Romford	1948		
Watford	1948		(45)
Welwyn Garden City	1948		(29)
Worcester	1948		(14)
Muswell Hill	1949		(174)
Kenton	1949		(52)

1950	1960	1970	Remarks
742	700	519	
748	713	543	
633	799	467	
279	357	340	
617	640	492	
941	1092	1270	
275	227	85	
215	327	396	
454	648	663	
1015	1270	1357	
782	1220	1242	
308	361	248	
375	555	545	
410	431	313	
683	1092	1937	
652	791	821	
176	218	259	
158	202	231	
150	170	135	
301	538	703	
94	98	88	
90	126	108	
296	594	1016	
215	261	245	
91	133	202	
126	163	148	
96	69	41	
126	368	484	
209	204	208	
199	661	984	
	—	—	Closed 1955
53	87	82	
57	30	42	
103	148	227	
28	22	23	
74	135	226	
83	146	142	
53	77	105	
31	59	66	
15	18	11	
203	255	354	
98	534	1007	

Synagogue	Date of Admission	1950	1960	1970	Remarks
Mill Hill	1950	65	267	374	
Slough & Windsor	1950	58	60	35	
Epsom	1952	(30)	28	21	
Hainault	1952	(51)	55	—	Amalgamated with Chigwell
Harold Hill	1953	(78)	99	77	
Barnet	1954	(50)	65	175	
Marble Arch	1954	(58)	341	467	
Boreham Wood & Elstree	1955	(49)	92	165	
Putney & Wimbledon	1956	(19)	46	76	
Chiswick	1957	(42)	95	53	
Hemel Hempstead	1957	(22)	20	30	
Enfield & Winchmore Hill	1963	—	(118)	114	
Chigwell (& Hainault)	1965	—	(48)	220	
Belmont	1966	—	(77)	141	
Potters Bar & Brookmans Park	1968	—	(20)	20	
Newbury Park	1968	—	(129)	217	
Bushey	1970	—	—	48	

LISTS OF SYNAGOGUES SHOWING DATES OF ADMISSION
INTO THEIR RESPECTIVE CATEGORIES

	Constituent		*District*
1870	GREAT	1927	MILE END & BOW
	HAMBRO		WEST HAM
	NEW	1931	RICHMOND
	BAYSWATER	1932	EALING & ACTON
	CENTRAL	1934	FINSBURY PARK
1873	BOROUGH		(Wembley)
1876	ST JOHN'S WOOD		(Willesden)
1877	EAST LONDON	1935	(Finchley)
1878	NORTH LONDON		S.W. LONDON
1879	NEW WEST END		PALMERS GREEN
1885	DALSTON	1937	(Hampstead Garden
1890	HAMMERSMITH & WEST		Suburb)
	KENSINGTON		(Dollis Hill)
1892	HAMPSTEAD		UPTON PARK
1897	HACKNEY		ILFORD
1903	STOKE NEWINGTON		(Edgware)
1905	BRONDESBURY		N. FINCHLEY &
1913	BRIXTON		WOODSIDE PARK
1922	GOLDERS GREEN	1948	KINGSBURY
1931	CRICKLEWOOD		S.E. LONDON
1935	HENDON	1949	REGENT'S PARK Z &
1939	WILLESDEN		BELSIZE PARK
	HAMPSTEAD GARDEN		EAST HAM &
	SUBURB		MANOR PARK
1946	DOLLIS HILL		HARROW
1950	FINCHLEY		HIGHGATE
1954	EDGWARE		MUSWELL HILL
1956	WEMBLEY	1952	STANMORE &
1961	MARBLE ARCH		CANON'S PARK
			COCKFOSTERS &
			N. SOUTHGATE
		1958	STREATHAM
		1959	KENTON
		1960	SOUTH TOTTENHAM
		1960	MILL HILL

Affiliated

1931	(Willesden)	1949	BARKING &
	(Wembley)		BECONTREE
1932	HIGHAMS PARK &		HORNSEY &
	CHINGFORD		WOOD GREEN
	(Dollis Hill)		(Kenton)
1933	(Edgware)		Poplar ∅
	(Harrow & Kenton)		VICTORIA and
1934	(Palmers Green)		CHELSEA
1935	(Highgate)	1950	SLOUGH &
1936	(Kingsbury)		WINDSOR
	(South Tottenham)		(Mill Hill)
	(Ilford)	1952	EPSOM
1938	(Regent's Park & Belsize Park)		HAINAULT +
	CATFORD	1953	HAROLD HILL
	EDMONTON &	1954	BARNET
	TOTTENHAM	1954	(Marble Arch)
1943	(N. Finchley)	1955	BOREHAM WOOD
1945	HOUNSLOW	1956	PUTNEY
1946	STAINES	1957	CHISWICK
	(Stanmore & Canon's Park)	1957	HEMEL HEMPSTEAD
	(Streatham)	1963	ENFIELD
	SUTTON	1965	CHIGWELL +
1947	RUISLIP	1966	BELMONT
	ST ALBANS	1968	POTTERS BAR
	WANSTEAD &	1968	NEWBURY PARK
	WOODFORD	1970	BUSHEY
	BARKING =		
1940	(Cockfosters & N. Southgate)		
	Dunstable ∅		
	ELM PARK		
	HIGH WYCOMBE		
	KINGSTON & SURBITON		
	PETERBOROUGH		
	PINNER		
	ROMFORD		
	WELWYN GARDEN CITY		
	WATFORD		
	WORCESTER		

	Associate X
1902	(Poplar) ∅
	(East Ham & Manor Park)
	(S.E. London)
1907	(West Ham)
1916	(Richmond)
1917	(Victoria & Chelsea)
1920	(Hornsey & Wood Green)
	Walthamstow & Leyton*
1921	(Ealing & Acton)
1922	Sandys Row*
1923	(Upton Park)
1927	Hoxton & Shoreditch ∅
	(Becontree) =
	(S.W. London)

NOTES

Synagogues whose names are shown in brackets ( ) have since achieved higher status.

* Seceded from United Synagogue.
∅ Closed down.
X Associated Synagogues Scheme terminated 15 August 1949.
Z Now known as SOUTH HAMPSTEAD.
+ Amalgamated 1968. Now known as Chigwell & Hainault.
= Barking and Becontree amalgamated, 1948.

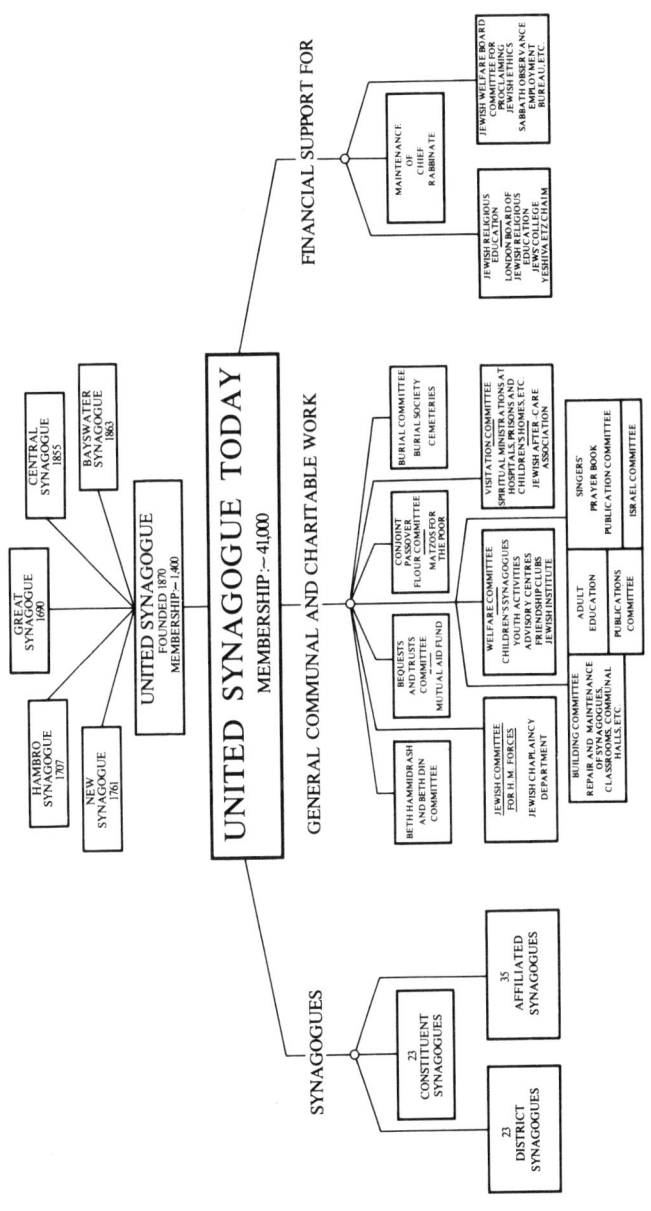

MAP 1

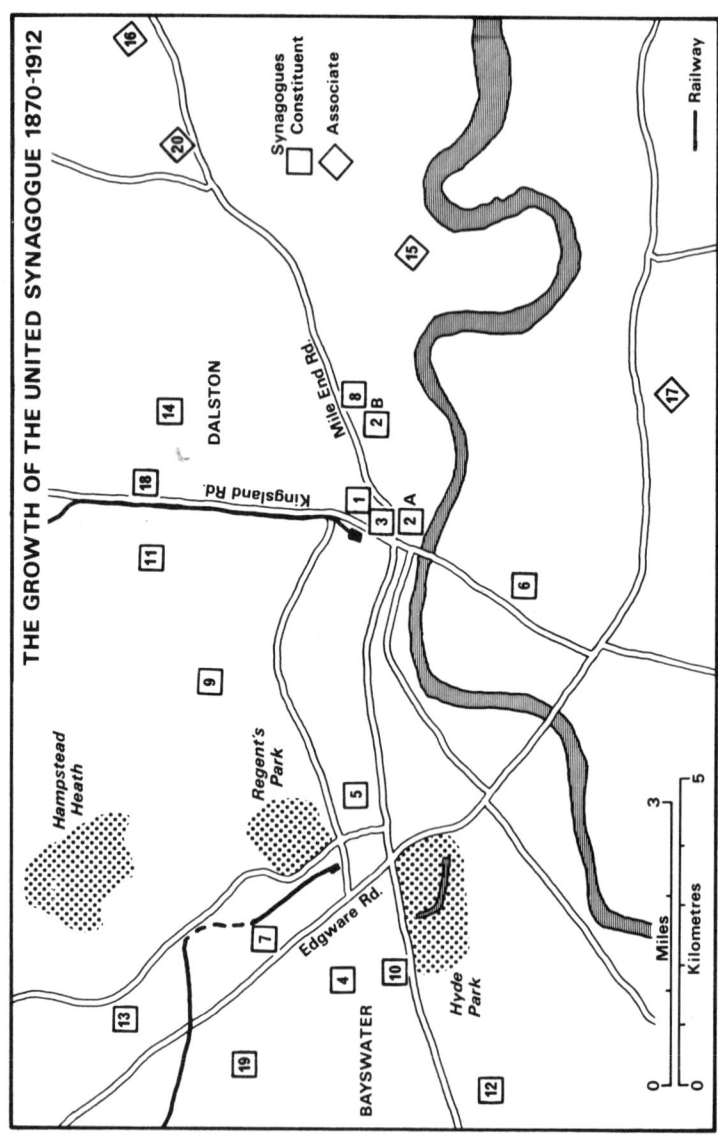

THE GROWTH OF THE UNITED SYNAGOGUE 1870-1912

Synagogues
Constituent
Associate

Railway

16
20
15
17
DALSTON
14
8
2 B
Mile End Rd.
18
Kingsland Rd.
1
3
2 A
11
6
9
Hampstead
Heath
Regent's
Park
5
7
Edgware Rd.
13
4
10
19
Hyde
Park
BAYSWATER
12
3
5
Miles
Kilometres
0
0

MAP 1

KEY

No. on map	Name of Congregation	Date of Admission	Status on map
1	GREAT	1870	Con
2 A/B	HAMBRO (moved 1899)	1870	Con
3	NEW	1870	Con
4	BAYSWATER	1870	Con
5	CENTRAL	1870	Con
6	Borough	1873	Con
7	St John's Wood	1876	Con
8	East London	1877	Con
9	North London	1878	Con
10	New West End	1879	Con
11	Dalston	1885	Con
12	Hammersmith and West Kensington	1890	Con
13	Hampstead	1892	Con
14	Hackney	1897	Con
15	Poplar	1902	Ass
16	East Ham and Manor Park	1902	Ass
17	South East London	1902	Ass
18	Stoke Newington	1903	Con
19	Brondesbury	1905	Con
20	West Ham	1907	Ass

MAP 2

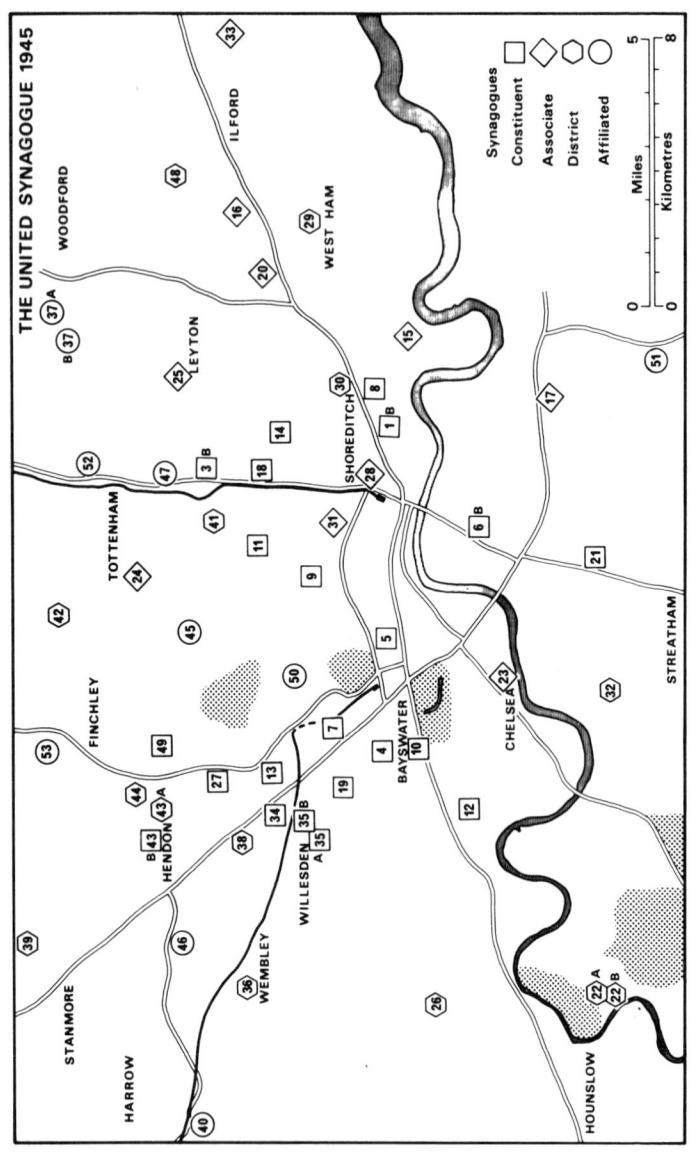

228

MAP 2

KEY

No. on map	Name of Congregation	Date of Admission	Status on map
1B	GREAT (moved after 1941)		Con
2	HAMBRO (amalgamated with Great 1936)		Con
3B	NEW (moved 1915)		Con
4	BAYSWATER		Con
5	CENTRAL		Con
6B	Borough (moved 1927)		Con
7	St John's Wood		Con
8	East London		Con
9	North London		Con
10	New West End		Con
11	Dalston		Con
12	Hammersmith & West Kensington		Con
13	Hampstead		Con
14	Hackney		Con
15	Poplar		Ass
16	East Ham & Manor Park		Ass
17	South East London		Ass
18	Stoke Newington		Con
19	Brondesbury		Con
20	West Ham (ch status 1927)		Dist
21	Brixton	1913	Con
22A/B	Richmond (adm Ass 1916) (ch status 1931) (moved 1938)		
23	Victoria & Chelsea	1917	Dist
24	Hornsey and Wood Green	1920	Ass
25	Walthamstow & Leyton	1920	Ass
26	Ealing & Acton (adm Ass 1921) (ch status 1932)		Dist
27	Golders Green	1917	Ass
28	Sandys Row	1922	Ass
29	Upton Park (adm Ass 1923) (ch status 1937)		Dist
30	Mile End & Bow		Dist
31	Hoxton & Shoreditch	1927	Ass
32	S.W. London (adm Ass 1927) (ch status 1935)	1927	Dist
33	Becontree	1927	Ass
34	Cricklewood	1931	Con
35A/B	Willesden (adm Aff 1931) (ch status (Dist) 1934) (ch status (Con) 1939) (moved 1939)		Con
36	Wembley (adm Aff 1931) (ch status 1934)		Con
37A/B	Highams Park & Chingford (moved 1937)	1932	Af
38	Dollis Hill	1932	Dist
39	Edgware (adm Aff 1938) (ch status 1939)		Dist
40	Harrow & Kenton	1932	Af
41	Finsbury Park	1934	Dist
42	Palmers Green & Southgate (adm Aff 1934) (ch status 1935)		Ass
43A/B	Hendon (adm Dist 1935) (ch status 1935) (moved 1935)		Dist
44	Finchley	1935	Con
45	Highgate	1935	Dist
46	Kingsbury	1936	Af
47	South Tottenham	1936	Af
48	Ilford (adm Aff 1936) (ch status 1937)		Af
49	Hampstead Garden Suburb (adm Dist 1937)		Dist
50	Regent's Park & Belsize Park	1938	Con
51	Catford	1938	Af
52	Edmonton & Tottenham	1938	Af
53	North Finchley & Woodside Park	1943	Af

MAP 3

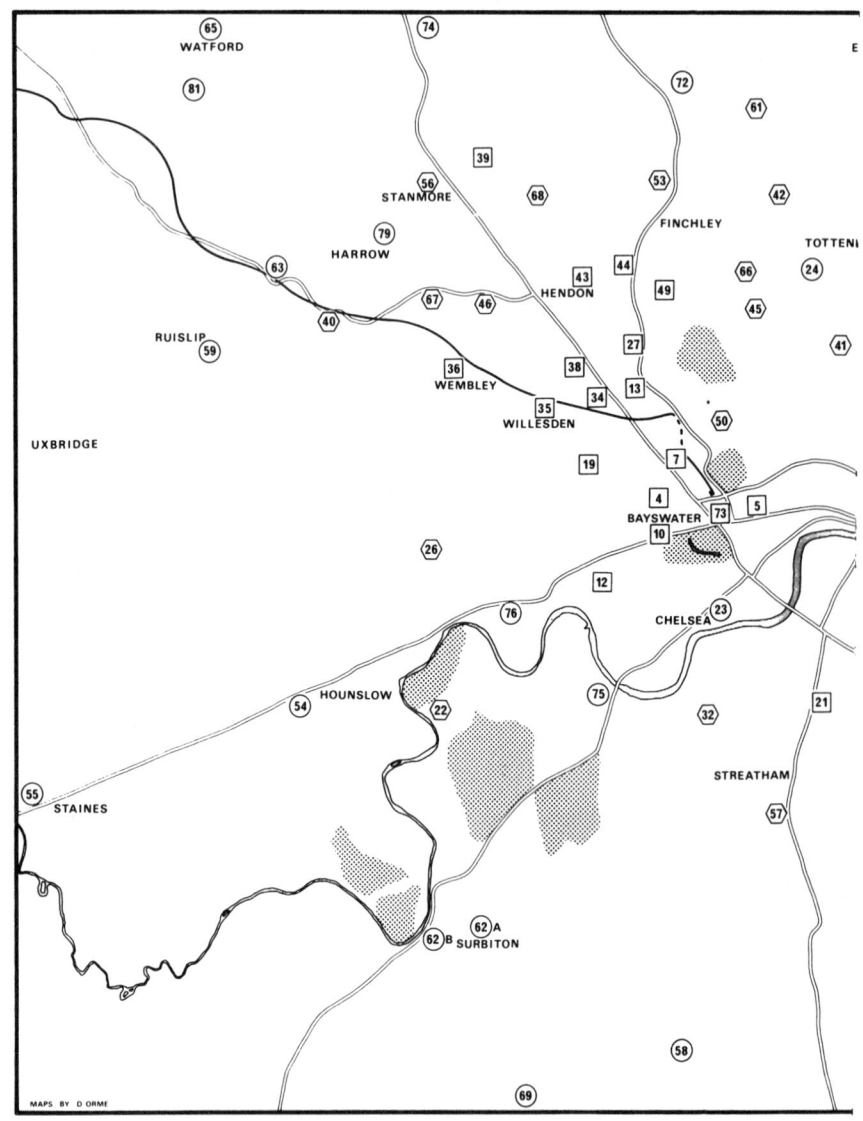

MAP 3

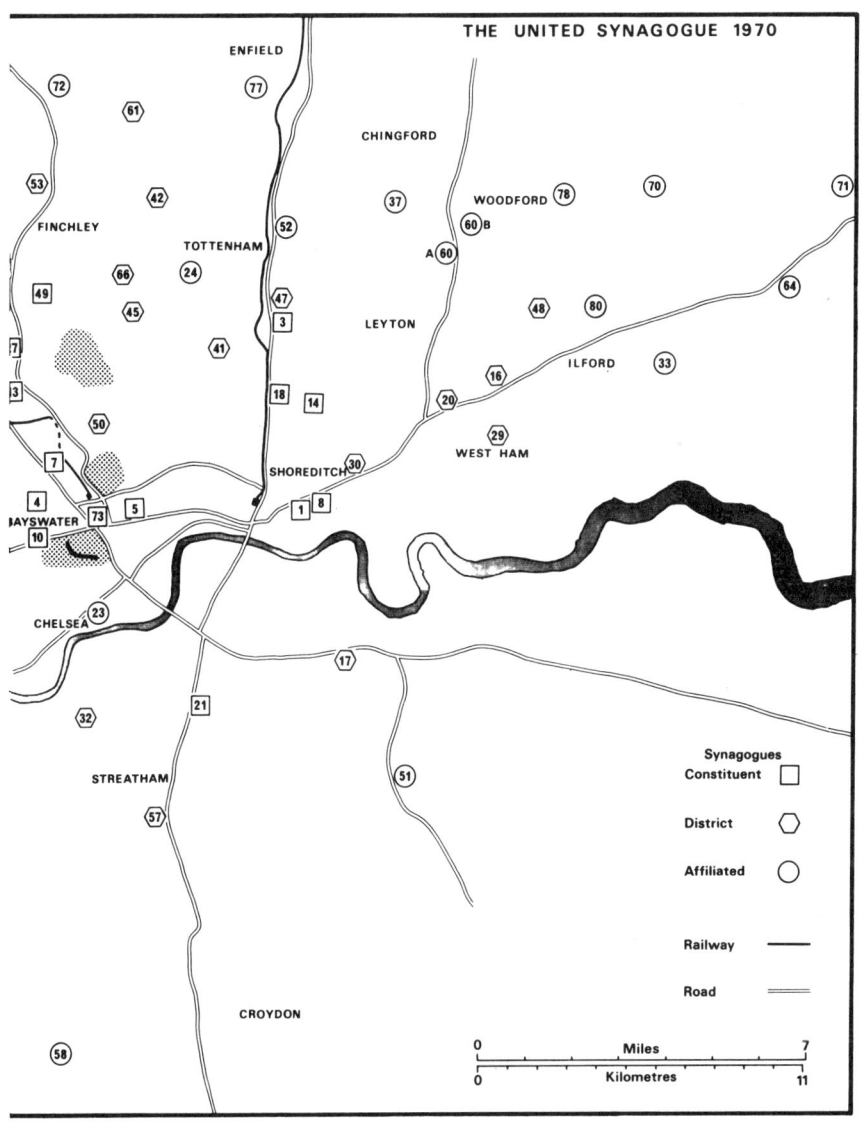

THE UNITED SYNAGOGUE 1970

MAP 3

KEY

No. on map	Name of Congregation	Status on map
1	GREAT and HAMBRO	Con
3	NEW	Con
4	BAYSWATER	Con
5	CENTRAL	Con
	Borough (amalgamated with Brixton 1961)	—
7	St John's Wood	Con
8	East London	Con
	North London (amalgamated with Dalston 1958)	—
10	New West End	Con
	Dalston (amalgamated with Stoke Newington 1967)	—
12	Hammersmith & West Kensington	Con
13	Hampstead	Con
14	Hackney	Con
	Poplar (closed 1951)	—
16	East Ham & Manor Park (ch status 1949)	Dist
17	South East London (ch status 1948)	Dist
18	Stoke Newington	Con
19	Brondesbury	Con
20	West Ham	Dist
21	Brixton	Con
22	Richmond	Dist
23	Chelsea (formerly Victoria & Chelsea) (ch status 1949)	Aff
24	Hornsey & Wood Green (ch status 1949)	Aff
	Walthamstow & Leyton (seceded 1949)	—
26	Ealing & Acton	Dist
27	Golders Green	Aff
	Sandys Row (seceded 1949)	—
29	Upton Park	Dist
30	Mile End and Bow	Dist
	Hoxton & Shoreditch (closed 1949)	—
32	South West London	Dist
33	Becontree (now Barking & Becontree)	Aff
34	Cricklewood	Con
35	Willesden	Con
36	Wembley (ch status 1956)	Con
37	Highams Park & Chingford	Aff
38	Dollis Hill	Con
39	Edgware (ch status 1954)	Con
40	Harrow (ch status 1949)	Dist
41	Finsbury Park	Dist
42	Palmers Green & Southgate	Dist
43	Hendon	Con
44	Finchley (ch status 1950)	Con
45	Highgate (ch status 1949)	Dist
46	Kingsbury (ch status 1948)	Dist
47	South Tottenham (ch status 1960)	Dist
48	Ilford	Dist
49	Hampstead Garden Suburb	Con

MAP 3

No. on map	Name of Congregation	Date of Admission	Status on map
50	South Hampstead (formerly Regent's Park & Belsize Park		Dist
51	Catford		Aff
52	Edmonton & Tottenham		Aff
53	North Finchley & Woodside Park (ch status 1947)		Dist
54	Hounslow	1945	Aff
55	Staines	1946	Aff
56	Stanmore & Canons Park (adm Aff 1946) (ch status 1952)		Dist
57	Streatham (adm Aff 1946) (ch status 1958)		Dist
58	Sutton	1946	Aff
59	Ruislip	1947	Aff
	*St Albans	1947	Aff
60A/B	Wanstead & Woodford (moved 1954)	1947	Aff
	Barking (adm Aff 1947) (amalgamated with Becontree 1948)		—
61	Cockfosters & North Southgate (adm Aff 1948) (ch status 1952)		Dist
	Dunstable (adm Aff 1948) (closed 1955)		—
	*Elm Park	1948	Aff
	*High Wycombe	1948	Aff
62A/B	Kingston & Surbiton (moved 1954)	1948	Aff
	*Peterborough	1948	Aff
63	Pinner	1948	Aff
64	Romford	1948	Aff
	*Welwyn Garden City	1948	Aff
65	Watford	1948	Aff
	*Worcester	1948	Aff
66	Muswell Hill	1949	Dist
67	Kenton (sep from Harrow, adm Aff 1949) (ch status 1959)		Dist
68	Mill Hill (adm Aff 1950) (ch status 1960)		Dist
	*Slough and Windsor	1950	Aff
69	Epsom	1952	Aff
70	Hainault (adm 1952, amalgamated with Chigwell 1968)		Aff
71	Harold Hill	1953	Aff
72	Barnet	1954	Aff
73	Marble Arch (adm Aff 1954) (ch status direct 1961)		Con
74	Boreham Wood & Elstree	1955	Aff
75	Putney & Wimbledon	1956	Aff
76	Chiswick	1957	Aff
	*Hemel Hempstead	1957	Aff
77	Enfield & Winchmore Hill	1963	Aff
78	Chigwell (amalgamated with Hainault 1968)	1965	—
79	Belmont	1966	Aff
	*Potters Bar	1968	Aff
80	Newbury Park	1968	Aff
81	Bushey	1970	Aff

* Not included on the map.

INDEX